Radical Human Centricity

Radical Human Centricity

Fulfilling the Promises
of Innovation Research

By Paul Hartley, PhD

ANTHEM PRESS

Anthem Press
An imprint of Wimbledon Publishing Company
www.anthempress.com

This edition first published in UK and USA 2022
by ANTHEM PRESS
75–76 Blackfriars Road, London SE1 8HA, UK
or PO Box 9779, London SW19 7ZG, UK
and
244 Madison Ave #116, New York, NY 10016, USA

British Library Cataloguing-in-Publication Data
A catalogue record for this book is available from the British Library.

Library of Congress Cataloging-in-Publication Data
A catalog record for this book has been requested.

ISBN-13: 978-1-83998-571-3 (Hbk)
ISBN-10: 1-83998-571-2 (Hbk)

ISBN-13: 978-1-83998-568-3 (Pbk)
ISBN-10: 1-83998-568-2 (Pbk)

This title is also available as an e-book.

CONTENTS

ACKNOWLEDGMENTS

This book is the result of more than 11 years of experiences, mistakes, problem-solving, and learning. I first want to thank my excellent colleagues at the Human Futures Studio because each of them has played a role in developing the perspective and processes described here. None of this would have been possible without Dr. Morgan Gerard who took a chance on me all those years ago. Special thanks go to my principal partners in crime, Mat Lincez and Dr. Shane Saunderson. Thank you to Antti Mäkelä at Embassy of Design for coining the phrase Radical Human Centricity and letting me use it. The biggest thanks go to my wife, who has supported me through the writing of this book and in all other things.

FOREWORD BY ALEXANDER MANU

Uncoded in academic jargon, authentic and bold, and most of all necessary, Paul Hartley's book delivers a roadmap to courageous creativity and offers an approach to the vision, complexity, and scale necessary to make qualified observations founded on rigor, sensitivity, and knowledge.

As the title suggests, commercial research is in need of radical change. There is an immutable truth in his observation that design and market research are not equipped for learning the semiotic system another person uses to understand the world around them, or their purposeful behavior. The lack of context and awareness is the root cause of the current commercial research's inability to produce reliable results. Hartley is endeavoring to make individuals understand that research into human behavior is much harder than advertised and also that it requires a specialist practice to achieve its intended purpose. What separates the people we call experts from those who are creative thinkers and skilled planners? Experts are people who know what to do. I find this Bill Maris (founder of Google Ventures) quote entirely appropriate in illustrating the point Hartley is trying to make in the book: *"those of us who know what we are doing, know what we are doing!"*[1]

The essential components of Radical Human Centricity are framed by a structure that is both pragmatic and compelling. The book is a lively and fascinating the exploration of the transforming power of specialized knowledge and research. Radical Human Centricity unravels the intractable need for adaptive experimentation, human centricity, and learned human excellence in research. It suggests we can entirely dismiss the limitations of mere rationality in navigating the complexity of innovation through an absolute commitment to human-centeredness, specialized research guided by constant intellectual curiosity, focused creativity, and critical thinking.

The scope of Radical Human Centricity expands and develops into both a philosophical account and a practical manifesto, one that guides a radically new vision and the commitment to uncovering the skillful work that lies behind understanding people's motivations and actions. That framework supports a radically new form of critical reflection—one sorely needed in commercial practice. Its potential is astonishing: enabling the transformation of our worldview and giving businesses the knowledge to develop tools that can successfully process information about human behavior in the context of the development of products and services. Hartley illustrates a wide range of principles, methods, and notions for research and development, and a fundamentally different way of thinking and acting is needed in the context of design and business strategy. A more radical approach requires learning to prioritize the empirical approach of commercial research that needs to become fully integrated into a methodology that creates alternative structures and a disciplinary human-centric approach that will shift to a more profound vision of design research.

Radical Human Centricity addresses the shortcomings of more traditional methods. It seeks to provide improved ways of communicating with the research participants themselves, rather than the researcher's ideas. Hartley's work builds upon the established ethnographic research tradition to become a more innovative, human-centric way of working in social science research. It offers new approaches, new methods for understanding the context of human experience, and new ethical principles for presenting data and describing and describing ourselves.

Hartley describes radical human-centeredness as an approach to better understanding and designing for complexity and scale. He asserts that simple solutions are deeply problematic. His emphasis on a nuanced understanding of the radical complexity of the "world as it is" and its challenges lead him to suggest ways to bring the richness of honest complex solutions to human-centered design. In particular, radical complexity demands that companies generate a rationale for their need for research and creativity in the context of the complexity of the future's challenges.

There are many people in design that have good skills in the methodology of thinking. However, there are very few that use those skills very effectively and that has the focus to apply them to solving problems. This process needs a lot of experience and expertise. There is a considerable gap in the traditional methodology of design research. The design process does not work the way that most companies think. In truth, it may be unreasonable for the traditional methods of thinking to be applied to design challenges in the first place. It takes much skill to understand customers, how they think, and how they can be convinced to live differently.

With this in mind, Hartley notes that "design thinking, design research, and human-centric approaches were all developed to overcome the lack of detail, abstractions, and measurement biases in older forms of market research or to meet the needs of an innovation process that seeks to change the way people live their lives by adding new products, services, or experiences into the system. But instead of correcting the core problems, practitioners of design research, in-house innovation teams, and innovation consultants papered over the cracks in thinking and practice and continued as usual."

This trouble seems to have started when psychology entered the lexicon of design researchers in the field. Design researchers reasoned that designers would then create the design by using only the observed behavior patterns of a person in the marketplace. However, the problem with thinking abstractly was that users of that design would not be emotionally connected to the product. Moreover, they were essentially now designing for people who do not exist. The changes were superficial and quickly evaporated. Over time, market research practices crept back into the system. Marketing teams, designers, and engineers still prefer statistics or abstracted, simple views of people to make the strategy and innovation decisions, when their thinking should be rooted in the details of the real lives of their customers.

The lack of a mechanism for developing a fundamental understanding of their research subjects is one of the reasons design researchers solve the wrong problems and are incapable of even comprehending what is happening, never mind understanding what it means or how it is expressed. Hartley exposes the inadequacy of the current empathy research and design practice in a single and most clarifying illustration: in etic viewpoints, behavior is studied from outside of a particular structure and as an essential first step to understanding an alien system, while in the emic viewpoint, behavior is studied from within. Current forms of design research are only capable of capturing etic detail and miss the emic perspective entirely.

His argument crystalizes in his critique of the problem of empathy in design research. What is empathy, and how does it relate to research? Empathy refers to a consciousness toward another person. Empathy is a heightened consciousness—the point where you experience your own life as an experience that another person experiences. The point at which you feel empathy for someone is not that you experience their life but rather that you are experiencing it deeper. This level is our stage of expression, awareness, and experience—our personal stage. In empathy research, we engage in dialogue, asking questions—inquiry. We observe some signs and acts in other people to find the signs that define the intimacy of our exchange.

The challenge for research on a topic as complex as empathy is to move beyond superficial descriptions of characteristics, stimuli, and behavior. Empathy requires that we understand the sign language used by another person to signal what they are hearing or seeing together with the structuring context. Often, we do not have the sign language to communicate with people from other cultures or different parts of our own.

Hartley argues that to gain an understanding of another person's perspective, the first step is to understand what it is that makes their perspective unique. The first step is the acknowledgment that we are separate people. What we do is essentially personal action of the most basic kind. We need our own space to come to terms with the world around us and for our individual experiences to emerge. Ethnographic research is simply a human response to the reality of *reality*—a response to our own momentary experiences and their meaning. As human-centered social theorists, we cannot presume what it is like to be a child, a student, a struggling family, or a homeless person. That would not be our reality or personal experience.

Radical Human Centricity helps us explore how much more can be done with new techniques, principles, new ways of communicating, and understanding to help us become more mindful students of the human condition and human beings. Our understanding of ourselves is only ever a reflection of our values and those of others. In RHC practice, the question is not how far away the truth is from what we are doing, but where the truth lies and in what shape it is ultimately expressed.

Radical Human Centricity provides a way to describe, understand and transform our reality as human beings as part of radical human studies. It is more than an intellectual exercise, but a way of being and transforming reality by reorienting values in the scientific and technological processes. Radical Human Centricity is a step toward radical design and a radical human future for business. We all need more of it.

Alexander Manu

Note

1 Retrieved from: https://www.businessinsider.com/bill-maris-explains-why-gv-didnt-invest-in-theranos-2015-10.

INTRODUCTION

There is a problem at the core of commercial innovation research. The tools and methods companies, consultancies, and even governments use to research human thought and behavior promise an understanding of the world that they cannot deliver. They cannot deal with complexity honestly. They cannot provide the detail suitable to make true design or strategic decisions. And they cannot help companies understand their customers with enough depth to meet the requirements of human-centered design. They claim to, but they cannot. Consequently, there is a wide gulf between what commercial research is asked to do and what it can deliver.

This problem exists because most commercial research is still stuck in the past. Despite claiming to be cutting edge, most commercial research methods are still grounded in market research practices and rely on outdated theories or misapplied research practice. None of these patterns of practice are suitable ways to feed into innovation efforts. Current commercial research is simply not able to understand the world in enough detail or complexity to provide a comfortable foundation for creating empathetic, sustainable, and truly innovative products, services, or experiences in an increasingly complicated world. Human-centricity promised a solution to this, but ultimately left more unfulfilled promises.

Commercial research is still broken. Ethnography has been coopted. Design research has been watered down. Any careful observer of commercial research and innovation already knows this. But what is less well understood is that the latest fashionable practices in innovation research, particularly many of the so-called human-centered solutions, also suffer from the same fatal flaws as the system they were meant to improve. Design thinking, design research, and human/patient-centric approaches were all developed to overcome the lack of detail, abstractions, and measurement biases in older forms of market research, or to meet the needs of an innovation process that seeks to change the way people live their lives by adding new products, services, or experiences into the system. But instead of correcting the core problems, practitioners of design research, in-house innovation teams, and innovation consultants, simply papered over the cracks in thinking and practice and continued as normal. The changes were superficial and quickly evaporated. Over time, market research practices crept back into the system. Marketing teams, designers, and engineers still prefer statistics, or abstracted, simple views of people to make the strategy and innovation decisions, when their thinking should be rooted in the details of the real lives of their customers. Now, as we move into a time where we are trying to be more aware of the ethical, environmental, emotional, and practical impacts of our actions it is time for all of us working in business, innovation, and commercial research to leave behind the broken, unethical, and frankly weak thinking and methods in all these research approaches and embrace the alternations we need to actually be human-centric in commercial research.

It is essential that we do this. Product, service, and strategy innovation is now so influential and deeply ingrained in business practices, that it shapes a lot of our daily, lived experiences. Few of us live without the minute-by-minute interventions of a designed product or experience. Your smartphone, for instance, is a collection of these very things. Our expectations, relationships, social interactions, and even our very understanding of the world around us are all influenced by these designed experiences. It goes deeper. Governments and NGOs are now using innovation processes and practices to build and implement policy and guide their populations. It even has an impact on the climate because it shapes how we all understand the material world around us. Simply put, design and strategy innovation has become one of the dominant ideologies of our day and touches almost everyone on the planet.

This influence is not without its problems, however. The lack of clear, well thought out research practices means design and strategy innovation operate without the full knowledge of their impact. Design and innovation practitioners are largely ignorant of the world as it actually is and make a number of mistakes in their work as a result. They are functionally blind to the realities of the world because the theories, methods, and practices used to study the world and the people who live in it were developed to simply and reduce for the benefit of the designer or innovator. Consequently, the world is rendered as an idealized system built on simple rules, rather than the complex web of interconnections, variety, and contradictions it actually is. Because the entire approach is unable to handle the complexity of real life, it cannot prepare people to anticipate impact beyond the immediate effect of the design intervention. Consequently, many opportunities are being missed, and people around the world are suffering because of the unintended consequences of designed experiences and poorly thought-out business strategies.

The time has come to do better in our commercial research practices and approaches to innovation. It is necessary not just to have more realistic human insights in commercial research, but also to improve the standards of our design and strategic innovation efforts. If we want to design a better world, be more sustainable, and generally do less harm, we must be sensitive to the complexities of real life. We must work with a model of the world that preserves the rich differences in gendered, national, racial, historical, and other identities, for example. We need to do this to have an innovation practice that does not bulldoze these details in favor of a view of the world with a simpler user experience for the designer or engineer. If we want an innovation process that is capable of addressing the practicalities of correcting the climate crisis, we need to stop depending on a system that assumes growth-capitalist models explain the world at every level of detail. If we want to understand people's "needs," desires, and beliefs, we need to stop casting human action as the "non-technical problem." If we want to deal with the realities and nuances of lived experience and understand the world through someone else's eyes in the most empathetic way possible, we need to start to make the most of the 180-year tradition of real ethnographic research and change the way knowledge is created during innovation research. We need to strive to be truly human-centric and work for real human beings and not idealized, sanitized versions of our fellow humans. In short, we need a radical rethink of what research should ground innovation processes and business. We need what I call a Radical Human-Centric approach, based in the traditions and cutting-edge advancements of the social sciences, but tuned to the particular needs of a commercial audience. We need to fulfill the promises of human-centricity and respond to the richness and complexity of the world as it is. If we do not, we risk continuing down the path where our innovation efforts contribute to short-term gains but long-term problems.

The Problem of Human-Centricity

The first step is to take a long look at the problem of the idea of "human-centricity" itself in commercial research. Of all the buzzwords in business none is more problematically empty than "human-centric." Most often, it is a fuzzy concept used to refer to a kind of research only used in technology companies or in innovation consulting sales copy. The "human" in "human-centricity" is meant to be a modification of the usual focus of research and development in these contexts: the product itself. However, putting the "human" aspects first is really about making products and services more useable and reducing the time it takes to refine a product in user testing. As a research approach— it is not a methodology—human-centricity is a Frankenstein's monster cobbled together using scraps of research ideas from software design, psychology, market research, and human–computer interaction. The result is something that does not put humans at the center because it is nothing more than an alteration to past practices which never considered the user at all. It is "human" because it is less designer-centric or engineer-centric, but none of these approaches are actually human-centric.

Moving to the full phrase, what does "human-centricity" really mean? The phrase itself is usually found tacked on to some action-oriented term, like process, approach, research, or design, but this does not give us much to go on. The phrases, "human-centered design," "we take a human-centric perspective" and its variant "our human-centric approach" are all too common on corporate and consulting websites. Their use signals only the ideological intentions of its users. They are not there to demonstrate that the idea, product, service, or experience has been developed with the help of rigorous research and careful thought, at considerable expense. It indicates only that it was developed "with the customer in mind," but this could mean almost anything. How is the customer in mind? Which customer? How is this perspective built in the first place? The idea of keeping the customer first, or considering their "needs," separates one development process from one that does not. Human-centricity almost never indicates *how* this is accomplished, and there lies the problem. How you consider humans and human behavior is more important than merely being "empathetic" or "needs-based" in the process. "Human-centricity" is only a placeholder, and because it can mean anything, and everything, it does not guarantee rigorous deployment of the real work that must be done to study people, understand them, and explain them. We know this because true human-centricity—what I take to mean understanding people and their lives on their own terms—is very hard and engrossing work. This kind of research takes experienced, specialist researchers, a wealth of background knowledge, and rigorous practice.

As things stand now, the ideology, structure, and processes of business thinking, design thinking, and innovation are not human-centric. They were never intended to be. Most contemporary business approaches, in design, strategy, or management, work by eliminating the very detail that a truly human-centric approach reveals. In fact, most of the research methods commonly used in business today are the very structures and approaches human-centric innovation processes were developed to correct or replace. But instead of changing how we do business, human-centricity was reduced to jargon, and the system continues as it was before. Human-centricity is just an idea that has not yet been fulfilled.

We need true human-centricity in design, innovation, and business practices. This half-hearted version is creating a host of problems by preventing all of these areas of activity and though from actually connecting their work to the realities of people's lives. It is creating a set of problems, like devolving the social contract of politeness in daily interactions, increasing dependence on "walled garden" style offerings, intractable privacy problems, opportunities for invasive surveillance, and a continuing reticence to play any role in handling the climate crisis. It is wasting time and money with iterative processed that could have been shortened by honest, rich engagements with real people. It is providing a new way to sell consulting services that have not changed in 25 years.

Business leaders, not-for-profit entities, and governments now operate in a world of ever-increasing complexity, but they are invested in avoiding this fact. Simplicity is still their goal. They prefer to reduce people to data points because it is much easier to handle. What is lost in this process is profound. The only way to manage the complexities of an interconnected world filled with non-human social actors like AI, sophisticated software experiences, and robots, is to understand people even more closely and in their full richness and complexity. But to understand people's lives, businesses must also make what they learn relevant for themselves.

Today, business is conducted on at least two scales simultaneously: at scale (global, relevant to many, and interconnected), and focused on individual experience (idiosyncratic, limited, and personal).[1] The days are gone when a product could simply satisfy an easy majority at first and then be honed over many series of iterations. Now it is essential to provide an individuated experience to every customer/user and to provide this immediately to as many people as possible across the globe. And this must be done with considering the impact on a single person or on the environment. This challenge will not be met using research methods that eliminate the essential details of people's lives or those that cannot connect these two scales of human experience (the idiosyncratic and the globally common).

This is a problem for every business trying to create new products, services, and experiences. The rules for competing and thriving in this world have changed drastically. For instance, venture capital has created a new working environment where money is used to scale businesses well beyond their natural potential in order to erode older industries.[2] Advances in communications technology have brought flexible digital experiences to anyone able to purchase a device capable of accessing the internet. And the rise of a new entrepreneurial cultural order has guaranteed that there are several iterations of a new idea in the works at any time. Together, these forces have put pressure on traditional business and strategic programs, requiring business leaders and R&D teams to look for alternatives in how they respond to the world and design or strategize a new way of doing business. Of all the conceptual and practical alternatives, human-centricity and design thinking have provided a needed intervention. They aid businesses to consider aspects of their customer base that they never had before, despite not requiring much from them.

As an intervention to traditional business thinking and practices, human-centricity and design thinking processes offer a deeper connection to a businesses' customer. They are supposed to bring customers' way of thinking, their desires, and quirkiness into the product development process. But if you review what has been written about human-centric design, and design thinking—which we will in chapters two, three, and four—you quickly see that both of these "approaches" are still designer-centric. In practice, all of these methods and processes are really about creating good ideas. There is a clear process from ideation, to concept generation, to iteration and refinement of the new product, service, or idea. However, there is almost nothing said about how to capture the intimate details of real-life and know them well enough to explain how they combine at scale. There is little to them that can bring the complexity of real-life into the development process.

This problem is amplified in the technology industry, where there is a reliance on a normative, mechanical view of people borrowed from social psychology. In the tech space, the dominant knowledge culture is a modification of the cultural systems learned in STEM programs, mostly in American universities. This sub-cultural framework draws almost exclusively on models of human behavior developed in a search for human universals by the laboratory-based practices of psychology. Social psychology, in contrast to more open-ended qualitative practices like anthropology and sociology, studies human behavior as a universal object—what is common to all of us. Because of this focus, they struggle to study life lived on the ragged edges of culture or social behavior, or in the idiosyncratic development of identity, meaning, or ideologies. Instead, they study behaviors in individuals and reduce this complexity to arrive at universal explanations, like the basics of perception, or the instinctual causal pathways in stimulus/response contexts. People are understood as bundles of responses to stimuli, or as examples of a universal behavior that can be leveraged in the development of a new feature or product. This requires strict research protocols that eliminate the failures and idiosyncrasies in individual behavior, cultural constructs, and experience. In a practical sense, it means using laboratory conditions to eliminate all of this "noise."

Because companies that develop technological products, or new business strategies, are more comfortable with this way of studying people, they are lacking the humanizing information that these research practices eliminate. They do not have a solid understanding of how culture structures our thinking, how social order shapes behaviors, how ideology changes the way that we think about everything, or how experience is not universal, but unique to each of us. Because all of these are modifiers of even the most basic, and universal human behaviors, they do not see how universal behavior is particularized.

They cannot fully understand behavior in action, out in the real world, where these normative explanations fail to explain what actually happens. They look for descriptions of people based on the causal inferences you can draw from characteristics, for example, because someone is tall, brown-eyed, university educated, and 45, they will like their coffee with cream and may buy apps to locate spiced lattes. Further complicating things, because they are also businesses, they are also using the prevailing business thinking to respond to their limited view of humans and our behavior. This means the tech world works with borrowed models that insufficiently describe how people live in the world and respond to this knowledge by further eliminating the detail of this world to make it simple enough to make a business decision. In many cases, this is still referred to as "human-centric," despite it being nothing of the sort.

But before we begin a full critique of these problems, we must realize that it is not individual researchers' efforts that are the problem, it is the patterns of practice that are at fault. The culture of business analytics itself prevents any shift toward real human-centricity because it requires the way of working to adhere to specific beliefs about the world. These assumptions, guiding structures, and acculturated beliefs shape research programs and obscure the way forward. Business culture and its patterns of practice value quick and practical approaches over rigorous and thoughtful ones. The older systems of knowledge and research that provide these quick, practical answers are not up to the challenge of managing experience and cultural design at scale—they are barely adequate to address the simplest marketing questions. But they are maintained because they align with the expectations of how the world should work. The entire system is trapped by the belief that business is not complicated, and one just needs a simple framework and some actionable insights to make the right decision.

This means companies and commercial entities of all kinds rely on a conceptual model of the world so divorced from reality that it is becoming harder and harder to conduct business without falling into false beliefs about the world. They believe in the rational, competitive *homo economicus* of nineteenth-century economics theory. They believe in simple explanations of complex things. They believe in causal models of stimulus and response. They believe the world can be described in terms of segments, and 2 x 2 models, and demographics. Thus, they see the world as reducible to easy-to-understand pieces—which it isn't. The world is a wild, woolly, complicated, and messy place of interconnections and contradictions. The result is much of the actual work of innovation teams, strategy groups, and marketing departments are grounded in an error-prone philosophy and skewed insights. They are inefficient, inflexible, reactive, and myopic as a result. A better understanding of the world around them would improve almost everything they do.

This division between the way business practitioners are taught to understand the world of their customers and the real world filled with human beings is largely the fault of decades of poor research training and practice. And I am not referring to badly executed research. I am meaning to say that the research that has been done was built on the top of theories about human beings and their behaviors that were incapable of providing a realistic view of what people do when they live their lives and act as customers/consumers/users. The theoretical underpinnings of the conventional business mental model are corrupted from the beginning. The evidence processed through these models fits just well enough to allow the entire practice to continue. But because there is a prejudice against true theorizing in business and innovation, these theories could not be critiqued, so they persisted. This has contributed to a situation where the way business is conducted in most major corporations is incompatible with real, theoretically sound research.

The fault does not lie in the business thinkers alone; this myopia is learned. It is a symptom of the failure of their knowledge apparatus, and the entire knowledge system surrounding business thought. It is one of the reasons businesses behave in a way that is often detrimental to the health and wellbeing of people and the planet. Ultimately, this is about how we understand the breadth, depth, and variety of the natural, social, and cultural worlds around us and how we make sense of it so that we can produce ever more successful products, services, and experiences for people to use. But if we lack the ability to understand this world in its full majesty, or to understand the people who are our customers, we have no way to innovate properly, and no ability to design or strategize properly. We must undo the endemic, systemic failures of a research paradigm that is now entirely unfit for purpose. We have to save business research from itself in order to help business leaders, thinkers, innovators, designers, engineers, and entrepreneurs from creating and recreating a world that is divorced from itself. If we do not, this false world will overtake the real one, and the environment will be permanently damaged, human life will be challenging, and vulnerable populations will continue to suffer. No exceptional device or service providing surprise and delight is worth this. But we can have it both ways if we build these innovations, products, services, and experiences on models of real-life that are grounded in lived reality.

We must fulfill the promise of human-centricity and fully develop the intent and method behind it so it can make the change it was meant to accomplish. I am proposing we reorient how all of us in commercial innovation think about people, develop better methods to research their lives, and push human-centric design and strategy to allow everyone to take the turn and design and innovate in a way that does not oversimplify or distort the beauty of real life. I am proposing a *Radical Human-Centricity* that actually puts the person/customer/user first and abandons all of the practices and thinking that are preventing us from engaging in the world as it really is while we try to develop new strategies, products, solutions, and experiences at scale.

I do not intend to suggest that we replace one empty buzzword for another. A true Radical Human-Centricity needs to be a philosophy, an approach that guides all methods, and a practical set of tools, frameworks, and processes. But more than anything else I am suggesting we begin with a radical overhaul of the way all of us in commercial innovation think and reassess the way we approach every step of our work as researchers and practitioners of commercial research. It requires us to wash away some of the old ways of thinking and doing. We must learn to be unafraid of complexity. We must learn to stop seeing a division between theory and practice, and we must start putting people and their complicated lives at the center of the decision we make in business, policy, and innovation. We need to start building for a future that is better for everyone and not one that is tactically advantageous in the short term. Radical human-centricity is radical because it offers a break from our past and provides a way of engaging with the details of real-life in a thorough and practical way. It will mean leaving behind old research practices that efface the humanity of the individuals we encounter when we study culture, behaviors, experience, and society. It necessitates committing to always engaging with their world when we build and create for it. And it forces us to do what is right for everyone, including our planet, before we do what is easy. Radical human-centricity is what human-centricity was supposed to be: putting people first, understanding context, and dealing with consequences of what it means to create new things for a rich, complicated environment.

We need this because until now the emptiness of human-centric approaches has led otherwise well-meaning practitioners to conduct weak, inadequate research. Because they are the eyes and ears of their business, governments, or just individual innovation teams, they are providing an inaccurate view of the world, built on false comparisons, problematic assumptions, and unchallenged ideologies, to people who create products and services serving only the company that makes them.

At scale, these small failures, and troubled decisions, are amplified beyond their initial intentions. As we take one perspective on the world and scale it up to serve as the foundation for a product with tens of millions of units, its problems, failures, omissions, and prejudices are scaled too. This is the same fear lurking in the problem of how algorithms can be racist or the cause of media bubbles that bend people's understanding of community. If we do not take time, experience, scale, and impact into consideration then we are not designing, innovating, or providing anything that is actually human-centric. Instead, we are just developing something that is minimally useful. In a world where technical innovations and their practical application in commerce can damage ecosystems and cause harm or suffering, we must begin to take a more measured approach to what we create. For all of the good they provide, things like plastics, smartphone apps, and engineered food are good for business, but when we see their impact at scale we see that they choke oceans, create debilitating addictions, and promote and complicate obesity epidemics. If we consider their application in a more human way, they may be able to do the good with fewer negative effects.

The intention behind radical human centricity is to provide a better way to work in innovation, design, and in human research. But I want to make it quite clear that I believe that in doing this, researchers, consultants, foresight strategists, futurists, designers, and innovation practitioners can have a lasting and positive impact on more than a product or an eighteen-month strategy. Radical human centricity is focused entirely on changing how we create knowledge about others and how that is applied in the act of creation. It is a new format for applied research. But within this, it contains a better way to do business—one that I believe is absolutely necessary at this time. This book is a statement of hope that a broken industry can heal itself and do better.

The Radical Human-Centric Approach

The radical human-centric approach is a new way of thinking and doing commercial and applied human research that actually puts the human story at its center but fits into knowledge systems and ways of working still stuck in older ways of thinking. It is a bridge between two eras in commercial research, one where humans were beside the point and one where human experience is the beginning, middle, and end of the story. It is a cluster of alterations to the thoughts, actions, and beliefs that define design research, UX research, patient-centricity, and market research. But it is not a wholesale demolition of these practices. Radical Human-Centricity is an approach, not a methodology or a process. It is something that can be used to humanize many ways of working.

Its strongest methodological orientation lies in the incorporation of real research methods like true ethnography into a research system unable to understand humans as they are. Its purpose is to develop insights into the human experience capable of supporting the most detailed and thorough design and strategic work possible. Only real research is able to answer the questions behind why people do what they do. By understanding the reasons why, it is possible to provide better solutions to the customer/ user. You need real ethnography to meet them on their own terms. Because real research is a departure from what is currently used in HCD (Human-centered design) it will require an alteration in how researchers, designers, and strategists live in the world around them. The change in practice requires a transformation in the researcher. This is not about new methods, but about making the best use of the practices common in HCD now. We will discuss this in greater detail throughout the chapters of this book.

This will require the industry as a whole to abandon many of its traditional methods, to combine insight with foresight and qualitative and quantitative practices, and to embrace professionalized, expert practitioners as the driving force behind the work. It is time to leave the DIY ethos behind and to squeeze more out of the research we are doing. If we can accomplish this then the fear that this will be too time-consuming and expensive will be easily allayed. Fundamentally, radical human-centric research provides a window into the real world and how real people live their lives that is richer and more capable of answering the kind of questions keeping designers up at night. It helps to answer the difficult questions like why we should design for them at all, how we can provide an experience that is better than the solutions they have now, and how we can differentiate our product, service, or experience from all of the MVP-led options that exist already. By being more connected to real life, radical human-centric research practices are ultimately cheaper, quicker, and more actionable than methodologies pulled from market research or design thinking. Insights produced through radically human-centric research are also easier to connect within an organization. A single study can answer more questions than those developed in lighter, thinner research and speak to more stakeholders within an organization. And because real research within the radical human-centric approach connects the past, present, and future, the insights will have a longer shelf life and will be easier to incorporate into longer-term strategic planning, thus connecting design to the problems facing the entire organization. Finally, more rigorously developed insights are testable and help to build a basis of knowledge, rather than provide a fleeting glimpse of something before being replaced by the next thin study.

A commitment to radical human-centricity is a commitment to all people, including those in your organization and your customers, or client. It involves a decision to work with people in the real world and to stop trying to exploit them for your own gains. It is also the only way to escape the cycle of mediocrity that is strategically damaging, financially wasteful, ethically dubious, and ecologically unsound. Radical human-centricity provides a new way of being in the world that is actually capable of transforming the relationship between companies and their customers through the development of products, services, and experiences that are sustainable and transformative in themselves. It can even be a way to introduce more advanced design principles, like subtractive design, into a world already saturated with quick, and easy commercial products. Ultimately, it is a covenant with your customers to be better and to try to improve everyone's lives with what matters more than a quick buck.

What is the book you have in your hands?

This book is not a business book. It will not be possible to find easy answers or frameworks that can be readily applied to existing practices. Rather, it is something between a call to action and a how-to manual. Each chapter will take a problem with human-centricity and turn it into something more through a thorough investigation of what will make things better and more productive. But the book is divided into three parts. The chapters in the first section provide a critique of current practice in commercial with an eye to improving the current state of affairs. Chapter 1 outlines the need for real research and explains what this can be. It explores the current thinking in anthropology and sociology, the two disciplines that invented and developed ethnography in the first place. Chapter 2 highlights the need to reclaim ethnography for real human-centric research. It also continues the critique of many existing practices in older, weaker commercial research practices. Chapter 3 explores the other shifts we need to make in order to realize a radically human-centric research approach. It provides a strong critique of the moribund practices in market research and outlines the tools and methods capable of being real research. Then it explores the problems of bias in rich qualitative practices and how to work it out throughout the design process.

In the second section, I explore the methods, practices, and ways of thinking that can immediately improve any research practice and make it radically human-centric. Chapter 4 looks past empathy as a goal toward the kind of things we should be concerned with when we study people and their activities. Chapter 5 explores the way we write about people and how we can push insights beyond the simple observations that usually pass for human-centered observations. It offers an argument on how to incorporate thick description into a design and development process more used to easy, tactical descriptions of humans and their behaviors. Chapter 6 provides a detailed reconfiguration of the standard working process for human-centric design and applied commercial research. This includes examples of how researchers, designers, and strategists need to change the way they think about people in order to get the most out of this new format of research.

The third section is devoted to showing how these alterations change a research program, and how to manifest them at each step. This section outlines the flow of a typical innovation research project and identifies where the RHC modifications can be made and why they are important.

The best way to read this book is with a skeptical mind—itself a key mindset in the radical human-centric approach. I hope that you will fight the arguments made in this book and try to find a way to make them work for you. Read a chapter at a time and look for things you agree and disagree with. Then try to figure out how what is presented here is equally true and functional as what you have found will work. You will find your way by resolving the tension between what you feel to be true, and the truths expressed in each chapter. The radical human-centric approach is a model for being in the world. It is not just a set of tools and practices. The intention here is for you to learn the skill of resolving this tension, because it is exactly that action that is the core of understanding the way other people live their lives.

Notes

1 The true revolution in business and technological change is not in its problem solving, but in the ability to bring scale to actions that have been around for a long time. The current partnership of technology and business is optimized to take something humans have always done and make it faster, cleaner, easier, work across larger distances, or include more people. We are not living in a technology revolution, we are living in time where action at scale is the focus. Technology is only the facilitator of this scaling.

2 This is actually what goes on during the process known as "disruption." It is money, not ideas that drive this ritual of technological advancement and growth-based capitalism.

Part I
THE CRITIQUE

Chapter 1

THE NEED FOR REAL RESEARCH

Our radical take on human-centric research starts with an acknowledgment that there are no shortcuts. Real research is hard, and often what may appear to be good research now actually has fundamental flaws. Once we admit this, we can begin our pursuit of a true human-centric approach to research by making a commitment to real human-centric research. But before we dig into what constitutes real research, we have to first explore what is wrong with commercial research today, in both it is market research and design research variations.

Not too long ago, I went to Shanghai to assist a research team from a small strategy and innovation firm on a project for a major Japanese Camera manufacturer.[1] It was a difficult trip. I had just decided to resign from my post at my agency because I had realized I was uncomfortable with their approach to research. When I was being hired, they had claimed they worked within an anthropological model and that they were devoted to the tenants of real research. Instead, they were using what I can only call basic consulting research—traditional market research and design research approaches made to look like anthropologically inspired practice. While they claim they were human-centric, they were not. And I had decided to leave to get back to real research.

As I got on the flight to Shanghai, I reflected on why this project would not work out for the client. Most of the problem was rooted in a failure of research methodology and practice. The partners at this agency were forcing me to go on this trip to oversee a series of focus groups, complete with a moderator, translator, mirror-lined room, and a gallery of clients. I was told to "bring some anthropological flash" to the proceedings. There was little about the research plan that struck me as good research, let alone anthropological. As an anthropologist committed to only doing useful, rigorous research, the idea of running a set of focus groups was already making worry. I have worked in innovation research for over a decade, and this was going to be my first one. Mostly this is because focus groups are not meant to be used in the discovery phase of any innovation work.

They are a remnant of a bygone age. Using my credentials and presence to justify what I thought was a bad research plan, was just making it even worse for me. But I went to do my duty. What I saw was one of the most appalling spectacles I have ever witnessed, and it made me realize that there needs to be a revolution to replace market research, and its design thinking variants, with real research. It made me realize I had actually participated in the first step of this grand rethink at my first agency, Idea Couture, and my approach to research was drastically different from what is commonly done in commercial research.

My career as an innovation researcher began in the aftermath of the 2008 downturn. It was the waning days of my Ph.D. education, and I was beginning to realize I was not going to be a professor of anthropology or ethnomusicology (my area discipline at the time). My training and topic were too niche, and my timing was too unlucky. The banking crisis in 2008 had sucked the money out of university coffers, so jobs were few and far between. Most places were furloughing tenured professors, and the year I left school, there were exactly zero job openings in my discipline. Realizing it would be almost impossible to be a professor four or five years after graduating, I started thinking about where I could be a practicing anthropologist and do something that would be more meaningful than picking up a few adjunct courses at the local university. I had always been interested in design, and so my career as a design anthropologist quite literally began with a google search for "design and ethnography." What I found in that list of results was so exciting, I am, over a decade later, still thrilled every day. The first few hits were websites related to Ideo and design thinking. The next few were the websites of a few companies that touted ethnography and anthropology as specialties. One of these was Idea Couture in Toronto.

A few emails, resumes, and cover letters later, and I found myself in Toronto in front of Dr. Morgan Gerard, the chief resident anthropologist at Idea Couture. I now realize I was very lucky to be sitting there with Morgan, because almost anyone else might have sent me packing. But about halfway through our conversation, I looked at him and asked, "do you believe all of this business stuff?"

He stopped talking, looked me straight in the eyes for a few seconds, and said, "well, all of this business stuff is actually some serious stuff covered in a layer of bullshit. So, no. Of course I don't believe it, but I do believe we can help them be better."

I walked out of that meeting with a job and soon found myself trying to learn business culture and the design thinking culture all while trying to suppress my instincts as an anthropologist with academic training. What struck me immediately was the vast gulf between the kind of research I knew how to do and the kind of research those in business expected me to do. The former is about knowledge, and you take your time to get it right. Business research, on the other hand, is about nick-of-time foundations. Everything is quick. Everything is lean. Everything is expected to be delivered without complications or pretensions. And it can often be mostly bullshit, as Morgan said.

I saw that research for a business context is a collection of research practices that are convenient and efficient but are not really that good at creating knowledge or understanding. Business research is really more about ritualizing an engagement with "the customer," and generating some data points before one gets on with the work of being a businessperson—with the strategy, synergy, leadership, decision making, and so forth. Market research, the principal form of business research, is built around this principle. What we were doing at Idea Couture, under Morgan's guidance, was something altogether different. We were doing real research on behalf of commercial clients.

Idea Couture was almost unique in that its insights researchers were almost exclusively anthropologists. As a team of nearly 20 researchers, we spent nearly a decade developing ways of doing commercial research in an anthropological way. This set us apart from the majority of practitioners in the insights game who were still working in older formats and within the business-friendly methods of market research. This background made my transition to a different company after the sale of Idea Couture to a global IT outsourcing giant extremely difficult. I had to find a new job outside of the world of real research we had built at Idea Couture.

This meant I spent my time between leaving Idea Couture and founding the Human Futures Studio, experiencing a more traditional approach to research. I learned how the majority of research projects are executed in commercial research and just how far this was from real research. My new employers and their staff would write a proposal with promises of human-centered research rooted in market research methods and then run a program of focus groups run by freelancers or people with little research training, and no anthropological background. The approach to research I witnessed at this firm, and that day in Shanghai, is mostly standard practice for most of the so-called human-centric innovation research executed today. However, it was a shock for me. It was not what I did at Idea Couture, and it is a long way from how we run projects at the Human Futures Studio. At the time, I was only waking up to why it is a problem. I could feel there was a problem. Seeing the usual practices in action made me committed to making a drastic change in commercial research.

The project for the Japanese camera giant was troubled from the beginning, from the moment of its instigation. The entire process began with a problematic research brief written by a well-meaning gentleman whose 15-year career as a market researcher led him to believe there was nothing wrong with the usual approach to research. Objectively, it was a typical request from a company used to market research and only just beginning their journey down the path leading to design thinking. This Japanese camera giant wanted to run a set of focus groups and build a set of design personas to help them stop the loss of market share in Asia to Sony. You can see the problems lurking in this request immediately.

First of all, they asked for a process (focus groups) and did not begin with a research question. Then they asked for a deliverable format (design personas) without considering if personas are the right format for insights about camera uses. Design personas were certainly the wrong format for delivering the kind of answers they needed to understand why Sony is eroding its business. Next, it would be unlikely they could simply design their way out of what is essentially an enterprise-level question. Design is only one input to market share problems. Fourth, focus groups are the worst format to gather any of this information and connect these dots. Design personas require contextual knowledge. Strategic questions require market-level knowledge. A focus group yields neither. One partner at my firm had structured the research response improperly, and no one saw these problems in time to do anything about it. So, as I got off of the plane on that sweltering day in July 2018, I knew I was headed into a disastrous situation where I could do very little to help.

I do not speak Mandarin, which meant I was unable to run the research myself. That alone should have precluded me from being there. However, in commercial practice, it seems it is not a problem for the primary research to be unable to carry out the work. This work was to be run by a moderator who had not participated in the setup of the research and had very little power to change things. However, because I knew the moderator personally, she developed a plan to improve things. And we prepared for the day ready to make subtle changes to the entire process to make sure it was a better research plan than had been devised. However, our alterations were noticed and eliminated immediately. The work would carry on as originally planned. We would have three groups of five DSLR owners split into amateur, hobbyist, and quasi-professional groups (these were the client's categories). We would hold a two-hour conversation with each group of four photographers fitting the categories descriptions, during which we would complete two design thinking exercises intended to capture why they take photos, what they want out of a camera, and what drove them to take photos. Then we would travel to a camera market to do some "in-situ" investigation of the purchasing process. A keen observer would notice that at no time would we be taking photographs or actually going to see what they do when they take photos—the centerpiece of their hobby. Instead, we would be sitting behind a mirror and listening to people talk about why they take photographs and watching them complete a few written exercises in silence. Which, for the next 10 hours we did.

The sessions were built around the basic focus group format. They were carefully structured according to a discussion guide. This meant they were all the same and were easily comparable. However, the questions were not working, and the participants were clearly bored throughout most of the conversations. They also looked a bit trapped. Sitting in a badly lit facility and listening to other participants answer questions is not a great way to spend a day. But we could not change the questions because they had been reworked by the senior market research on the client's team. He insisted we stick to the rigid format provided by focus groups and would not make any changes to the discussion guide to preserve the "objectivity and comparability of the findings." So, instead of being flexible and correcting what was clearly not working, he sat in the dark, behind the mirror taking page after page of notes on people's awkward answers and digressions from the script. I was trapped myself, because I had to sit behind the mirror and support the note taker. But I felt horrible for the participants who had to endure this experience. The conversations continued at their slow pace, and we heard the same answers over and over again. But it was not just the big things that were bad. Many of the smaller moments showed me that a focus group is a horrible way to do research.

One important thing I noticed was the difference in the translators. We had one pair translating Mandarin to Japanese and another individual handling Mandarin to English for my benefit. I noticed that my translator was working harder than the Japanese translators. He was constantly correcting himself and adding context into his translation in order to help me understand the nuances. He probably was speaking twice as fast as the other translators in order to accommodate this extra information. So, right away, I found my client was at a disadvantage, lacking the extra pieces my translator was contributing to his narrative. This was confirmed in later discussions with the translators. The Mandarin to Japanese translators were just translating the dialogue. This meant the intensity and diligence my client put into his note-taking would not be able to compensate for the fact that his translators were not giving him very much information about what was happening in the setting. His data was compromised from the very beginning. This problem played a big part in our discussions later when he was unable to understand why a potential insight into Chinese visual culture was relevant to amateur photography.

Next, the gamified co-creation exercises failed. Two hours in a room with five strangers where one of them is trying to keep a stilted and strained conversation running is a long time. Sometimes it is just easier to have everyone draw some pictures on a piece of paper. And this is a very common feature of the design thinking variations of focus groups. In my experience, gamified exercises are fun, but rarely yield the kinds of insights a client needs. It is better to talk or simply hang out with them for a while— activities that are generally more efficient and insightful. These artificial "data gathering" practices in problematic environments are really just a way to kill time. They are often poorly conceived mechanizations of basic analytical procedures. In this setting, the client insisted we have them force rank (an exercise where participants have to assign a relational value to a list of options) several predetermined "photographic values" like "beauty," or "capture the moment." These were intended to help them understand which persona people should be in and what their core need was. While these games helped assign people to their persona, they did little to explain why, or to productively challenge the thinking behind the client's categorization. Given that they wanted to know why people in China were not buying their cameras, it was odd that the exercises did not challenge their status quo.

Once back at the office in Helsinki, I worked with another team member to make sense of what little we had collected in Shanghai, Japan, and the United States. We developed a set of insights that paired aesthetic norms and cultural differences to develop a contextual baseline for how people hunt for the perfect photograph. We then connected this to the feature conversations in order to develop a systematic view of how feature priority mapped onto the hunt for good photographs. We built the personas around this, emphasizing an if this, then that format for the designers. We put all of this into a PowerPoint deck and passed it to the partner who would pass it on to the client. We thought we had nailed it. We were naturally surprised when we were told the senior market researcher did not like our work because it did not connect simple demographic data to the three categories he had devised earlier, amateur, hobbyist, and quasi-professional. He was unhappy we had disproven his hypotheses and changed the definitional criteria for the personas. Our partner did not like the deck either because it was too insight-focused and not "market research-y enough." He was annoyed we had pointed to why their current camera portfolio was underperforming and not just developed the personas so they would feel more comfortable about their current practices. We had managed to create a set of insights to meet the brief but had failed to consider that no one cared about any of that. In the end, this was just a market research project designed to create abstract categories speaking only to a formalized business requirement. It was supposed to add data to a set of predetermined results.

This was supposed to be the company's first attempt at "human-centric" research. The project was designed, commissioned, built, and sold as a human-centric approach to customer research. Compared to how this Japanese camera manufacturer worked in the past, it is possible this was more human-centric, but like many commercial practices claiming to be focused on the human aspects of life, it was nothing of the sort. It shows how human-centric research needs to be pulled out of the past and away from market research and the gimmicks of design thinking, to actually be useful research.

Toward Real Research

The only real answer to this failure is to incorporate real research into commercial practice. I use the word "real research" to show that thoughtful research grounded in lived reality is a world away from the arbitrary traditions and practices common in conventional human-centric research, UX research taken out of its setting and bend to a new purpose, and traditional market research. It is "real" research because the focus is the real world and real people, not the convenient quantified or universalized placeholders studied in these more established commercial research approaches.[2] It is also real research because it avoids all the mistakes I observed in Shanghai and in other facilities and interview situations during my career as an innovation researcher.

To understand the difference between real research and this moribund approach, we must begin by seeing most commercial, human-focused, behavioral research as compromised research. Even though it is conducted with good intentions, there are many ideological, methodological, and ethical failures inherent in its current form. It will be necessary to work to replace it with better research practices, especially those working against the dehumanizing aspects of conventional commercial practice. But we must become aware of its shortcomings and its troubling effects. Conventional, market research-based work creates a false sense of security, where business decisions and design ideas do not have an impact on people, the environment, and society. It fails in this new environment because current commercial research practices in market research and design research are conducted using antiquated tools and methods. It is bad because many of the practitioners are not trained in the theories and nuances of good research, potentially turning a well-intentioned project into an ineffectual attempt. It is bad because little of the research done in commercial settings is actually human-centric or able to describe human behavior in realistic terms. A truly human-centric alternative is able to present the world as it is, in its richness and its messiness, and place innovators, business leaders, engineers, and designers in a position to work within the possibilities and limitations of this world. Real research connects people, whereas conventional practices seek to keep them at arm's length.

With this in mind, what is real research? Simply put, real research is a careful, rigorous, ethical, well-executed investigation of something in the world. Within the context of applied human-centric research, real research is a philosophy, a methodology, a value system, an educational system, a genre of communication, and a way for researchers to be in the world, all devoted to understanding human action, thought, belief, and feelings. As a philosophy, it should be based on rigorous, theoretically balanced epistemological principles that consider human experience, relativistic models of knowledge, and systems dynamics. As a methodology, it should combine the best practices from anthropology, sociology, cognitive anthropology, behavioral economics, and social psychology. In this regard, it should be a carefully considered form of ethnography, unrestrained by the damaging snobbishness and prejudices toward careful research, common in commercial settings, constraining careful, accretive research. As a value system, real research is an ethical practice that requires researchers to be honest, sensitive, vulnerable, and dogged in their pursuit of the truth.[3] As an educational system, real research should take on the best pedagogical methods to ensure that the knowledge it generates is accepted and learned by the audiences it addresses. Researchers should also understand how to use every media resource and channel available to communicate the results of the study. Sometimes writing is not sufficient, so real research practitioners need to also be able to turn to videos, computer game environments, and emojis to get the point across. Finally, real research requires a lot from those that practice it. Researchers must be curious, tireless, skeptical, and reflective in order to be able to do what is right, even when what is easy would be quicker and simpler.

Real research, in a human-centric context, must be grounded in an ethnographic practice (philosophy, theory, and method) that does not compromise its practice or ethics in order to deliver the results for its commissioning audience while protecting and respecting the people whose lives are the focus of the study. It is human-centric, in that it puts humans at the center of everything. It is not aligned with the buzzword version of "human-centricity" currently in use in the tech and business worlds. It needs to be ethnographic, because this is the only methodology that is capable of connecting design and business thinking to the real, lived experience of daily life. Ethnography is the most empirical human-centered method because it is conducted in the world of the people we are trying to understand. One has to be there to see it, touch it, and feel it in order to report about it in an ethnographic report. However, for radical human-centricity to shine, we must redefine commercial research's understanding of ethnography—a concept that has been coopted by design thinking and rendered in an overly simplified form.

But what is wrong with market research and the design research carried out under the human-centricity rubric? This is a very large problem, because it is not necessarily the practitioners or the practices that are at fault. The problem with market research and design research lies first in the cultures in which they are practiced. I have already described what problematic research looks like in my extreme example from Shanghai. It is now necessary to make a more productive critique of the distance between conventional commercial research practices and real research. In making this critique, we need to work hard to separate the failures of the research culture from well-intentioned practitioners. It is essential that we "hate the sin and not the sinner." This is because the turn to real research is actually something everyone can do. Indeed, I'm arguing it is something we all *need* to do.

Real research begins with a commitment to do better, always. Committing to conducting real research must begin with an honest appraisal of what you have done in the past and a desire to constantly improve. This is a state of being. Real research requires the researcher to be in the world differently, primarily with a reflexive view of the world that allows oneself to see the causes and effects of your own behavior. What this requires is someone with a healthy skepticism, because everything must be questioned, from your own beliefs to the methods you use. By skepticism, I mean the ability to see that just because something has always been done a certain way does not mean it is the best way or even the right way to do it. Then one must also be optimistic enough to trust that a better way can be found. With this honesty, skepticism, and optimism, you are prepared to dig into researching people in a reflexive, human-centric way. And this means putting their truth on equal or greater footing than your own. Our job as researchers is to know a way of being from the insight out, not to seek exploitable details and capitalize on them. This probably means you need to add patience and bravery to the list of basic characteristics.

The Radically Human-Centric Version

I want to return to what I saw in Shanghai and demonstrate how a radically human-centric approach would be different. As I said before, this project was conceived improperly at every level. The research approach was inadequate to meet the goals the client needed to achieve. The client, a Japanese camera giant, asked for a set of focus groups to build a set of design personas to help them undo the loss of market share in DSLR cameras in Asia. As I noted above, they asked for the wrong things, and my employer gave them what they wanted rather than what they needed.

A radically human-centric approach to this situation involves understanding a business problem as the result of human thought and action. A loss of market share really comes down to people preferring to buy and use other companies' cameras. There are many reasons why this can happen, different features, cost, a change in how amateur photographers understand their hobby, poor marketing, or even just changes in fashion can cause people to be interested in new products and less interested in old ones. The job of a radically human-centric approach is to not make any assumptions, but to discover which of these issues, and in what proportion, are causing the loss of market share. This involves talking to people and exploring why they take photographs, and how they do it, which means we have to set up opportunities to explore all of these issues during our time speaking to people.

An RHC (Radical Human-Centric) approach begins with an assessment and deconstruction of the problem, so we can understand what we should be looking for in our customer immersions. Deconstructing and understanding the underlying issues should be one outcome of the work. To do this, we will first spend some time studying the history and current state of the erosion, the design changes to their camera portfolio over this time, and that of their competitors. This work will help us see what research tool to use and how comprehensive the study needs to be—which in turn helps us understand the scale and scope of our research program. We then build a set of hypotheses to test with people who use these cameras and a set of key questions that need to be answered. In this instance, the portfolio was somewhat out of date, and their competitors were adding new features and making their cameras cheaper. It is possible our client's approach to UI is creating frictions, or their product portfolio has failed to capture a key element of new features or UI expectations. We need to explore why their competitors' cameras are more interesting and set ourselves up to discover how they fit into people's experiences taking photos. And we need to do this to uncover opportunities to design a solution based on a new perspective into the inner workings of hobbyist photographers.

The research format used for this project should have been focused on collecting open responses and experiential learning. The RHC approach would be designed around a participant observation method, where the researchers would meet with these amateur photographers and go out with them on their usual photography outings. This would help understand how they take pictures, why, and what they expect from their equipment, all while being able to watch them actually work with their equipment. While we are taking photos and talking about the joys of their hobby, we could also discuss what they look for in a new camera, what new equipment they have their eye on, and what they expect from new products. All of this would take place out in the world, while taking photos, and not in a dingy room in an office block.

Finally, the analysis would be organized to distill the details we glean from their actual practice of taking pictures, thoughts about equipment, purchasing decisions, and the reasons why they take photographs in the first place, into an honest assessment of what hobbyist photographers look for in a camera and what they want it to do for them. Since people naturally differ in their thoughts and reasons for doing something, we would compare their similarities and differences to develop a set of profiles that illuminate these divisions. These profiles would work better than personas because they are based on the reality of the situation and not on answers to predefined questions in a focus group discussion guide. Once this is accomplished, and all the hypotheses have been tested and the questions answered, we can then use these profiles to analyze the client's current portfolio of products, UI (user interface on the cameras), features, and services. This will help them understand what needs to change to provide for their customers better and thus make a case to them that their cameras are worth buying over the competitions.

Unlike my experience in Shanghai, this format would allow us to understand the lives and world of these photographers as it is. We would build the entire perspective from the details of their thoughts and actions. We would do this in their language with minimal fuss and allow them to lead us to the answers rather than prefiguring everything beforehand. It is also likely that everyone would have a better time.

Radical human-centricity is not complicated, but it involves rethinking many of the established practices in an industry that needs to control the conditions of research for its own benefit. Making this shift is challenging, but valuable. There is a world out there to discover, but we have to start with the human beings that shape it and avoid seeing everyone as customers or users.

The rest of this book is an exploration of the details of how all of this is accomplished and an identification of the areas in conventional commercial research that need to change to achieve a truly human-centric approach. But before I begin to describe some of the more practical concerns about how to make the radically human-centric alterations to commercial research, I want to first work through the theoretical considerations of why we need a new approach to human-centricity. I believe that we should always think first and act afterward. This means theory first, application second. I also believe business is not theoretical enough. If ethical or practical problems were considered before people acted, we would not need a book like this trying to argue for a correction to human-centric approaches—something which should have been a wonderful thing in the first place. So, first I will outline what I see as some major theoretical steps forward for human-centric research.

Following this, we will turn to the practical aspects of real research, from setting up a research exploration, through conducting the work, to writing it up and telling others about what we found. What will become immediately clear is how real research does not differ from weaker varieties in the broad strokes. Instead, the importance, and shift, of real research is found in the details and in the reflexive mode taken on by the researcher. Many of these alterations are small, but they are all powerful. Together they make a profound difference and elevate methods simple enough that anyone can do them into some of the most powerful tools available. These alterations shift everything, from basic conversation techniques to sophisticated analytical methods—even quantitative methods.

Notes

1　I am not going to *name names* right now because I do not feel the negativity is productive. The problems I am highlighting here are endemic in the entire commercial research system, and so singling out companies, consultancies, and individuals is putting the blame on people and not on the entire system itself.

2　I say placeholders because many of these practices are deliberately designed to simplify the messiness of real life and transform individual humans, and groups of people, into entities that can be more easily managed within the commercial context. Personas, segments, and idealized users are much less complicated, and working with these highly processed "people" makes life easier for everyone in a company. This is not a good thing, but it is a honest assessment of how people are "managed" in even the most human-centric study for corporate clients and many NGOs.

3　You will notice I did not say "empathetic." The full set of reasons for this is discussed at length in Chapter 4, but I will give you a quick overview to save you the trouble of skipping to it right now. Empathy is, and can be, only the first step in a human-centric approach. Emotions are not sufficient phenomena to ground knowledge in an innovation context, and so it is odd that everyone involved in design thinking has not realized empathy can only be a step in a much more rigorous process.

Chapter 2

RECLAIMING ETHNOGRAPHY

Real research is engaged with the world in the most direct, experiential way. It is conducted alongside the people we study, on their terms, and deals with this world as it is, without tools to simplify what is found.[1] There is no room for "good enough." There are no compromises, gimmicks, or shortcuts. A researcher doing real research is in the thick of things, working at the point where the line blurs between research and just living life. When studying people, their behaviors, and their thoughts, researchers live life with them. They eat their food, speak their language, dance their dances, shop in their stores, use their smartphone apps, and live as they do. Here, the researcher is also always thinking about their audience and how to explain the meaning and impact of these experiences to people who did not have the luck to be there in the thick of it all with them. What this means is that within a commercial context, real research begins with an ethnography inquiry. This is true even if it ends with a quantitative study.

To understand real research and working in a radically human-centric manner, we must come to terms with what it means to do ethnography. However, this is not as easy as it sounds. For many years, ethnography has been borrowed—a stronger way to put it would be appropriated—by design research and design thinking. This has not been good for ethnography because the practice and tradition have not been respected. The weaknesses inherent in these research processes have been covered by claims of the power of the anthropological approaches and ethnographic methods they try to employ. Few practitioners who claim to be proficient in ethnography have any substantive training. Few commercial researchers are actually doing ethnography. At most, they are using a very watered-down variation. In short, the human-centric research and design research world still do not really know what ethnography is. So, to explain the ethnographic underpinnings of real research, we must first cut through some hype and misinformation and claim the practice back for human-centric research. Once we understand a little bit about ethnography, we will be able to see how it provides the framework for real research and a better approach to human-centric innovation.

Understanding Ethnography

Ethnography is more than a method, and it certainly is not just interviewing people or UX observations during home visits. Anthropologists call it "a way of being in the world." And while this sounds like a zen koan, it is actually quite simple. If you want to understand how people do something, why they do it, and what is involved in doing it, do it alongside them. This is the only path to understanding. This is true when you want to understand how to conduct a religious ceremony, how to play a game, and how people make consumer decisions in the middle of a supermarket. The ethnographic principle of being in the world is the first commitment to real research and in radical human-centricity. Go out. Explore. See the world. It's as simple as that.

Applied ethnography, which includes commercial research, is a more complicated thing than pure ethnographic research. It is often assumed that applied work, especially commercial research is easier or simpler to execute. It is actually *more* complicated because it is ethnography at its most lean and utilitarian. It is less forgiving and there is little room for error. Instead of attempting to understand as much as possible about a particular context and people, applied ethnography is a more limited, goal-oriented affair, where the researcher is trying to answer a specific question for an even more specific reason. Applied ethnography has clearly establish limits of time. It is commissioned to achieve a particular task or answer specific questions. It studies the whole in order to explain a small part. It is also intended to engender change in an audience that does not go to field with you. Unlike its more open cousin, applied ethnography has to connect this audience with what was learned as quickly and effortlessly as possible. This means the stakes are higher for applied ethnography than for many kinds of pure ethnography, where time and the difficulty of the audience are less pressing concerns. It is strange that ethnography has become a smaller, less powerful too in the hands of commercial practitioners. It is perhaps because of not having the training; they do not fully understand the implications of what they are doing.

This opens an important point for us to consider, ethnography is a much larger concept than what most people involved in commercial research believe. Doing ethnography is not just about interviews. It is not just doing in-home immersions. It is not just a set of data gathering and management practices. It does not contain a single analytical procedure. And it is not a single communicative medium or genre of writing. No. Ethnography is a complete approach to being in the world and coming to terms with what one sees, while also doing all of those other, more social things. This means it is everything I just listed and more—much more. Ultimately, ethnography is about understanding a particular context as completely as possible, understanding how people behave in this context, and then being able to function in that space as an insider would. This means the task is huge. Technically an entire commercial project examining people's behavior and designing something is ethnography. Everything in a design thinking process, agile design, or product roll-out is part of the ethnographic effort. The product launch itself is not the end of a process, but the middle of the ethnographic engagement. Design and strategy are really about operating in a world one should already know a great deal about. This reversal of emphasis away from design and business strategy towards using ethnography to engage with people is one of the first steps in using a Radical Human-Centric approach to commercial research. We will get to the practical implications of "being in the world" shortly, but first let's have a quick word about just what ethnography is, and what it actually means.

Ethnography: Writing About People

I have found the misconceptions about ethnography in commercial research are due to a general lack of understanding of its history, its purpose, and its various forms. Many researchers in commercial and design research roles even use the word ethnography without even knowing what it actually means. And this is revealing because "ethnography" does not even mention interviews, deep-dives, or shop-alongs. Even just understanding what it means would reorient people away from the weak version common to conventional human-centric and design research.

The term Ethnography has two words in it. They break down into "ethno" and "graphy." The first half comes from *ethnos* (ἔθνος), meaning a group of people or a nation, while the second half is *graphy* the English suffix rooted in the Latin *graphia* (itself transliterated from the Greek γράφω) meaning writing. This means the true definition of ethnography is so far from interviewing it does not even reference talking. It literally means writing about people.

ethno		graphy
	[analysis]	
people	interpretation	writing

In practice, much of what ethnography is sits between the two terms "ethno" and "graphy." There is an implied analytical component, making ethnography a practice of understanding the details of other's socio-cultural experience and explaining that to another group of people who were not there with you. Therefore, it is actually an act of double translation, where the researcher learns and translates what they have learned for themselves and then retranslates that knowledge for a wider audience who were not able to participate in the study. What this means is that ethnography is as much about communicating something as it is about studying it and learning it. A poorly communicated ethnographic insight is not very useful and is almost worse than a badly researched one. This is true whether it is the high-grade professionalized version of ethnography or the amateur variety. The difference between these two lies in how these translations are performed and how successful they are.

What this means then, is that there are actually three basic actions in ethnography: learning about the world of another person, understanding this for yourself, and then explaining it to someone else. A quick, business-friendly version of this might go like this: observe, analyze, explain. Each of these phases requires a researcher to have a deep knowledge of the possible methods and procedures needed to complete them and the skill to use each one well when necessary. A weakness in any one of these categories can damage the success of an ethnographic study. Consequently, any ethnographic research requires a well-trained, professional researcher—a fact that is a long way from the DIY ethos of the design thinking world. But it is worth it. Any true human-centered research will depend on ethnography for most of its insights into human beings. The quality of the ethnography determines the quality of everything that follows—you cannot build quality products on the understanding provided by terrible ethnography. As we say in innovation consulting, "shit in, shit out." The implications of this are clear, the ethnographic encounter must be carefully planned and skillfully executed to ensure the success of the entire project.

ethno		*graphy*
	[analysis]	
people	interpretation	writing
Observation	Analysis	Communication

Practically speaking, applied ethnographic research has three basic phases, observation, analysis, and communication. They closely follow the three actions of any ethnographer: learning, understanding, and explaining. However, while considering what I just said, these three phases cover everything found in the standard innovation process from commercial innovation. All of the commercial frameworks, like the one from design thinking, fit into this three-part process. You can see how the various ways to break this down in the design research literature "observe, generate, activate;" "*empathise, define, ideate, prototype, and test;*"[2] and "*frame a question, gather inspiration, generate ideas, make ideas tangible, test to learn, share the story*"[3] all share the same basic outline.

Regardless of how you parse these phases, the ethnographic versions span every one of these processes. "Empathise," "frame a question," and "gather inspiration" are all aspects of the learning through observation in the ethnographic procedure. Then when it is time to analyze what you have learned, "generating ideas," and "defining" are part of the insights development process. Then all of the "ideating," "prototyping," "making ideas tangible," and "sharing the story" are all about the final act of explanation, getting what you've learned out to others so they may benefit from it. The only parts that do not neatly match the ethnographic process flow are the final testing phases in the true design thinking model. But if you understand ethnography as a continuous process that never stops, reengaging with the field is common and necessary. Therefore, going back to ask questions and making sure that you have it right, is both good manners and good practice.

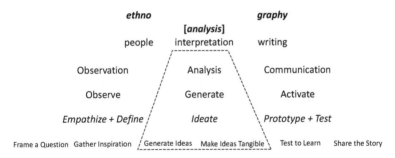

Technically, the entire design thinking method neatly fits into the applied ethnography format—even the prototyping and testing. It fits so well, that it might be better to see design thinking as a subset of ethnographic practice and not the other way around. Ethnography does not have to be an independent process relegated to a single phase. It can provide the backing for the entire process—something which would be an immediate shift towards fulfilling the human-centric promises. Designing is closely related, if not an extension of, of the analysis and communication processes in ethnography, the most human of empirical methodologies. For ethnography to take its rightful place in a radical human-centricity, it needs to be seen as the overarching research approach. But to do this, we have to first overcome the false belief in business thought that ethnography is subjective and therefore suspect.

What Being There Means: Empiricism, Subjectivity, and Objectivity

It was the anthropologist Clifford Geertz who coined the term "being there." He did so to identify the primary way in which knowledge is created in human-focused research. He also pointed out "being there" is essentially the only way to guarantee the empiricism of a study.[4] His point is that direct experience is the foundation of any ethnographic study, and it ultimately trumps any other method. However, it comes with a problem; in "being there" one can end up being too close and losing the objectivity of the moment. Anthropologists have struggled with this since the first of us conducted real ethnography. Many contemporary ethnographic methods are devoted to overcoming the problems with slipping off the knife's edge and into a world of biased subjectivity.

The risk is more than overcome by the gains. Direct experience is still the only way to "know" anything about how other people live. It is empirical in its fullest meaning. And this is one of the important changes brought about by human-centric approaches. But the training designers and other nonacademic human-centered researchers receive is lacking the tools and methods to mitigate the problems of "being there" and preserve the empiricism. Ethnography requires total effort from the initiation of the project to the final presentation. To understand the experience of others you have to throw your whole self in. You must experience it firsthand. You must learn to think as they do. This is not possible in a few two-hour interviews. This requires you to devote your whole self to a process of *participant observation*.

What is great about this is that it also means a skilled ethnographer is the best piece of equipment available in the ethnographic process. Because ethnography is empirical and studies the details of lived experience, it is messy. Ethnography is fun. It is uncomfortable. It is hot. It is cold. It is smelly and unpleasant. It is filled with light and color. It is sometimes quiet, yet often loud and boisterous. As an ethnographer, you need to be able to use every sense available to you to learn. You must experience everything. The human experience is not something that is communicated over a table in a qualitative research facility or over a video chat. It is experienced by dancing, sweating, driving, eating, laughing, gossiping, and even napping. What this means is that to be human-centric, it is necessary to actually be human, and not some form of organic-based research robot programmed to conduct a deep dive into customer needs. Naysayers will argue that it is too expensive and out of scope to do anything more than a quick, tactical exploration. But to answer real questions, like how a product or a service will be used by real people in their real lives, it is necessary to actually understand as much as you can. Even in a short amount of time, real ethnography can provide answers to more questions than any quick, tactical piece of market research. Being in the world is the only way to understand how others live in the world.

This is important because the way they are in the world explains how their experience of it colors their understanding.[5] Yes, people of different cultures and societies can share the same spaces. But it is likely their culture has organized their experience differently—meaning that they create knowledge differently, they "see" differently, and they expect different things from people and the nonhuman world around them. We study experience through experience because it is the best window into how culture and social constructs color knowledge, and how this makes people behave according to different logics. These experiential differences are what contextualize and situate behavioral observations. Unless we can understand how someone's experience is similar or different from our own, we cannot hope to explain anything about what they do or say to anyone else.

In one RHC study, I conducted several years ago, we were working to understand the experience of patients with chronic conditions treated by advanced biologic medications. We were exploring the experience of rheumatoid arthritis and how biologic medications, delivered through subcutaneous injection, changed the experience of their body, disease, and treatments. One key aspect of this study was pain. And although this is a common feature of many healthcare studies, we took an RHC approach to understand pain through an experiential lens. We decided to not prefigure the terms we were using to see how people would describe their pain. We allowed them to try to convey their experience of both the disease and the injection. What we found was that people in different countries and even in different socio-economic brackets used very different terminologies when describing pain but tried to convey a similar experience. Some said their hands "hurt," and that the injection "smarted." Others describe the pain in their joints as it as "unendurable throbbing" and the injection experience as something "burning like lava in my veins." Pain is a notoriously difficult concept to measure objectively because it is grounded entirely in a bodily experience which cannot be shared. One person's description might be idiosyncratic and tied more to their intention in communicating something rather than their actual experience. These individuals might have been trying to downplay or emphasize the nature of their suffering for effect. However, once we began to spend some more time with these individuals, and get different descriptions of the same experience from them, we were able to bring all of this together into an insight to explain some of the discrepancies.

What we noticed were that there were several countries where it was more common for people to use hyperbolic language to express pain (the United States, Italy, Israel), and those where people consistently chose more muted language (United Kingdom, Denmark). What we had encountered was a roughly shared experience with a different way to express pain. We took these findings back to our respondents and they agreed that the difference in the intensity of expression was likely due to cultural differences in how pain is expressed. Once this was acknowledged by everyone, we were able to dig past these cultural structures and get closer to the lived, idiosyncratic experiences. What made this a radically human-centric approach was we avoided pushing our assumptions onto our new friends. We let them speak for themselves. We spent the time to keep delving into their experience. And we returned to them with our findings to let them reassess their own experiences and reconsider how they talked to us. We were able to let their experience guide our understanding, and then let our experience guide them. We were able to uncover a real insight by digging into how experience is expressed, how culture structures both the experience of pain and how the behavioral rules about the appropriate expression of this pain govern what they say.

Studying experience and behavior together, instead of just studying behavior, gives you access to a set of explanations of why people do the things they do. Studying behavior without experience is studying effect without a cause. It is like trying to understand a goal in football (soccer) without any understanding of the rules of the game or the events leading up to it. When you understand how someone else experiences the world, the way they behave can be seen as a direct, logical action within a set of possibilities. A researcher who has come to understand some of the experiential details surrounding a particular action can explain why someone does something, and in extreme cases, predict what they will do. Only real ethnography can get you there.

As I said earlier, real ethnography is an entire constellation of practices, tools, methods, traditions, and philosophies. There are many things an ethnographer does that help to make sense of theirs, and others', experiences in field. I want to focus on a few areas where commercial, human-centered research has coopted or distorted several of the key actions in ethnography and make some recommendations about how we can improve them. Here I am effectively outlining the sub-practices of a radically human-centric ethnographic practice. I will deal with these as a set of suggestions for better practice or a shift from one way of thinking or doing to another. I will cover interview techniques, data capture, scaling a project, recruiting, the role of specialist researchers, and fieldwork ethics.

Interviews ≠ Asking Questions to Gather Data

Interviewing is an important part of the ethnographic process. In anthropology and anthropologically inflected fields, we are trained in a wide range of interview techniques, many of which are quite different from the others. Different research questions and different outcomes require drastically different approaches to interviews. In fact, there is little in common between a socio-cultural linguistic interview and an ethnomusicological one trying to understand how alterity is manifested in listening to technical death metal. Both are anthropological interviews. Both are part of ethnographic studies. But they are not the same because the outcomes require different approaches with different emphases. One requires knowledge of the language and the underlying structure of human communication. The other requires a deep knowledge of music and listenership. The interviews, consequently, focus on very different things and record drastically different data. So, to make the necessary corrections to human-centric processes, one needs to appreciate that there are *many* interview methods in an ethnographic interview. There is not just one. Here, we return to the idea of real research bringing flexibility and many more methodological options into the mix. We also see, again, why a trained specialist is so necessary. One needs to know all the available options to select the best tool for the job.

It is not necessary to explore all of the possible options here. There are many excellent books on field techniques and interview methods.[6] Nevertheless, it is important that we explore at least one example of how interview methods typical in market research and human-centric design are inadequate for the task. One key example comes from what one should do in studies where a person's experience needs to be a central focus of the study. This kind of study is typical when understanding how different disease states affect a person's ability to take medicine or use a medical device. It is also important when looking for new opportunities to design a technologically mediated alternative to a common task (read: a new tech device to clean floors, open doors, drive the car, do laundry, cook food, or watch the kids). Typically, these studies are conducted as a search for unmet needs—a deeply troubling concept despite its ubiquity in business thinking. The interview is built to first place the person into a particular segment based on demographics and attitudinal criteria. Next, the interviewer conducts a "deep dive" that captures some information about needs and desires that can be attached to this profile and establish the different segment's needs and desires. This allows the researcher to establish a list of problems, desires, and little niggles that are all open to design interventions.

Conventional best practices dictate the format of these interviews, where discussion guides guide the interviewer and interviewee through the list of questions that will elicit the responses necessary to assign and categorize the respondent's statements and fill these categories with content. But there is little human-centric about this because the interview and the responses are preconditioned, just as they were in the focus group I saw in Shanghai. The discussion guide creates a format that everyone must follow, pacing the answers and presupposing the focus of the interview. However, it also implicitly organizes the content of the answers before the respondent has even entered the mirror-lined room by strictly controlling the topics of conversation. Experiential information is only captured in anecdote, and it is only allowed in conversations that usually begin "what are your biggest problems?" and "how does that make you feel?". Moreover, by adhering to the discussion guide subtly indicates to the respondent what the power dynamic is in the session—whoever has the discussion guide papers is the one in control of the conversation.

By contrast, the RHC real research variant of an experiential interview is based around a cyclical format and is designed to allow the respondent the space to guide the conversation. The first basic change is to jettison the discussion guide altogether. Anthropological ethnographic researchers working in an RHC format use topical guides to help them keep track of what might be discussed. But this is memorized, never seen during the interview, and never shared with the respondent. It is merely a tool for ensuring that a sufficient breadth of conversation has been achieved and key points have been discussed. What is important is to allow for three things to happen: build a rapport, learn about how the person expresses information, and learn what they want to tell you.

A cyclical format allows the researcher to constantly return to similar topics from different angles. This allows them to seamlessly test prior statements, learn more about specific topics, clarify misunderstandings, and dig deeper into the experience of the person they are interviewing. The cyclical format eliminates the linear topic-by-topic unfolding of a conversation. This means that a respondent has a chance to talk about a particular issue they may have, and then upon their return to it, make a meta-critical assessment of what they just said. They then become a guide to help the researcher understand what they meant. Yes, it is true that a discussion guide can be formatted this way as well, but it is unlikely that a discussion guide can manage the conversational twists, turns, and dead ends that have to happen to get there in the end.

The example I gave above also serves as an example of how this cyclical format works in an interview and in an entire research practice. We began with open-ended conversations about the experience of rheumatoid arthritis and the injection of biologic medications, but let our respondents lead the flow of the interviews. We then went back over the experience of pain, again and again, from different angles in order to find different ways to convey what we heard. Then after coming to terms with what we heard across the globe, we went back and went over the same topics again. This allowed us to collect many expressions of pain, understand how this can change in different cultural contexts and individual circumstances, and then return to the issue and overcome these differences to discover a new level of similarities. The cyclical method takes time, but it allows people to speak for themselves and allows researchers to make sense of it all with the help of their respondents. Consequently, it is inherently human-centric.

Adherents of conventional commercial research practice are uncomfortable with almost everything in this approach. Most of the interview techniques employed in market research and formal human-centric design research are there to maintain control and the appearance of scientific principles. The belief that these totally arbitrary methods are "scientific" comes only from this appearance of control. They are not any more scientific than an unstructured interview carefully managed and recorded. But the controls are there for the researcher, not for the benefit of the research. Moreover, these controls turn one-on-one interviews into structures to eliminate all of the experiential detail so that a person's utterances can be comparable to others. The connection between interviews is all those conventional interviewers are interested in. Consequently, they cannot study the impact of individual, idiosyncratic experience because they are not interested in the individual as themselves, merely as an example of a generalized type.

Fieldnotes: Capturing the Field Experience

Another major problem common in conventional human-centric research is one of a lack of control over what is captured. Within human-centered research training, there is very little emphasis on the data capture techniques of the ethnographic encounter. Market research outlines practices that are much better at this than design thinking variations. The notes you take, the recordings you make, and the photos or videos you take are all opportunities to overcome the tendencies to slide into subjectivity. But if you are not prepared to make the most of these recording practices, you will just limit your ability to capture, and understand, the nuances of daily life and personal experience.

However, before we can consider the radically human-centric practices for writing fieldnotes and creating visual representations of what was found and experienced, we must first consider how notes, photos, and video are often used now. Once again, conventional market research, innovation research, and human-centric design research struggle to use any of these assets well. Practitioners often fall into abusive practices, especially where the video is concerned.

There are two reasons to record field experiences. The first is to make a research record that can keep the details of what was seen, experienced, discussed, and felt fresh for the researcher. The second is to capture assets that can be made into representations of the field experience in order to enhance the presentation of the insights to people who were not able to attend the research.

Creating a good research record is an essential piece of the research process. But very often fieldnotes are not part of the commercial practice, largely because it is time-consuming and can distract the researcher from the other duties of a consultant in field, namely entertaining the client. There are many approaches to creating fieldnotes and many good training manuals explaining how to do it.[7] But these seem to have been largely ignored in commercial research, particularly in human-centric design, where most of the processes are just notetaking.

A fieldnote must be several things at once. At a minimum, it must be an accurate record of an interview. It must also capture important contextual details, the outline of the conversation, and provide the timestamps for the recording to facilitate the initial review of the audio. If it does all of these things, it is still incomplete because it must go beyond these basic details. It must capture features of the interview that will be needed for the analytical stage. Principally, it must detail what the researcher was thinking and the assumptions that were made as they guided the flow of the conversation. These are essential points because they explain why all of the questions were asked. This allows the researcher to mitigate any bias and understand their impact on the story more fully. And this must be done near the time of the interview because you can never rely on your memory for this kind of information.

This is part of the radically human-centric approach. But the conventional commercial research method falls slightly short of these ideas. Of all of the fieldnotes, I have seen from human-centric design projects most are simple capture templates on one side of a sheet of paper. For the most part, the information captured are things that can be found in the screener responses or at the beginning of the audio recording—usually the basic demographic information with quotes. At most, they will capture some outlines of major points in the conversation with a few observations. What they capture are some details of the conversation that the research team has decided were important. This is less problematic after many interviews, but if you begin your fieldnotes this way, you are guiding the development of insights too early by selecting the essential details that are "worthy" of capture.

The radically human-centric outlook positions fieldnotes as tools to aid recall and guide the development of insights by providing connections between conversations. They should not be an opportunity for the researcher to edit the conversations into something that is more "tactical," or just a collection of interesting quotes. Fieldnotes should also be a connection to the other recorded media, helping quick reviews and giving some context to what is in them.

Now, this brings us to field recordings, which present another set of problems. The taking of photographs and videos in human-centric research is where some of the most egregious casual abuse of participants occurs in conventional research. Recordings of any kind, be they audio, video, or photographic, should only be used for reference purposes. However, they should only be made if absolutely necessary—that is, only if the project outcome requires it. A radically human-centric approach to field recording should be grounded in the idea that you take only what you have to and try to do no harm. Conventional commercial researchers often abuse the fragile relationship between researcher and participant by taking too many photos, making video recordings when they are not needed, and making recordings and then never using them. This is often made worse by using these recordings in ways that were never communicated to the participants. Recordings are an invasion of a person's privacy and an act where they become research subjects to be examined and dissected all too quickly. They have a right to control this process and to limit the number and type of recordings made if they should feel uncomfortable. But the fact that it is paid research, and business clients like to see photos and videos to make them feel "that they were there," or to serve as proof that the project was human-centric. Consequently, researchers are obliged to take photos or videos when it is not necessary and then deliver them to clients who often do not follow any ethics rules to protect the privacy of the individuals. In full-length noncommercial ethnographic settings, this kind of behavior might destroy the project because people would eventually learn to distrust the researcher. The radically human-centric approach looks to preserve trust whether it is a short-term or long-term study, and researchers avoid collecting unnecessary videos or photos.

The only way to actually be human-centric is to be strict with the materials policy of the project. Do not ever take a recording when one is not needed to achieve the goals of the project. Do not provide recordings to anyone not immediately involved in the research. And allow participants the final say on the recordings that have been used. The $200 they receive to participate does not pay for total compliance.

The Possibility of a Micro-ethnographic Practice

Real ethnography usually takes a very long time. In a "pure" format, mostly used by academic anthropologists, studies take years. One of the reasons why it is not more prevalent in commercial research is the fact that real research is often not cheap or brief enough to be comfortable. The answers to many questions concerning issues like experience, identity, or social structure must take months, if not years, to produce. This is not useful in a business or policy context where the situation can change in a matter of days or weeks.

To be completely useful in a commercial context, a radically human-centric approach to applied research needs to be able to work within the constraints of shorter timeframes and be affordable, without giving up very much. This means a rigorous, but practical, micro-ethnographic approach is needed, provided it can be developed with no compromises in the epistemological, ethical, and actionable requirements of radical human-centricity.

The "micro" in a micro-ethnographic method refers to the scale of a particular study. The ethnographic approach remains unchanged— much of what one does is not affected. What does shift is the way the study is framed. The scope and scale of the study and the expectations placed on it need to be carefully considered. This means if a study needs to be a month long, then you cannot expect it to explain how people create personal identities or form complicated social formations. Those issues are simply out of scope for a project of this duration. Conversely, if you need to understand how to design new autonomous delivery systems for an urban environment, you need to scale up the research phase to accommodate the complexity of this kind of problem. The "radical" quality of this lies in the acknowledgment that most commercial studies are micro-studies and cannot address major human problems and experiences with a few hastily organized interviews.

Radical human-centricity employs micro-ethnography as a key practice. But instead of focusing on abbreviated field experiences, or reducing the size of the respondent pool, the major focus is on "right-sizing" the limitations of the study with what can be expected to come out of the research. In essence, this is avoiding "boiling the ocean," but it is also about setting expectations. In my role as a consulting researcher, I am always helping my clients understand what they can expect as outcomes within the time and financial constraints we all must work in. I often find myself reducing the scope of a project or helping them to understand that their needs exceed their constraints.

The rules of thumb in setting up a research program in a micro-ethnographic mode are to limit the number of research questions you ask, talk to enough people in field so that the last few interviews or participant observation sessions are repeating what was seen, heard, or felt in the first sessions, and to always report what you found, not what is desired.

Finding the Right People: The Problem of Commercial Recruiting

In a commercial context recruiting appropriate respondents is a difficult task. There are a number of commercial recruiters who are able to find people to talk to. They usually identify individuals in their existing lists of potential participants who match the criteria a research team has hypothesized will be suitable respondents. If they do not, they have people to call a large group of possible individuals to find the right sample. However, there are two problems with this process that makes the exercise less than human-centric—one theoretical, and one practical.

The theoretical problem is the recruitment criteria. In a typical project flow, researchers, or even a commissioning client, will create a list of characteristics they assume will sufficiently identify appropriate participants. These criteria are usual demographic details with a bit of attitude sprinkled in for good measure. These criteria are used to create the screener, a list of questions designed to elicit responses that categorize the respondents into people that are right for the study or not (at the very least). But these criteria are usually nothing more than hypotheses, which would not be problematic except that in a typical commercial study there is no time or space to correct any problems. The people are recruited and that is it. The hypotheses behind these criteria are not tested or troubled in any way, and they are not altered when reality hits. This means the study is based on a guess—educated or otherwise—at the beginning of the process.

Compounding this issue is the practical one, the fact that the lists of commercial recruiters are people who have self-selected into participating in these studies. This means that issue of the "village idiot" problem appears in every study. Now, before you panic, I want to clarify what this means. Early in the development of the ethnographic method, anthropologists, sociologists, and ethnologists realized that there was a problem regarding who you speak to when you begin a project.[8] These early studies commonly took the form of an anthropologist arriving in a village with an intention to study the lifeways and social structure of non-Western peoples. That this was inherently problematic is a conversation for another time. The first order of business was to find people to talk to and start to learn the language. But there was a problem.

As someone who is an outsider, most people in the village would suspect the intentions of this outsider and avoid them. The anthropologist would languish on the margins of this social order for some time, even as their language skills improved. Often, the only people who would speak to them at first were themselves marginalized individuals. When the purpose was to study the social structure from within the "native" perspective, the outsiders were not the best place to start. This problem is commonly referred to as the "village idiot" problem—which is perhaps not the most sensitive term ever devised. I prefer the term "first respondent problem" and will use that going forward.

This issue is amplified in commercial research because of the tradition of relying on market research recruitment partners and practices. They maintain panels of people who are easy to find, and as a consequence are convenient sources of people to interview. But their methods lead to the problem of the "professional respondent" who supplements their income by participating in as many research projects as possible. While these are usually people with good intentions—they are not looking to deceive people, just mildly game the system—it is necessary to question their usefulness in a study. People who sign up to a panel before being found for a research study, are not necessarily representative of the group we hope to study. It produces the same problem that has weakened the strength of many social psychology studies.

One of the findings of the reproducibility project, a collaborative retesting of 270 major psychology studies begun by the Center for Open Science and its cofounder, Brian Nosek in 2011, stated that psychology's dependence on using college students seeking a quick 50 bucks as research subjects meant that many conclusions could not be representative of humankind, as research psychologists claim.[9] In the context of commercial research, we must think the same way. Market research, and any study that depends on market research recruitment methods, study a sub-set of people, not a general population. This sub-set is defined first, and foremost, by people who want to get paid to participate. Thus, we are facing the "first respondent problem" in the extreme.

Most people would choose not to participate in such a study, even when paid to do so. So, while these people are not "idiots" they are possibly compromised individuals from the standpoint of a research trying to get to the foundations of a particular way of being. We must question their status within this group, regardless of how well they fit the demographic criteria.[10] This problem stems from the permanent lists managed by the professional recruiters. People sign up to be contacted if they are eligible. When working with these recruiters, you always have to work through the group to make sure that everyone is there for the right reasons.

In an ideal world, we would avoid commercial recruiters altogether. The speed and convenience they provide rarely compensate for the compromises we have to make in the research design. The only solution we have that fits into a radically human-centric system is to find ways to recruit through existing networks of people (often called snowball recruiting) or to spend more time with people so that we can first verify people's suitability and then explore more deeply. This involves breaking the study up into an initial verification phase followed by a deep-exploration phase. The first phase tests the validity of the recruitment criteria and helps to hone the approach needed to investigate the problems that instigated the study. The experimentation phase digs into the details of people's lives and provides the basis for the insights that will be produced. This need not take too much time or be too expensive. What it requires is flexibility and patience on the side of the research team.

Remote Research: Working in a Pandemic and Postpandemic Reality

The global COVID-19 pandemic forced a rapid change in countless areas of human life. A notable shift was the service industry's move online. This alteration in working life affected a group of office workers, innovation workers, and business consultants who were lucky enough to be able to do their work from home without the risks of workplace exposure to COVID-19. But while working life was tolerable online, the situation was impossible for researchers practicing real ethnography. This is because real research, including most of the sub-methods of ethnography, require actually being present, and being able to meet people face-to-face. This is obviously impossible while we need to collectively avoid spreading a dangerous and deadly virus.

For some researchers and research consultancies, this was not that much of a problem. They simply scheduled their interviews as usual and ran them over video chat. This made the process of human-centered research even easier because now it did not involve travel or jetlag. Some have declared "remote research" to be the future of HCD and design research and are making noises about never going back.[11] But for a radically human-centric researcher this was not so simple. Remote interviews are nothing more than interviews in a more limited medium. They are not a replacement for ethnography in any shape or form. I agree with my colleague Daniel Mai when he says, "virtual ethnography" is a contradiction in terms and [is] an expression of commercial researchers misappropriating the halo that accompanies the original toolset. If it is virtual, it is barely ethnography, and thus we need to consider it as a different, lesser form of qualitative research. Countering the overall enthusiasm for new digital tools and the virtual human interactions they enable, we must therefore point out the drawbacks of remote qualitative research and call out those who pretend otherwise.[12]

And so we have to understand these drawbacks. Video chat technology does not add to a conversation. Almost all of us know this quite well. The technological problems, video and sound problems and lack of stability all contribute to an experience that is barely tolerable. The format precludes any extra conversation or chit-chat. People click on the link, have their say, and leave. If you have ever been on an ethnographic visit, that means about half the conversation—all the parts that are off the record—are missing. This means there is less time to build a relationship. There is less time to experiment. And adding to this problem, people are always distracted at home. This is why ethnography always has to expand beyond at-home visits. People take video calls in one of two places, at-home, with all the distractions, or somewhere totally inappropriate for the call, like a coffee shop. None of this is conducive to a good conversation, let alone good research.

Daniel Mai continues his critique with an important point. He says, "The general aim of ethnography is to understand 'What is going on here?' To reach such as understanding, it is necessary to look beyond what is obvious and embrace the coincidental."[13] There is nothing coincidental in a semi-scripted conversation over video chat. So much has been conditioned and controlled that this encounter is actually more filtered than a focus group.

All of this contributes to an inescapable conclusion. We do interviews remotely only when we have to. But to consider them human-centric is folly. They are anything but and should be avoided whenever possible.

Specialists Do Good Things: It is Time to End DIY Research

One key flaw in any human-centered design or design thinking research project is often the unwillingness to incorporate specialist practitioners into the research phase. Design thinking has always had a DIY approach to everything, which is one of its greatest contributions and flaws. The positive side of this DIY ethos is clear; it is what allows everyone in the project to have a direct, unmediated connection to the content that is studied and the work that comes out of it. This is good for selling books and cornering a market. Its dark side, however, is quite problematic because it has led to the research in most human-centric design projects to be underdetermined, poorly executed, and badly written up. This in itself is responsible for much of the current crisis in commercial HCD research.

This is a difficult point for me to make. At the beginning of my career in commercially applied human-centered research, I believed that any study should only be built and conducted by someone with a Ph.D. I thought that the Ph.D. was the only credible marker of a researcher who had matured to the point that they could be trusted with this kind of work. My argument was that the writing a long-format dissertation was the only way to encounter the problems faced by an ethnographer. Experiencing the problems of squeezing several years of ethnographic study into a single article or book chapter teaches one more about the pitfalls of ethnography than anything else. Holding a Ph.D. is then a guarantor that one has had to go through this rite of passage, whereas a master's thesis is insufficiently large to learn these lessons completely. Later, I convinced myself I was wrong and that this was a snobbish way to think.

However, I have returned to my original way of thinking, be it snobbish or not. I strongly believe that human-centered research is so difficult, and the outcomes so important, that only highly trained individuals should be doing it. It is simply too easy to do it incorrectly and the stakes in commercial innovation are too high. There are certainly enough highly trained sociologists in the world to ensure the business world will be well covered. It strikes me that to leave this work to someone with only a semester's worth of practical training, or less, seems to be a net-detriment to commercial research. It is better for the research, and therefore everyone involved. By using an expert, it is easier to manage all of the subtleties and nuances that are part of any high-quality human study. By contrast, the DIY approach reduces these complexities very quickly because they are not captured or properly understood.

A Radical Human-Centricity holds that specialists are key to managing the complexity and intricacies of the subject being studied. People are not simple creatures. A deep understanding of their actions, thoughts, and experiences requires a virtuosic approach to research. It also requires experience, a foreign language or two, and a lot of trial by error. Thus, a Radical Human-Centric approach suggests that if you want to understand people, you are better served with a trained, skilled specialist doing the work.

From a company insider's perspective, a radically human-centric research program involves finding the right researcher and employing the right research methods for the job. Real research requires specialists and demands that we find the most effective and efficient way to meet the objectives of the project. First among these is the imperative to meet the participants on their own terms. This means the research who conducts the interviews, develops the insights, and works with the designers or strategists must speak the participant's preferred language. There is no substitute for someone who can catch the nuances of language use in a conversation and understand the embodied communication (body language) like a native. If you do not have someone who speaks Russian when studying in Russia, or Japanese in Japan, or Borqueño in Albuquerque, then find someone or change the parameters of the study.

This is a radical departure from conventional practices, I know. But to conduct real research, we have to eliminate the convenient trappings of market research and its failures—at least the features that are unconnected to good research practice and are really only there to be expedient and easy. Moderators and simultaneous translators are just barriers to understanding and should not be used except in the most extreme circumstances. They are usually excellent people, but their roles in a study are relics of a moribund form of market research designed to be convenient for executives to go on "customer safari." The most obvious reasons why we should do away with these roles are twofold: the subtleties of ethnographic research require that the researcher understand the participant's worlds directly and unmediated, which means they need to communicate well and be able to avoid the inevitable game of telephone that clouds the communication of experiential insights from participant, to moderator, to translator, to researcher, to designer/strategist, to client. Adding a stranger into the mix who has no responsibilities for the final ideation and design process is just a crutch for a lack of language skills. It is better to hire an expert who can do the work from the beginning to the end in the local language. So, hire an anthropologist or sociologist who has excellent language skills and deep cultural knowledge of the context in which you need to do the work. Easy.

Setting up a research study devoted to providing insights for design or strategic innovation requires creating space and opportunity for accidental discovery and simple observation. Ethnography should never be limited to just one kind of engagement. Ethnography is not just interviews, for instance. One of the major tenants of an ethnographic study is participant observation, meaning the research must be able to feel and experience what participants feel and experience. You need to see and do it for yourself to know it. This means going well beyond interviews.

In commercial research, participant observation is usually viewed as too subjective, too biased, to be useful. But it is impossible to truly *know* something without experiencing it yourself. No amount of conversation can make up for direct experience. In a radically human-centric approach, we see participants as experts in their own lives. Within a radically human-centric practice, we try to encourage participants to guide us through an experience that approximates their own. We encourage them to be phenomenological (study of experience) tour guides who help us learn to live the way they do.

This can be feeling the problems that arise from a particular vacuum design or feeling the burn of frustration from an app misfiring. To create space for these experiential observations, we must release ourselves from the stultifying structure of the discussion guide and fill the time with explorative experiences which involve our bodies too.

Considering Impact: Ethics Before, Ethics After, Ethics Between

The last practical shift involves an application of ethics and demands an understanding of one's responsibilities while doing research in field. Both are sadly something that is often completely lacking in the development of many commercial research projects. A human-centered approach, radical or otherwise, must always work to protect the individuals participating in a study. This goes for everyone but is even more important when studying vulnerable populations like children, anyone with a medical condition, or any marginalized or disadvantaged person. This responsibility is all-encompassing and can, and sometimes should, result in refusing to do the study in the first place. Usually, what this means is scoping a study so that you are not asking people to divulge unnecessary information or disrupt their lives in ways that they do not want to.

The ethics of this situation is often blurred by the mercenary tendencies of commercial research relationships. The fact that we must pay people changes the encounter immediately and is one of the major sources of bias in the entire system. It may not be an exaggeration to say the payment "buys" a certain kind of engagement and facilitates a type of answer. This assumes a well-paid interviewee is much more interested in spending the time to dig deeply. While this might be the case, it does not exempt us from our responsibilities as researchers. We cannot pay our way to personal details and interesting insights. We must try to study a situation, and the people who inhabit it, with minimal residual impact. This means we must limit ourselves to what we need to know. If we were conducting a full ethnographic enquiry into people's lives, we would live with them, eat with them, and write about them. But we would engage as equals, and they would have a say in how far we get and what we get access to. The purchasing of their time asserts a kind of power that should not be forgotten. To be radically human-centric means to apply the golden rule "do unto others as you would have them do to you" at all times.[14]

This means scoping the study also means the timeframe and expectations should be adjusted accordingly. It also means that the people involved in the study should be prepared to limit their access to people's lives in order to protect and preserve the privacy of the people who participate. These are often heretical ideas in commercial research, and the limitations we should be putting on our work are often dismissed by many who lack true ethnographic training.

The duration, format, and number of interviews are all points that need to be considered at this stage. A project examining the intensity and issues related to the experience of self-injecting medication requires a completely different approach than one testing the viability of design changes in food packaging. A general rule of thumb is that the complexity of the problem dictates more in all areas—longer interviews or engagement with a single person, more talking, and more interviews allow us to better understand difficult circumstances. But in the self-injection example, we are talking to a vulnerable population, and so their moral needs and vulnerability should be considered when scoping and setting up a project. This may mean several short interviews rather than long ones. It may also mean making do with what you can get. The duration and number of interviews are in a direct relationship with each other. If you have a lot of short ones, this may yield similar results to a few long ones.

Ultimately, scoping a project within a radically human-centered system means establishing the conditions for flexible encounters. Mechanically working through the 20+ interviews you scheduled with a rigid discussion guide is usually never valuable, or good research. You have to be able to change in response to what you learn from the people you are meeting. If they collectively signal that shorter interviews are better, then you follow their lead.

The final note about ethics is about integrity. One key feature of a radically human-centric approach to ethnography is an unapologetic adherence to best practices, rigorous research, and maintain the highest ethical and quality standards. Anyone, even a fully trained anthropological ethnographer, can make a mess of commercial research if they let their standards slide. This is sadly all too common. Making sure to maintain one's integrity as a researcher, even in the face of opposition from business leaders and market research practitioners, is an essential quality of an RHC researcher. But it is not easy. Commercial research has too many ethical and methodological loopholes and slippages as it is. To ensure a radically human-centric ethnography we have to resist the temptations to make things quick and easy.

Conclusion

Reclaiming ethnography involves returning it to its roots in pure research. As I have shown, this means putting the rigor back into the system and avoiding the temptation to make shortcuts or to rely on the compromised practices of market research. Because this makes ethnography difficult to do, it puts it outside of the skill set of an untrained practitioner. This is not a problem, however. There are plenty of well-trained ethnographers available for this kind of work.

The reason why this is important is because of ethnography's centrality to experiential learning. It provides the context, framing, and methodological organization for experiential learning. This is key to any human-centric approach. But within a radical human-centric approach, ethnography becomes the driving force for everything, from experiential learning, analysis, to communicating the results. Because ethnography is a dialogic and discursive practice—that is, it depends on the reciprocity of sharing and caring through word, action, and thought—it also has the power to establish the kind of relationships with current and future customer/user/patients that design and strategy rely on. When used in its fullest form, real ethnography provides a degree of understanding and engagement in the world far beyond the wildest dream of users of market research practices. But there is more to it than just using a few ethnographic tools. Real research in radical human-centric approaches also requires several shifts away from some of the bad habits and erroneous beliefs plaguing commercial research. I will discuss how ethnography can be further amplified through these shifts in the next chapter.

Notes

1 When we think and talk about real research, there is no space for a distinction between commercial practice and academic practice in real research. They both have to adhere to its principles. So we really need to leave this distinction behind.
2 https://www.interaction-design.org/literature/topics/design-thinking.
3 https://www.ideou.com/pages/design-thinking.
4 Geertz, C., 1988. Being there: Anthropology and the scene of writing. *Geertz C, Works and Lives: The Anthropologist as Author*, pp. 1–25.
5 There has been a lot of talk about phenomenological hermeneutics in business research recently. This is a good thing, but it is a massive and complicated topic. Because it is the study of experience and its connection to knowledge, it is impossible for it to be easily productized or operationalized into a business framework. Thus, it is best to be wary of any attempt to do so.
6 Malinowski, B., 2007. Method and scope of anthropological fieldwork. *Ethnographic fieldwork: An anthropological reader*, pp. 4–25. ; Robben, A.C. and Sluka, J.A. eds., 2012. *Ethnographic fieldwork: An anthropological reader* (Vol. 23). John Wiley & Sons.; Okely, J., 2020. *Anthropological Practice: Fieldwork and the Ethnographic Method*. Routledge.
7 Emerson, R.M., Fretz, R.I. and Shaw, L.L., 2011. *Writing ethnographic fieldnotes*. University of Chicago Press. ; Walford, G., 2009. The practice of writing ethnographic fieldnotes. *Ethnography and Education*, 4(2), pp. 117–130.
8 Barley, N., 2000. *The innocent anthropologist: Notes from a mud hut*. Long Grove , IL: Waveland Press.

9 Open Science Collaboration. 2015. "Estimating the Reproducibility of Psychological Science." *Science*, 349(6251).

10 The idea that they can then be studied in "scientific" surroundings like focus group facilities and this somehow preserves objectivity or the precious "naive response" is doubly suspicious. But this is market research's problem, not theirs.

11 Again, I do not feel it is fruitful to "name and shame" here. A quick keyword search will give you all of the websites of agencies claiming to do remote ethnography you need. What is disheartening is the number of agencies and innovation teams who have decided that online interviews are something to be celebrated and not simply endured for the short term.

12 Daniel Mai. 2022. "Missing Fieldwork: Why "Virtual Ethnography" is Not Human-Centric." *Human Futures Magazine. July.* https://www.humanfutures.studio/articles/2021/7/27/why-virtual-ethnography-is-not-human-centric (accessed January 15, 2022).

13 Ibid.

14 Therefore, all things whatsoever ye would that men should do to you, do ye even so to them: for this is the law and the prophets. Matthew 7:12 KJV.

Chapter 3

RETHINKING COMMERCIAL RESEARCH

The Key Conceptual Shifts toward Radically Human-Centric Research

In the last chapter, I discussed the need to reclaim ethnography as a practice and a way of being in the world. This is the first, and most fundamental in the advancement of a radical human-centric approach. However, a rehabilitated ethnography is only the first step in repairing commercial research. The radical human-centric approach to research must also solve the many problems lurking in the corners of conventional innovation research. It needs to provide an alternative to the antiquated ideas and practices in market research and corrects the gimmicks and weak research approaches that are inherent in design thinking and human-centric design. Since none of these frameworks and methods are up to the task of providing a solid foundation for innovative thinking and action, it will require making additional shifts in thought and practice. It is necessary to reconceptualize the underpinnings of commercial innovation research. We must shift ourselves away from the bad habits and poor theorizing that plague conventional commercial research and move towards a theoretical and practical foundation built on an approach to research capable of delivering what human-centric perspectives have been promising: an understanding of customer/user/patients and their contexts capable of grounding successful innovation and design. This means we need to nudge innovation research practice towards a more solid foundation. We need to make a series of conceptual shifts in the world of business thinking and commercial research so we can fully make use of real research.

The Radical human-centric approach to real research brings interventions to 10 dimensions of the conceptual models governing innovation. The first shift, multi-disciplinarity, encapsulates the key alternations in thought and practice necessary to embrace a balanced research approach and to build the perspectival foundations for a radically human-centric approach to business research. The other nine—time, change drivers, the subjects of study, complexity versus simplicity, positive skepticism, the idea of needs, growth and homeostasis, impact and barriers, and research at scale—allow us to focus on the conceptual shifts needed to release commercial research from the shackles of many of the outdated, insensitive, unethical, and downright silly practices constraining it today. In this chapter, we will explore each of these shifts and see how real research is achieved through a radical human-centric approach.

The ten shifts that ground radical human-centricity

01	From quant as the only tool	→	to using qual and quant together
02	From the past as irrelevant	→	to considering the past, present, and future
03	From static views of customers	→	to considering human change and agency
04	From idealized customers	→	to real people
05	From Simplicity	→	to an appreciation of complexity
06	From safety in frameworks	→	to a positive scepticism
07	From a theory of needs	→	to no need for needs
08	From a preference for simplicity	→	to embracing complexity
09	From growth at all costs	→	to an appreciation of homeostasis
10	From business at scale	→	to understanding impact at different scales

1 Multi-Disciplinarity: Qual and Quant as Real Research

Over the years, I have noticed that some people in the business have an irrational fear of theory. This is not a criticism, as such. It is simply an observation of the culture of the business. They are not unable to understand it, rather they fear it and avoid it wherever possible. Some even go as far as to mock it, calling analytical thinking or speech too "academic." They say they do not want to "overcomplicated the situation," or "do not need to know" about the human details they consider "out of scope." They are also afraid of talking about things in a way that does not involve "concrete examples"—although, usually this is because they struggle to see the pattern of the theory and how it maps over examples they already know. Ultimately, this fear leads to a preference for methods and research tools that are easy to use and designed to deliver data that is fit-to-purpose and do not "over-complicate things." But there are consequences for this attitude. Because they do not have a strong theoretical understanding of the practice of business and research for businesses, they do not fully understand the tools they are using. This misunderstanding leads to unrealistic expectations, problematic shortcuts, and in the worst cases, suspicion of research and researchers.

All of this contributes to the over-reliance on quantitative studies. Most often, their misgivings about any kind of theoretical thinking manifest as a belief that qualitative practices are somehow inferior to quantitative practices. Qualitative studies do often require people to be more thoughtful as they require the audience to imagine many new things—the quality needed for design inspiration. The thinking goes that numbers are more trustworthy than anything else because they require very little thoughtful engagement. At the very least, it appears as a belief that qualitative and quantitative research are somehow mutually exclusive from each other. Either situation usually leads to studies where the principal methods are not fully up to the task they have been set—very often quant studies fill in for work that should be done qualitatively.

"Quant is more scientific:" Or, People Misunderstanding Research Tools

The most extreme example arose in a conversation I once had recently with a potential client. They were interested in hearing about our approach to CX (customer experience) to see if we could help them with a problem that they are having with their customers. Their company is a large investment services company that manages a large retirement investment portfolio that is part of employer benefits packages for workers across the country. They exist in an environment where they have no competition. Their plan is legally mandated, and their membership consists of people who must use them as their pension plan or opt-out altogether. Because of recent financial instability in the market, their portfolio was returning at the same rate as it did in the past. They found that without their prior remarkable levels of return they have very little to offer their end-customers, or "members." They needed to think about how to provide a new customer experience to their members to try to help them understand the value of the payroll deduction and sticking with the plan.

Our conversation with them began with a discussion of their current state and the most pressing problems. They told us they have a serious deficit of data about their members, to the point that they are even lacking the most basic details beyond names, addresses, and financial data. While this meant that they are at the beginning of a new phase of CX understanding, it also meant that they desperately needed to learn a lot about their members before they could embark on developing a new experience and services.

My partners and I continued by asking about their appetite for researching their customers, trying to see if they were ready for a full ethnographic assessment of their members' lives and needs. They said that they were hoping to build a journey map highlighting the major life stages governing their members' lives as a way to map out how to address them and to solution for them. We asked about how they were hoping to fill in this journey map with experiential details explaining how people prepare for retirement, expect to use the money this company handles, and how they were hoping to frame the behavior changes resulting from the decline in the return on their members' investments.

This open conversation was cut short when they said, "well, we're using surveys to understand them, and we are about to begin conducting an NPS assessment." We asked what work they would like to do to discover more about their clients, trying to show them that neither a survey nor an NPS assessment can provide the insight needed for a new CX program. They did not respond well. They clearly thought that survey-based research culminating in an NPS score was exactly what they needed to build a new customer experience. We were unsure how to convince them otherwise.

From this point on, it became clear that they were only willing to use these traditional tools to understand their customers and that they did not understand how little survey, much less an NPS assessment, can help them truly understand the experiential environment they are facing. Their data deficit means that they do not have a solid assessment of who their members are, let alone what they would want out of a pension investment company. This lack and their desire to use surveys to do open-ended, discovery work means that they will likely never build a sufficient understanding of their customers to help guide their CX initiatives. When we tried to argue for an ethnographic approach, they dismissed our arguments saying that we were "using too much theory," and that they needed to focus on being "practical."

What this conversation exposed was how many companies are still struggling with their understanding of the world. And the problem does not come from an inability to understand, or a lack of willingness. It is the result of a basic lack of understanding of what kind of research is appropriate for their problems. Our attempts to convince them otherwise fell on deaf ears because what they heard pulled them out of their comfort zone. It did not matter that we were not using any theory at all to make our argument. It only mattered that what we were saying was dangerous and making the case for an approach that engendered suspicions.

Many who work in these companies have business training that conditioned them to insist on what they believe is empirical data. Their training also states that empirical data involves numbers. As a result, the quantitative survey is the most empirical way to know about the world outside of a company's doors—or even within them. This has led to an over-dependence on what should be a relatively niche tool. With this in mind, it is understandable their first thought was to turn to quantitative analysis to help them with their problem. But because business thinking is stuck in this mindset, they were not even aware of the potential of an entirely different set of research programs that would be more successful, and cheaper, in helping them learn about their members. To solve for a knowledge gap about humans, you need a human-centric program of research. In this case, this is something quant cannot deliver. The solution can only come with a widening of everyone's horizons and adding the idea that new forms of research are acceptable, if not preferable to the old ways. What they needed was a qualitative examination of their members followed by a quantitative amplification (a scaling of the results from a view of a few to many).

Radical human-centricity involves truly multi-disciplinary research. In practical terms, this means bringing qualitative and quantitative research into harmony with each other and using them when needed for their strengths. It also involves understanding that even quantitative practices need a solid quantitative component. Because the radical human-centric approach also requires practitioners to have a solid theoretical understanding, it means that the tools, methods, and processes used in a study have been carefully selected from a number of alternatives to be the optimal tool for the job.

The Fantasy of Objectivity: How the Qual versus Quant Division Hides the True Nature of Empirical Research

The borders between qualitative and quantitative practices are protected by an ideology that arose as we moved from a premodern way of thinking into the age of modern thought. The idea of a field of study called "science" began to grow as the European West moved slowly from the Middle Ages and into the Renaissance. Over a period of 200 years, we changed the models that helped us understand the world and developed new intellectual tools to examine the world around us. Natural philosophers, the scientists of the time, also spent time working out just what the areas of study should be.[1]

Their process of categorizing modes of knowledge and organizing the tools to create new knowledge was one of making distinctions based on differences.[2] Music, an equivalent to astronomy and philosophy in antiquity was cast out as our ideas around scientific disciplines hardened. As categories of knowledge developed, they accommodated some areas of knowledge creation and threw some out. As we developed a sense of empirical study, the fields that did not focus on the natural world were placed outside the fortress walls of "science." As the concept of the sciences evolved, several lucky fields like chemistry, physics, biology, astronomy, were cast as "hard science," whereas others were relegated to "soft sciences" or worse yet, applied sciences. And thus, a hierarchy developed that structured our thinking, organized our universities, and decided where one field of study stopped, and another started. This process pushed the humanities and social sciences outside of the "scientific" world, according to largely arbitrary distinctions. Neither explores the physical world exclusively, and neither employed the common scientific method of observation nor testing to create new knowledge. As a result, they were too fluffy, too subjective, to be sciences.

Now we fast forward many decades to a world where business has entered the ranks of knowledge generators. This is rather funny given that when the Harvard business school was opening its founders struggled to find donors because most people believed it was preposterous that one could teach or learn business, or that it was anything more than an innate skill.[3] In the twentieth century, business aligned itself with experimental psychology and experimental forms of "industrial anthropology" to develop ways of understanding human behavior. This aligned business thinking with the "scientific" way of examining the world around us.[4] These are the origins of market research.

The close association with psychology has meant that a "scientific" approach to studying people is best found in the model provided by mid-twentieth-century experimental psychology or economic models. This is the reason why we have focus groups, NPS scores, and an emphasis on "the numbers" over experiential data. It is also this close association that design thinking and human-centered design were supposed to correct. It is also why we have

Business thinkers are taught that quantitative practices and focus group laboratory settings are more scientific because they are more empirical and more controllable.[5] If they are not taught this explicitly, then they are acculturated into this way of thinking on the job. The most common critique I have heard about ethnographic practices was that they were too subjective to be believable and not objective enough. Here there is a bit of confusion. When these critics use the term "objective" but actually mean empirical. They did not believe the stories collected in an ethnographic encounter were representative of real life, and they could not be convinced that ethnographic studies are the most empirical ones can be. Seeing, tasting, smelling, feeling, hearing, and sweating in a world that is not your own is the most empirical an exploration can be. You literally (not just figuratively) live and breathe the world you study.

The assertion that ethnography is subjective is correct. What is not certain is that this is a bad thing. Subjectivity is present in any analysis from a particular perspective. Any research study is subjective. The issue is whether subjectivity is mutually exclusive to empiricism, which it is not. A deeply empirical study that is subjective in how it is presented is still preferable to a subjectively developed rational study (in this case, nonempirical) communicated through abstracted, and idealized, formations (read: a quant study delivered as a set of segments). In plain English, this means a set of human-centric insights about real-life developed from the perspective of an ethnographic research is better than the bar chart showing something pulled from a qualitative assessment of the same behaviors with only five data points represented.

What I am trying to demonstrate here is that qualitative research is no less empirical than anything else. Indeed, it is more empirical than most approaches. That it is sometimes subjective is really only a problem when it is done poorly. A strong ethnographic write-up will allow a reader to see through the potential biases of the researcher's perspective and will mitigate any of these problems. However, because quantitative reports are rationalized and their complexity reduced in the analysis and presentation, their subjectivities are hidden. They are, therefore, more susceptible to the manipulations the epithet "subjective" is meant to expose. The history of scientific thinking built a hierarchy that divided subjective, human-centric research practices and objective, numbers-based research into two mutually suspecting tribes. Those who see qualitative research and ethnography on the wrong side of the line dividing science from nonscience, are fooling themselves. They are themselves. Good research is good research. There can be good qual and good quant. There can be terrible versions of both too. What makes them empirical, useful, and trustworthy is the care the researchers took to present the world as they found it. The constant fight over what is more objective, and whether or not subjectivity is a problem, is really beside the point.

Through the perspective provided by radical human-centricity qual and quant are not opposed to each other. Rather, practitioners of radical human-centricity try to use both in an appropriate sequence or in parallel to compliment and support the other approaches they are using within a study. If the purpose of the study is to get closer to some kind of "truth," then it is better to use the best tool for the job and to maximize your chances for success. The radically human-centric research working with the rules of real research uses the best tools available and knows enough about each of them to be able to manage their strengths and weaknesses.

A radically human-centric practice must accommodate a multi-disciplinary approach to research. What this means is real research has space for collaboration between expert practitioners working within their area of expertise. Statisticians, data scientists, anthropologists, sociologists, foresight practitioners, social psychologists, and other researchers can— and should—work together to tackle common problems. And they should do so outside of the disciplinary squabbles common in academia and commercial research alike. The reason for this is because a radical human-centric approach to real research cannot end at simple description. Its value in applied projects, commercial or not, is to help others, be they designers, strategists, policy makers, executives, or other researchers, find ways to help other people. This means we cannot just make observations and report them.

No. Real research has to describe, explain, and even predict wherever this is possible. And these insights must come from working together.

2 Time: Considering the Past, Present, and Future

Time is a difficult construct because it is only detectable as it passes us by. Recognizing its passing, and describing this phenomenon depends on experience. This means, at the human level at least, concepts like the past, present, and future are not based on scientific laws, but on how we, as human beings, experience time. The passing of time is counted in units but illuminated in the stories we tell about ourselves and our changes over time. The past is usually relegated to the view of historians. Even a cursory inspection of their internal conversations demonstrates that how we understand the past is a patchwork of interpretations. There is no solid "truth" in what the past was, or how it speaks to us now. The present is a fleeting, ephemeral experience that leaves as quickly as it arrives. It is entirely unique and multiple because it is experienced differently by literally everyone on this planet. The future is perhaps the most difficult of these three concepts, because unlike the others, it has no basis in reality. It does not exist, and we cannot study it as we would anything else. The future, as we understand it in the early twenty-first century, is the product of a slow period of intellectual development. In the nineteenth century, people did not look to the future as they do now. It was not a place populated by increasingly more complicated technologies as it is now, or even the location of hope and promise—all of this came later as we began to refine how we tell stories about what will come. Thus, it may be better to see our view of what the future is as one of the most significant inventions of the twentieth century. It is a new kind of myth, structured in reverse so that mythical ideas eventually become real, that says more about how we understand ourselves now than it does about any possible future state.

Of the three, only the present and the future feature in business thinking. The past is past, and therefore left to case studies, which are examples of prior action to be emulated or avoided. However, human experience is lived across all three. The stories we tell about each one, whether personally or as a collective, occur simultaneously. Thus, in lived experience the past, present, and future are simultaneous. Linear thinking, like business strategy, cannot manage this simultaneity easily, and so prefers to array time out as a continual progression towards a goal. This means that business strategy is structurally different from the way that actual humans live their lives. It is an oversimplification that works to organize companies around a collective effort, but leaves them blind to how people, cultures, and societies see and experience themselves.

Beyond this, business thought is also obsessed with looking for ways to impact things over time. Business thought is heavily dependent on causal logic. Key terms such as "drivers," "levers," and "indicators" demonstrate a belief in single-causation, where a single factor directly creates the conditions for a result. In practice, this means looking for the phenomena that "drive change," or that can serve as "levers" for reorganizing a particular circumstance. Human-centric studies run within this way of thinking look for "needs" that drive customers to do something or seek out the "key drivers" that will change people's behavior.

Radical human-centric research has a more realistic view of time and how change unfolds. We prefer the messy, human understanding of time rather than the linear constructs needed in strategic thinking. RHC considers every aspect of human behavior in its view across time, from the past, to the present, and into the future. It recognizes that change unfolds at different rates and has multiple, often competing for causal factors. And it understands change as the effect of systemic alterations, many of which cannot be identified in a single study. What this means is that a radically human-centric perspective begins with an acknowledgment that the world is temporally complicated and that change cannot be traced with tools developed to identify single-causal features or simplified into easy descriptions.

Real research, however, is not constrained by conceptions of time. If a project needs to have a historiographical explanation of something, then it will have one—preferably developed by a historian. If it needs to expand into understanding the future, then there will be a foresight component run by a foresight strategist or speculative anthropologist.[6] In most cases, the focus of any applied project should involve both the past and the future to some degree. This is because any applied project intended to make something new—to innovate or create a product, service, or experience—is really about change. Understanding change in detail is the only way to understand how to innovate more successfully.

Insight, Foresight, and the Fantasy of the Technofuture

A radical human-centric perspective assumes that behavior does not stay the same. In fact, to understand pretty much anything that people do, you have to be ready to also come to terms with how they change. Importantly, this means finding a way to merge applied anthropological ways of working with foresight. Foresight is really a social science too. But for the most part, few of its practitioners have woken up to this idea, even in the academic corners of the discipline.[7] However, it is not that difficult to merge the two. Over the past several years, I and a few colleagues, have been developing an anthropologically inflected approach to foresight that we call Human Futures.[8] We consider it so powerful, that we named the company, the Human Futures Studio, after it.

The technofuture is any story of future change told through the perspective of the development and application of new, or existing technology. You may notice that almost every story of the future told today is a technofuture. This is partially because we are acculturated to see this kind of story as the best, and even only, example of human progress. The idea of progress as we understand it now, began in writings from antiquity, the birth of the discipline of archaeology, and in the justifications of the rapid technologization of the industrial revolution. We began to measure progress in the past through the tools left by our ancestors—noting the passing of the stone age into the copper age, and bronze age, into the iron age. By the 1950s cold war ideology and science fiction finished the job and history became the story of technological progress from agriculture to metal working, through an industrial revolution, and into the fourth industrial revolution.[9] Progress was inextricably connected to technological innovation. Now the technofuture reigns supreme because it is the descendent of this approach to understanding the passage of time and rating the achievements of those who lived in the past against the people who live today.

The central pillar of any technofuture is the belief that technological change drives social change. Initially, we developed the Human Futures perspective to counteract the dominance of this idea. But it gradually shifted when we realize that few foresight projects are able to place human agency and human action in a network with weak signals of change.[10] This was odd because most, if not all, weak signals are merely symptoms, or resultants, of human action. Not only was the central belief of the technofuture backwards— it is actually human action that pushes technological change—the research mechanisms we have developed to understand how this change unfolds cannot handle the human half of change. So, we began building Human Futures as a methodology capable of tracing change through the stories of human action.

3 Change Drivers: Understanding Agency and Change

It is easy to see that any human-centric perspective must put humans and their actions first. The shift here requires us to move away from understanding people according to a set of definitional characteristics— demographic and psychographic markers—and towards a view of human agency and change. Human action, choice, and belief must be central to real research. This is the only way to truly be human-centric. If we continue to view humans as clusters of definitional characteristics and try to predict behavior by assigning categories to describe these clusters, we are staying within the confines of market research and current business thought.

A radical human-centric model of understanding people incorporates an understanding of change as an integral part of the work. We do this because people are not static. They are always changing, pushing limits, and experimenting, so we must be able to trace this in our explorations of their culture, thoughts, actions, and beliefs. It only follows, if people change over time, as researchers we must have a way to study that and its impact. To do this we must use a synchronic, (with time) perspective. We must consider change as it occurs in time. We must consider human action as a focus and an agent of this change. This means combining our view of the current state with potential future states. We have to begin to anticipate the effects of change. Doing this depends on an using the Human Futures perspective to follow human behavior as time progresses. It means crafting insights that speak about now and what might be true in the near future. The adaptations of the Human Futures approach bring ethnographic methods, foresight modeling, and critical theory into an existing commercial research process that has been blindly positivistic, operationalized, and lacking in the kind of reflexivity needed to conduct rigorous analyses of human behavior and change.

As we saw in the discussion about technofutures above, it is all too easy to see humans as more passive social actors than they actually are. Certainly, people are affected by the world around them, but most, if not all, of those changes are due to the actions of other people. Smartphones and Twitter do not change social behavior, the way people use them changes how others behave. The belief that technology drives social change is only one example of how traditional commercial research practices and design thinking miss the point that humans have agency. Humans make decisions. We omit things. We make mistakes and correct ourselves. We work to impact others. All of this means we are able to enact change in our environment through belief, thought, and action. Putting human agency back into insight and foresight models makes them much more complicated, but it is a necessary change to see the world as it is. The added complexity is not really a problem because it improves the final outcome of the study. It provides a better basis for design and strategic decision making. However, it does mean the searchers doing the work need to be diligent and rigorous enough in their practice to compensate. It also means that a Human Futures style project will never end in a simplistic trend report, or in a set of scenarios built solely out of a 2×2 model. It will always end with a description, explanation, and prediction of what is happening, what might happen, and what can be done about both.

The Human Futures approach to studying now and studying the future involves understanding change in context. We must first understand the rate at which change factors are evolving. It is impossible to understand the impact of an observed change or a weak signal of possible change without understanding that the future unfolds unevenly. So, to create rigorous explanations of change, a Human Futures practitioners must examine how change unfolds as we move from the past, into the present, and then on into the future. This means that longitudinal analyses are essential components of the Human Futures method and for Radical Human-Centricity.

It also means that the designed response to these kinds of insights needs to be radically different from what is practiced now. Our recommendation is that instead of inspiration-based, creative-led design, that those wishing to work within a Radical Human-Centricity use the Transition Design approach to enacting change, be it in a product, service, experience, or social level. Transition Design is the work of Terry Irwin, Gideon Kossoff, and Cameron Tonkinwise, and Peter Scupelli, at Carnegie Mellon University.[11] Like our radical human-centered view, transition design "applies an understanding of the interconnectedness of social, economic, political and natural systems to address problems at all levels of spatiotemporal scale in ways that improve quality of life." It is the design approach that is the natural counterpart to radical human-centricity because it is an action-based design approach that also understands the impossibility of continuing with our current application of unsustainable, tech-centric design processes and rapacious, late-capitalist business methods.

The goal of transition design is to design within a program where one also tries to make positive, permanent changes in the context the designers are designing for. Within a strict set of ethical parameters, transition design also looks to transform the way groups of people work together and live in the world. The best examples of this would be helping people transition away from throw-away culture and into a world where a DIY ethic is combined with skills and well-made products that will last for years. Transition design guides the design of these new products and helps to prepare the social world in which they are valued more highly than their disposable predecessors.

These two approaches two go hand in hand. A radical human-centric study uncovers the signals indicating how people are changing over time. It provides a deep analysis of what is changing, how this might affect people, and how quickly this will happen. This provides a grounding for a deliberate response. The transition design methods provide an outline for how to thoughtfully respond to these changes, and how to achieve a set of goals that can be derived from understanding where people might be in the next three, five, or seven years' time.

4 Subjects of a Study: Real People versus Idealized Customer/Users

Who and what do we study when we do research on human behavior in a commercial setting? This question is difficult even for anthropologists and sociologists. It is a complicated problem. It also poses a number of questions. What is behavior? How can we study something that moves through time? Are we taking a large enough view of the context to explain what we see? However, in business, even in human-centric ones, these questions have been quietly, tacitly answered. We are only supposed to study customers or users and the behavior that is directly related to a particular company's business. Anything else is out of scope.

The problem here arises when you question what customers or users are. If a customer is a person engaged in a commercial interaction, or some act of consumption, and a user is someone who is actively using a product or service, then they are people who are doing only one of the many things they will do that day. What I mean is that a customer, or a user, is only a social role—one that is inhabited for a short time and then left behind just as easily. It is one of the many hats we all wear in a day and is not reliably connected to who we are as a person. Being a consumer could be a learned social role, like a soccer referee, or a TV host, and not really connected to who that person is during the rest of their life.

This reveals a problem, because business thinking contains a part-for-whole mistake, where leaders, market researchers, and design thinkers mistake a customer for a complete person—essentially someone wearing one of their many hats. A customer is someone fulfilling a social role in the act of evaluating or making a purchase—that is, being a customer in order to illicit a particular response from a company, retailer, or even shop clerk. But they are much more than that. They lead a full and rich life filled with many social roles and a few contradictions. They are a complicated, complete person, who is only a customer a few times a day at most. They are also a parent, a child, a friend, a worker, a voter, a church goer, a citizen, a member of society, and many other things all at once. Studying them as a customer/user is only customer-centric, or user-centric, it is not human-centric. This part-for-whole error haunts most human-centric work because much of the detail of their other-selves is eliminated out of hand, even before the first interview is held.

But why should we study a human being, rather than just a customer? The argument against a human-centric view would suggest we are only interested in the moments where they are a customer. We must for the same reason that knowing one part of something does not guarantee that you understand the whole. Here we are confronted with the old story about blind people trying to understand an elephant.[12] Each of them scrutinizes a different part of the elephant, and consequently has a different explanation of the nature of the animal. However, they are all wrong because they know only a small part and do not fully understand the whole. If they were able to see the whole animal first, then their close examination of a small part would be given context and greater meaning.

To understand people either as complete individuals or just as customer/users, we have to begin with their context. We must then study their lives, thoughts, desires, and behaviors considering their surroundings and the other people in their lives to make sense of any of it. This means more than just conducting an interview in their homes. What this means is understanding the context of their actions and the implications of their efforts. This is difficult to capture and is largely left out of the kind of short-term work done in innovation research or design research—to say nothing of the limited practices of market research and design research.

It also means that researchers doing this work must resist oversimplification. More traditional human-centric approaches usually involve some form of light ethnographic work that results in a design persona. This persona is similar in its intention, if not its form, to the segments used in traditional business research. It is a profile that designers and strategists can use to ensure that they are being customer or user-centric. But both are oversimplifications. Neither is a complete portrait of a real person. A persona is not a sufficient profile of a real person because it is an abstraction made for the benefit of the designer. It is inherently designer-centric.

If a persona is not detailed enough—and they never are—then it becomes a simulacrum[13] of the person; it stands in for someone but is not actually representative of them. A simulacrum is a representation of something that resembles it but becomes a replacement for it and loses any connection with the original in the process.[14] It is a false representation of a thing. This process also involves a sleight-of-hand, where the real person is replaced by an artificial one that is easier for the designer and the business strategy to handle. Any gains made for the designer are offset by the loss of reality in the model. Consequently, this is not really a human-centric process, but one that is designer-centric.

The implications of this are important enough to repeat. The application of personas—a hallmark of human-centric practices—is inherently not a human-centric practice. Because the details of the context and the whole person are mostly lost as data is transliterated into a persona. The process is actually a mechanism to do this, and little, to no, consideration is made in what is lost. Once a persona leaves the context in which it was built, i.e. the research process, and moves to people who were not involved, or aware of how they were created, then all of the remaining detail is lost forever and the persona becomes more "real" than the person or persons it was based on. Any empathy that someone may feel for this persona is based on conjecture, and grounded only in the appearance of reality. More empathy is never a bad thing, but we are still talking about improving research, so here it is not that helpful. The idealized person described in the persona replaces any real people for the rest of the design process. While this is convenient for those working on the project, it is not actually good science.

While persona development can be improved by adding more detail into the mix, it is ultimately the over-simplification and idealizing of real people that are to blame for its problems. It is better to do away with them and work with contextualized, detailed explanations of real people, with all of their complexities and contradictions. The approach we advocate within an RHC model is to avoid them as much as possible and eliminate the need for a persona altogether. The solution to this comes through intertwining the research and concept design stages. At its core, a persona is nothing more than a communicative tool, to transmit details of the field to the designers and engineers who use it to guide their decision making. If they participate in the research alongside the researchers, it will then become easier for them to use richer, more detailed accounts of the customers/users/patients who are the focus of the work.

5 Complexity versus Simplicity

The root of this persona problem lies in the fear of complexity in commercial research and business culture. The conventional human-centric research/design process is organized to aid the designer in developing something that is suitable for this task. The first step is to understand the customer/user/patient. But this is done using practices and tools that have been developed to reduce the complexity for the researchers and designers. This is understandable because complicated situations require time and effort to study and understand. Designing for them is equally, if not even more, complicated. However, instead of meeting complex contexts with solutions that are in scale, the most common approach is to simplify the situation and develop an MVP (minimum viable product) as a first attempt at providing a product or service that people can use. This means that the entire process is devoted to developing a simpler model of what is going on and addressing only a sliver of the issues that are found.

While the data is collected empirically, this reduction is accomplished *a priori* (rationalized without direct experience or evidence) in several ways.

First, it happens when the customer/user/patient research projects are designed so that they are too focused to gather contextual information or anything beyond a limited set of questions. Second, it happens when researchers use methods that reduce the amount of human detail captured— quantitative analysis in place of qualitative methods, limited, highly structured discussion guides, focus groups, low sample sizes, drastically shortened timeframes. Third, it happens when information from fieldwork is made to fit frameworks developed before the data was captured or outside the confines of the research study—a major feature of processes that use STEEP-V[15] or PESTL[16] categorization schema and any application of 2×2 models.[17] Fourth, information that is captured in field is reduced through the production of oversimplified personas and other simplified models. Finally, a sensemaking process that involves clustering details into categories and then never considering the details again.

All these problems are common to the human-centric design model as it stands now. These mechanisms of oversimplification are driven not just by poor research practice, but also by an overarching belief in reducing the complexity at every step. Often, this is an unexamined belief and enters into a research program as an unnoticed factor of processes taught to practitioners in school. So, while they are breaks in process, they are features of the philosophical underpinnings of what we are doing when human-centered researchers conduct research on humans in applied contexts. These problems can render human-centered design research merely a process of simplifying the world for the designers' convenience. And unfortunately, it often veers into oversimplification—a cause for failures and a need for iteration.

A radical human-centric approach works against these tendencies. At its core is a certainty that the world must be studied "as it is" to be properly understood. This makes it the researcher's and designer's responsibility to address the world as they find it with an equivalent level of complexity in how they design for it. This means there is no reduction in scale, scope, loss of context, and a requirement that big problems are met with effort. The implications of this are not always comfortable. Research programs must be designed to let the subject matter and the individuals in the field site guide how long the engagement must be, which can mean longer field trips. The sensemaking process is organized around systems modeling and away from easy, causal explanations. Additionally, analysis is governed by a mandate to not fictionalize the circumstances by imposing overly simplified categorical frameworks. Every insight is tested, and every recommendation is contextualized, so that they remain connected to the world, and people, they came from.

6 From Frameworks to a Positive Skepticism

Business thinking is filled with countless frameworks and models. Most business books provide a new "how to" guide to conducting business more successfully by applying a novel framework for action or reconsidering the model through which something is structured. They feature titles like *The Synergy Solution: How Speed Dating Teaches us about Running a Multinational,* or *The Ten Habits of Cool People: Learn to Innovate Like a Hipster.* But like most self-help book, these frameworks and approaches are usually just a rehashing of common sense. The actual framework is irrelevant provided you think logically and consider the order of operations for any task carefully. If you cannot, then the framework provides the scaffolding for the application of common sense. Most sensemaking procedures are perfect examples of this as they too are rules for organizing thought and action.[18]

However, functional these frameworks may be, practitioners usually do not have a theoretical awareness that allows them to understand how these frameworks obscure or bake-in their unspoken, tacit assumptions and beliefs (biases). Our assumptions and beliefs structure the way we understand the information we are given and how we choose to respond to it. We learn these structuring pathways by becoming acculturated to them when we are young. But the unconscious nature of these "structuring structures"[19] renders the problem unavailable to most. Thus, people know *how* to work through a particular situation or process, but do not understand *why* they should do so. It also means the frameworks are just bolstering thinking that should be questioned, deconstructed, modified, or eliminated altogether.

The RHC shift here is to move away from simplistic, easy frameworks, and to commit to being skeptical in the work we are doing. If you are using a framework capable of rigidly maintaining your perspective, assumptions, or beliefs, then you cannot benefit from this outcome. If you do not understand the framework you are using, like the basic service design process, or design thinking protocol, then you risk it becoming a rigid structure capable of obscuring the very thing you should be looking for. The implications of this are clear. Frameworks should be questioned. They should not be followed without carefully considering the implications of their use. They can be used effectively to manage the act of collaboration, but they should never go unscrutinized.

Skepticism is a positive trait in a researcher. It allows one to take stock of the appropriateness of your resources, including the strengths and weaknesses of tools, methods, and practices. This skepticism must be grounded in the acknowledgment that the process does not guarantee success. Unquestioningly moving through a framework only orders the steps one takes; it does not create excellent results. I am not suggesting that we move away from frameworks as a way to organize and collaborate, rather that we stop believing the idea that they provide certainty. The emphasis has to move away from the actions to the thinking and expertise of the people doing the work.

7 Theorizing Needs = The End of Unmet Needs

Within the current thinking about human research, one of the most problematic examples of this papering over reality is the search for unmet needs. Simply put, unmet needs are a myth, and Maslow's day has come and gone.[20] Yes, it is true that there are many people who suffer in poverty and face a lack in many basic provisions of a comfortable life, food, money, healthcare, position in society. But few businesses are interested in these problems[21]—the only things that qualify as unmet needs in the lives of people who are many steps from starvation. I understand this is a contentious point. Most conversations within the business about customers and users involve a discussion of their needs. This is because, in business thinking, an unmet need is an opportunity for business. It is a point where a new product or service can restructure how people do things so that they become customers/users of the company selling this option. Within this construct, an unmet need is just something that is a minor problem or gap that can be addressed by creating something new. All of this works well enough for the most part. But if we are trying to create even more complicated products to fit into even more complicated circumstances, an AI home assistant, for instance, this will no longer be adequate. It has to be said that in most cases the unmet needs uncovered in design thinking research are nothing more than breaks in a previously designed product or service. They provide keys to iterating on something that was already a created situation. To improve commercial research, we must reassess the idea of the unmet need. Here, it is the idea that they are "unmet" is the problem, because the entity that would "meet" these needs is always going to be a business.

Unmet needs do not exist because the vast majority of people not suffering the privations of poverty live complete lives. They are able to get through the day perfectly well without any new innovations, be they products, services, or experiences. In fact, their lives are already saturated with solutions. So they have no unmet needs, only desires or points where they can be convinced to live and work in a different way.

What this means is that any new product or service is not something that fills a gap in someone's life, but is actually an intervention into a complete, self-regulated system. The new product is not a benign solution to heal a lack. It is a novel introduction that must come with an argument of why someone should change what they are doing and switch to a new way of getting something done. This means that designing for unmet needs is about creating interventions into a fully functioning life—this is not something that is altogether human-centric. The shift here involves abandoning the belief that innovation and design fill holes in life and adopting a view of innovation as a process of changing the parameters of what is going on in a particular context. Instead of meeting a need, innovation is about making an argument about why a different way is better. This will help innovators and designers respect the human lives they are messing with.

8 Growth and Homeostasis

Growth, the model used in contemporary capitalism to outline its fundamental purpose, is at odds with the way the world really works. How, in a finite ecosystem, is continuous growth possible? It isn't. Yes, the various mechanisms allowing for the movement and development of global capital provide a way to literally create money out of thin air. However, when we consider the growth potential of products and services, we encounter a limitation in available resources.[22] We now know that natural resources such as water, food, wood, oil, minerals, and topsoil are finite, and rapidly depleting.[23] Our insatiable appetite for goods of many kinds is straining our plant to its breaking point.[24] Even space is now at a premium, with population increasing and viable land decreasing. All of this brings us to ask if continual growth is possible. Everything, even digital resources have an environmental impact. Our approach to growth seems doomed because very soon there will be nowhere to grow into.

While economic growth presents a very real threat to the way we live now, it continues as a fundamental concept and basis for business thinking. Theories of growth lead us to believe that economic activity always has more headroom—a resource of untapped potential.[25] But following the same pattern of sleight-of-hand, the conflation of economic activity and human activity, this idea contributes to a tacit belief that the domain of human activity operates with the same headroom. There is always room to add more into the system, and these additions will improve the quality of life for all.

This philosophy is quite dominant in the technology industry, where design thinking organizes people's efforts into development and creation. The very idea behind the design thinking process, or indeed, human-centric design is that something new and innovative can be developed to make the world a better place. There is very little consideration of whether another new solution will be ultimately useful, or if removing something might be a better approach.

Humans live in a relatively homeostatic manner, meaning that our fundamental societal and cultural structures are slow to change and can absorb a lot of alterations. This is one reason why it takes a long time for cultural or societal change to happen. There has been little radical change for millennia in many of our behavioral systems. Languages change very slowly. Our sense of ethics and morals change very slowly. And while there is a great deal of evolution and entropy changing the surface details, we live much as people have for many thousands of years. We eat, sleep, procreate, work, fight, and entertain ourselves much as our ancestors did—despite the more rapid changes in the technologies we use to do it. The proof of this comes in how we subsume new technologies for old purposes. The penny post, telegraph, telephone, mobile phone, email, and text apps are all radically different technologies, but they are all used to do the same thing: talk to one another about the goings-on in our lives.[26] What we have gained in speed and convenience has not radically changed what we do with the communications. All of these technologies have been brought into a communicative purpose that they cannot affect. Within this homeostatic behavioral system, there is only a little space for change and innovation. At this scale, is no place for growth, because a homeostatic system has no headroom for change. It is naturally self-righting and self-sizing.

What this means is that when growth is a pillar of a particular knowledge system, like in human-centric design, this system is immediately divorced from the way that our behavioral world works. Additive design fueled by a belief in growth simply adds to a system of options but cannot affect the baseline behaviors, rendering new innovations in communications systems merely an alternative to technologies of the past. The behavior will be basically the same, although the way we have to interact with this new technology might have to change. This reveals the fact that the theories behind business and human-centered practices consider human behavior at a level much smaller and incomplete than any attentive behavioral study. Human-centric perspectives cannot accommodate a larger frame of reference.

A radical human-centered model acknowledges the fact that human behavior is found in a relatively homeostatic context, where behavior does not change that quickly. It seeks to provide insight into this system with the understanding that design should be a practice of participating in this world and not trying to change it in one go. Making positive changes in a homeostatic system means pushing for change at many levels, something few businesses are equipped to do. By abandoning growth models of business, a radical human-centricity also provides a framework for developing sustainable change that is not always directly connected to the small wins of commercial success.

9 Impact: Understanding the Complexity of Homeostasis, its Inertia, and Barriers to Change

The theoretical shifts involving needs, complexity, and homeostasis combine to provide an indication of what should actually be studied in human-centric commercial research: impact.

As I suggested earlier, design and innovation do not exploit real gaps. Rather, they make interventions into a context where people are already managing by themselves, or where designed products, services, or experiences are failing to live up to their promises. Real people live in a context or system that is complete, functional, and homeostatic. Their lives and the way they do things have their own inertia, and there are no gaps because the system is complete and self-managing. What this means is people have always had complete lives and were perfectly able to manage without the next big technology or service. It may not be efficient, but speed is not everything. When we design a new product, service, or experience, we are not exploiting gaps or addressing needs in this complete, static system, we are changing it—sometimes for the better, sometimes not.

If we shift our thinking and our practice away from needs and gaps and towards understanding how changes will impact a complete, functional, homeostatic system, we take a big step towards correctly understanding what is going on in someone's life. We also begin to grasp exactly what the design world is doing. It is making changes to how we live according to a new system of logic. It is changing the rules to suit the efficiencies and benefits a technological intervention can bring.[27] The radical human-centric shift involves understanding this and seeing the intervention as something that might be positive or negative. It involves exploring how design and innovation can improve the situation by amplifying what is already good in it, and avoid destroying things just to make the context conform to the dictates of a device or "digital thinking."

With this in mind, a radical human-centric approach to research looks for the affordances of this system, the pathways and behaviors that can be amplified or modified by a designed intervention, and the socio-cultural barriers that will prevent people from accepting the changes. It must also focus on understanding the context and behavioral system in enough detail to predict the impact any design interventions may have. You can see these are all very far from "needs" and "gaps," and this is because neither of those things exists in real-life. They only exist in business thought.

The ethnographic process must then be a study of the complexities of a self-replicating, rich, and homeostatic system—complete with conscious and unconscious structures, behaviors, and human and nonhuman social actors.

Research studying such a construct must understand people as agents who maintain these processes and search for their conscious and unconscious alterations of what is going on. Their ethnographic process must also include an assessment of what is possible within the affordances and constraints of this context. A method called the ethnography of the possible has emerged from design anthropology theory and practices to help here.[28] Essentially a blending of co-creation interview and ethnographic encounter, the ethnography of the possible is a way to engage with the context's inhabitants— that is, the people you are there to study—and have them speculate on what changes might be possible, positive, and impactful in their world. It is a way to simultaneously assess what they care about and what they would like to see happen after the designers and prototypers have completed their work.

Cultural barriers are the keys to these systems, because they translate directly to design briefs. However, they are bafflingly absent from most commercial human-centric, or design research. The reason for this is they are not to be found in positive action—that is, what people do or say— but rather in the spaces between individuals, in the place where culture lives. This means, importantly, that human-centric research has to consider more than the person in front of you. It has to consider what people build together and how these communal values and structures might resist a bunch of designers from changing things.

10 Impact at Scale: The problem of Global and Local Perspectives

This discussion reveals another problem confronting anyone wanting to do honest, rigorous behavioral research in applied contexts. This problem one of scale, experience, and perspective. Human-centered research must be able to accommodate several levels of experience and understanding even when trying to study simple things like UI interaction. This is necessary because human beings do not perceive the world in a uniform way. Our view of reality changes drastically depending on which perspective we are using. This means individuals do not have a uniform view of things themselves. We are able to view the world around us as a member of society, as a member of a group, as a member of a family unit, and as an individual simultaneously. This simultaneity makes studying human experience quite complicated because the view from each of these levels can make the world look very different. Priorities shift. Explanations change. Even memory diverges. There is a parallax problem here, where even a single concept or object appears different when viewed from a global level or an individualistic one.[29]

So, when studying human experience, the scale of that experience needs to be considered. In contemporary human-centric approaches, it is not.

Scale also impacts what can be studied because many global phenomena may not exist at a local level at all. Things impacting individuals in their homes might not have any impact on global affairs. What this means is that design decisions based on a solution for a micro-level issue, might, or might not, impact meso (middle layer) or macro-level conditions differently. Designers of a social media app like Twitter likely created something that worked very well for an individual user. In fact, if they did not, the app would not be particularly useful. What they clearly did not consider was the impact it would have on politics when tens of millions of users were able to use it on a global scale. The app had to be redesigned and the interactions monitored to control the kind of debate that grew on the platform.[30]

Issues arising at different scales require different scales of responses. Global problems like climate change or social reform require an enormous effort from a large number of people and institutions. For an individual to make a change to the way their community runs requires less effort and resources. The same is true when designing or innovating for people. Life is not very complicated at the level of a customer/user and requires very little effort to change when compared to larger-scale experiences.

One task in any study of human behavior is to identify the scale of experience that a particular issue or phenomenon operates within. This is not easy because it involves understanding the total context sufficiently before this comparison can be made. Understanding the impact of changes made at one level on the circumstances at other levels is even harder to understand. Despite the difficulty, this is precisely what human-centered research must do. Currently, there is little acknowledgment of this problem within human-centered research and design practices.

The radical approach I am advocating not only acknowledges the implications of different registers of experience, it actively demonstrates how designed changes will fit and what impact they will have at all levels. This provides for a deeper understanding of the design challenge and what the innovation will do once it is out in the world. It will also allow policy makers, designers, and strategists access to issues and problems that might be out of view if the research study were only studying experience and behavior at a single level of experience.

Conclusion

There can be no complaints about theorizing. Engaging in theory is a process of making what is unspoken clear and obvious to any observer. By revealing what is going on—or at least what you believe is going on—allows you to understand it more. But more importantly, it helps you understand if you are correct, and if your method for understanding it is the right one. Willfully ignoring theory is folly, because it is only through the process of theorizing what good research can be will you understand what real research should be. Once you have a handle on what research should be, and what you need to shift to set yourself up to succeed in this world, you can move on to the practical aspects of doing research. We will get to the details of this in Chapter 7. But first, we need to discuss the practical shifts needed to push our research practice towards real research in a radically human-centric way.

By now, it is clear how a radical human-centric approach differs from what is commonly practiced today in commercial human-centric research. To put it simply, the major points of difference stem from the compassion and flexibility that provide ground for every choice a researcher makes during the execution of the study. The theoretical underpinnings leave behind many of the impediments to good research, including the professional in-fighting, prejudices against theory, and arbitrary disciplinary boundaries that keep commercial research from learning from practitioners who are pushing the limits of what ethnographic practices can do.

Our brief examination of a few practical points demonstrates that a radical approach has to depart from conventional human-centric practices by becoming responsible for the people we work with in field. This analysis is incomplete, however. All of the chapters that follow continue our critique and push the story of how a radically human-centric approach to commercial research can actually fulfill the promise of being human-centric. We've looked at how to get into field more compassionately and thoughtfully. The next chapter focuses on how we can be more rigorous once we are there.

Notes

1 Foucault, M., 1994. *The Order of Things: An Archeology of Human Sciences.* New York: Vintage Books.
2 Foucault, Michel. 1972. *The Archeology of Knowledge and the Discourse on Language.* New York: Pantheon.
3 Lepore, Jill. 2014. "The Disruption Machine: What the Gospel of Innovation Gets Wrong." In *New Yorker,* June 16.
4 Moore, D.G., 1988. Industrial anthropology: Conditions of revival. *City & Society,* 2(1), pp. 5–18. ; Jacoby, S.M., 1986. Employee attitude testing at Sears, Roebuck and Company, 1938–1960. *The Business History Review,* pp. 602–632. ; Schwarzkopf, S., 2016. In search of the consumer: The history of market research from 1890 to 1960. In *The Routledge companion to marketing history.* London: Routledge, 61–83.
5 Xu, J., 2005. *Market research handbook: Measurement, approach and practice.* iUniverse. ; van Hamersveld, M. and de Bont, C. eds., 2007. *Market research handbook.* John Wiley & Sons. ; Edmunds, H., 1999. *The Focus Group Research Handbook.* Stamford, CT: The Bottom Line.

6 A speculative anthropologist is an anthropologist with additional foresight training. Foresight and anthropology have a long history together, with some of the most cogent articulations of a speculative anthropology coming from Margaret Meade.

7 Metz, Ashley and Paul Hartley. 2020. "Development as a Valuation Practice: Implications for practitioners and fields. *Technological Forecasting & Social Change,* 155:C. ; Miemis, V., Smart, J. and Brigis, A., 2012. Open foresight. *Journal of Futures Studies, 17*(1), pp. 91–98.

8 Hartley, Paul. 2017. "What is a Human Future Anyway?" *MISC: Human Futures* 25:6.; Hartley, Paul. 2017. "Towards a Human Futures Perspective." *MISC* 25:117–125.

9 The fourth industrial revolution is an idea popularized by Klaus Schwab, the founder and Executive Chairman of the World Economic Forum. His assertion was that "The First Industrial Revolution used water and steam power to mechanize production. The Second used electric power to create mass production. The Third used electronics and information technology to automate production. Now a Fourth Industrial Revolution is building on the Third, the digital revolution that has been occurring since the middle of the last century." (https://www. weforum.org/agenda/2016/01/the-fourth-industrial-revolution-what-it-means-and-how-to-respond/) This was taken up by many in the technology industry because it supported their position as the focus of the economic, social, and technological lives of us all.

10 A weak signal is an indicator of change found in the subtleties of human activity and natural change today.

11 https://design.cmu.edu/sites/default/files/Transition_Design_Monograph_final.pdf.

12 This is an old story that may have its origins in Buddhist, Jain, and Hindu theology. Its purpose is to demonstrate the failures of understanding something without an appropriate context.

13 Baudrillard, J., 2020. *Simulacra and simulations.* London: Routledge, 230–234.; Deleuze, G. and Krauss, R., 1983. Plato and the Simulacrum. *October, 27,* pp. 45–56.

14 Baudrillard describes this simulation as "the generation by models of a real without origin or reality: a hyperreal," on the first page of his book. Although there is an entire book that follows this sentence, what he is succinctly saying here is that a simulacrum is a simulation of the real that resembles it enough to replace it despite being built on nothing. It has no relation to the real and can easily replace it so we are unable to tell the difference. A persona is one such form of representation. They are often built on weak foundations, barely resembling the people studied, and are then used to replace that person in the mind of the designer.

15 STEEP-V is a foresight format for categorizing weak signals. It stands for social, technological, environmental, economic, political, and value.

16 PESTLE is also a foresight categorization for organizing weak signals. It divides the world into a slightly different format than its cousin STEEP-V. It stands for political, economic, social, technological, legal, and environmental.

17 This is a major problem in the qualitative approaches common to foresight.

18 Chan, J., Dang, S. and Dow, S.P., 2016, May. Comparing different sensemaking approaches for large-scale ideation. In *Proceedings of the 2016 CHI conference on human factors in computing systems* (pp. 2717–2728). ; Boland, R.J., 2008. Decision making and sensemaking. In *Handbook on Decision Support Systems 1.* Berlin and Heidelberg: Springer, 55–63.

And

Rylander Eklund, A., Navarro Aguiar, U. and Amacker, A., 2021. Design thinking as sensemaking—Developing a pragmatist theory of practice to (re) introduce sensibility. *Journal of Product Innovation Management.*

19 This is a phrase use by sociologist Pierre Bourdieu in his book *Distinction.* With it, he is referencing the learned structures we use to make distinctions between things in our cultural world: good/bad, classy/basic, etc. These distinctions are the results of the kind of processes I am describing here.

20 Hartley, Paul. 2020. "Beyond Design Thinking: Can Design Research Education Unlock a New Foundation for Design?" *Applied Arts Magazine*, April 8. (https://www.appliedartsmag.com/blog/beyond-design-thinking-a17631/).

21 This is a major problem, because they should be.

22 Oberle, B., Bringezu, S., Hatfield-Dodds, S., Hellweg, S., Schandl, H. and Clement, J., 2019. *Global Resources Outlook: 2019.* International Resource Panel, New York: United Nations Envio.

23 Ibid.

24 Ibid.

25 Barnett, H.J. and Morse, C., 2013. *Scarcity and growth: The economics of natural resource availability.* Routledge. ; Roys, N. and Seshadri, A., 2014. On the origin and causes of economic growth. *The Social Systems Research Institute (SSRI)*, pp. 4–5.

26 Standage, T., 1998. *The Victorian Internet: The remarkable story of the telegraph and the nineteenth century's online pioneers.* London: Phoenix.

27 Ellul, Jacques.1964. *Technological Society.* New York: Vintage Books.

28 Halse, J., 2020. Ethnographies of the Possible. In *Design Anthropology* (pp. 180–196). London: Routledge.

29 Zizek, S., 2009. *The Parallax View.* Cambridge: MIT Press.

30 Liu, Y., Kliman-Silver, C. and Mislove, A., 2014, May. The tweets they are a-changin': Evolution of twitter users and behavior. In *Proceedings of the International AAAI Conference on Web and Social Media* (Vol. 8, No. 1). ; Rogers, R., 2013, May. Debanalizing Twitter: The transformation of an object of study. In *Proceedings of the 5th annual ACM web science conference* (pp. 356–365).

Part II

CORE CONSIDERATIONS

Chapter 4

BEYOND EMPATHY

When it comes to researching real people, current market research, design thinking, and human-centered approaches are actually quite poor guides for how to conduct research that is actually human-centric. They provide clear guidance on how to develop data for use within a business, be it market information, demographics and psychographics, or to fill design personas. But the methodological toolkit for how to do this research is surprisingly small. Design thinking and design research are especially lacking in solid research practices, preferring to focus on empathy as the grounding for solid research. The guidance on research practices that the majority of descriptions of HCR/HCD provide is approximately this: "[…] empathy is an approach that draws upon people's real-world experiences to address modern challenges. When companies allow a deep emotional understanding of people's needs to inspire them—and transform their work, their teams, and even their organization at large—they unlock the creative capacity for innovation."[1] This is all well and fine, but it hides the fact that empathy is neither a research methodology nor a gateway to knowledge of people. In fact, empathy is just table-stakes. It is the grounding every researcher should have to do any kind of research about people and behavior, from historiography to census taking.

A deeper problem reveals itself when people make methodological statements about design thinking and HCD. In the same article on empathy by several researchers at Ideo entitled "Empathy on the edge" the full definition begins this way: "The definition of empathy is the ability to be aware of, understanding of, and sensitive to another person's feelings and thoughts without having had the same experience. As human-centered designers, we consciously work to understand the experience of our clients and their customers. These insights inform and inspire our designs."[2] What is curious about this is the subtle shift that happens in this, and most, description of empathy in HCD. Do you see it? In the first sentence it says "feelings and thoughts without […] the same experience," and in the second sentence it says "experience of our clients and their customers." The first problem lies in the fact that the interior, emotional experience of an individual is not what people study when they do any form of UX (UX researchers are not interested in the thoughts of an individual). Secondly, that interior emotional experience is not the total experience of that person—something that requires a greater phenomenological study to understand. And third, the interior experience is not sufficient to provide an understanding "the experience of our clients and their customers."

While this is one of the most nuanced descriptions I was able to find, it is, from the first few sentences inadequate to the task. Emotional empathy is not the only route to understanding experience. There is a lot more to understanding someone else's experience than simply talking to them with an empathetic mindset—although this is undoubtedly step one. And emotional experiences are not the only experiences people have. Simply put, taken from the perspective provided by phenomenological theory, the authors' descriptions are both misleading and will likely create more problems than they will fix. These issues persist throughout the entire article because the authors make a flawed connection between empathy, emotions, and experience in practically every paragraph.

Empathy alone is not enough to build a methodology and practice of human-centered research. It is not even a sufficient feature of a study of experience. It is necessary and essential, to be sure, but it is insufficient to get to understanding by itself. With this in mind, the RHC approach focuses on developing and using methods that are about studying human experience and the complete contexts in which it is found. This means conducting the research to locate the details of how individuals and social constructs interact to foster interior states of mind. It also means operationalizing a relativistic perspective that allows us, as researchers, to understand how all behaviors and lines of thinking are equivalent. Their status as a "problem" or as an "error" is worked out later once the experiential model has been developed. We will discuss this more in the outline of incorporating cultural modeling into the methodology.

How Did We Get Into This Mess?

Human-centered design and design thinking arose as solutions to a lack, or if you will, a gap in business thinking. Both borrow from a designer's approach to creativity, problem solving, and product development to a business world suffering from an overly simplistic view of human behavior. As such, they offer an alternative to the quantitative-data heavy, positivistic view of human behavior typical in business thinking, and provide a way out of the operational, abstracted approach to humans we see in business or engineering thought. This was a necessary modification because most of the economic models of human behavior taught in your typical MBA program or business school are universalized descriptions of how idealized people behave in the limited arena of commercial exchange and do not offer any indication of how many of us live our lives. So, we can see the introduction of design into business innovation provided as an intervention into this way of understanding people and their lives and allowed new products and services to be grounded in a different stratum of the human experience.

Central to this philosophy is the concept of empathy, which is held up by Ideo and later design thinkers as a key pillar in designing for other people. On the face of it, trying to be empathetic in the practice of design is a good thing. It is always a good idea to empathize with others and try to behave according to the social and emotional bridge that empathy provides. However, the appeal to empathy common in most descriptions of HCD and design thinking is more problematic than anyone seems to realize. Even the evocation of the term "empathy" hides a clear lack of progress in the evolution of truly human-centric practices. Most D-school (design school) articulations of empathy demonstrate that the authors have little interest in human behavior or in the work that is required to actually empathize with someone.[3] Consequently, design thinking and HCD use empathy as an empty buzzword and render it devoid of practical meaning. Instead, it becomes a way to perform a saleable differentiator which makes it easier to sell design thinking processes to businesses that need a new product or design. We can see this in the descriptions of empathy themselves.

This version comes from Ideo's Design Toolkit, a key text in design thinking education.[4] The entire description is as follows:

Empathy is the capacity to step into other people's shoes, to understand their lives, and start to solve problems from their perspectives. Human-centered design is premised on empathy, on the idea that the people you're designing for are your roadmap to innovative solutions. All you have to do is empathize, understand them, and bring them along with you in the design process.

For too long, the international development community has designed solutions to the challenges of poverty without truly empathizing with and understanding the people it's looking to serve. But by putting ourselves in the shoes of the person we're designing for, human-centered designers can start to see the world, and all the opportunities to improve it, through a new and powerful lens.

Immersing yourself in another world not only opens you up to new creative possibilities, but it allows you to leave behind preconceived ideas and outmoded ways of thinking. Empathizing with the people you're designing for is the best route to truly grasping the context and complexities of their lives. But most importantly, it keeps the people you're designing for squarely grounded in the center of your work.[5]

Like the basic descriptions at the beginning of this chapter, the authors of this work describe empathy as just one of the "mindsets" of design thinking, with the others being "Optimism, Iteration, Creative Confidence, Making, Embracing Ambiguity, and Learning from Failure."[6] All of these mindsets, including empathy, preface or facilitate the design of a new product or service from a solutionist perspective that sees the world as a set of solvable problems and unmet needs, and goes about creating the solution for all of them.[7] This means that these are not really foundational mindsets, but are actually blinders to keep the newly minted design thinker oriented within this solutionist perspective. Leaving aside the validity of this solutionist view for a moment, I want to focus on what is going on in this description of empathy.

In their article, this statement about empathy from the Ideo team sits under the epigraph "Empathy: in order to get to new solutions, you have to get to know different people, different scenarios, different places." At first glance, there is very little wrong with the first few lines of the description that follows. Nevertheless, this epigraph shows the problems with evoking empathy. With this quick, introduction, we are already in confusing territory. It says empathy requires us to "get to know [...]" but knowledge and empathy are not necessarily the same thing. This suggests that empathy depends on gaining new knowledge. However, as an overarching mindset empathy must be prior to knowledge. They are actually different things. So, even the first few words are conflating ideas and definitions. This continues into the main body of the statement where empathy becomes a "capacity [...] to understand [...]" only to immediately be separated from understanding and rendered as a "stepping stone" to understanding.[8] Here the author further confuses the issue about what empathy is by making it a characteristic of the researcher and then suggesting it is a processual detail. In this statement, empathy is identified as a stepping-stone to knowledge. But what they are really talking about is learning about other people's lives, perspectives, and ways of dealing with the world. In this, I totally agree with them as this is the practice of research in the social sciences. However, I take issue with the idea that all of this fits under empathy.

Empathy, knowledge, understanding, and immersion in a world are all related, but they are not synonymous or interchangeable. They are all necessary components of good research, human-centered or otherwise, but they are not sufficient elements of a research practice by themselves. This means you cannot just have empathy and hope for the best—which is often implied in the way people teach DIY design thinking practices. Nevertheless, there seems to be a consensus in the design thinking literature that somehow empathy leads to knowledge. Eve Köppen and Christoph Meinel restate the same problem and even take it a step farther when they say, "design thinking authors are of the opinion that empathic [sic] insights are a form of extremely important knowledge that stems from concrete interaction with other people [...]. Indeed, three types of knowledge characterize design: technological knowledge, knowledge about user needs, and knowledge about product language [...] the two last forms of knowledge are rooted in an empathic [sic] understanding of other people."[9]

Here they conflate empathy with knowledge once again. Given that they are paraphrasing a number of design thinking texts here, this is not surprising. But instead of leaving it there, they define the kind of knowledge they are talking about. However, I am unable to see how technological knowledge or knowledge about product language are related to empathy, as these are products of a designer-centric perspective. Their point about knowing user needs is a pillar of design innovation, and more human-centric in its focus, but it is not rooted in empathy because it is part of a solutionist view of the world. Therefore, it is also mostly designer centric. This description of empathy is lacking both a functional definition of empathy and a clear statement about how it differs from knowledge.

Their next definition of empathy is much improved. "We understand the term empathy in its broadest sense as perspective-taking, including both the involuntary act of feeling with someone else as well as the cognitive act of placing oneself into someone else's position and adopting their perspective [...]. As a basic form of social cognition, empathy is the capacity 'to share, to experience the feelings of another person'.[10] Empathy is an ability that allows us to comprehend the situations and the perspective of others, both imaginatively and affectively. The aim of empathy is to construe mutual understanding."[11]

Now we are finally getting somewhere. This definition avoids many of the problems of the other two we have already seen. In this definition, empathy is prior to knowledge, and it is simply a facilitator for mutual understanding. It is not conflated with them. Empathy is the conduit to both. It is a skill, or capacity, held by the researcher that enables them to do their work and to bridge the epistemological and phenomenological (knowledge and experience) gaps that separate different people, different perspectives, and different cultures. But it is important to note, empathy is the first step or the first characteristic. It is not a guarantor of knowledge or understanding. Knowledge and understanding are not gained by adopting a "mindset" as Ideo's authors would have it, or just by inhabiting a perspective that is not your own (although this is important). They are generated through careful, meticulous, and rigorous research. Yes, this research must be "rooted in empathy," but it must also be introspective, reflexive, curious, detailed, and critical as well. It must also be grounded in solid practices and a clear understanding of the methodological and intellectual development of the subject matter at hand.

The problem with all of this is that people following the design thinking playbook often lack the necessary training in the social sciences to be able to do this. Thus, their evocation of "empathy" is insufficient to mount a rigorous, insightful research program. Design thinking and human-centered design lack a set of rigorous research methods for making the most out of this empathetic intent. At most, they put an empathetic veneer on the practices of the cold, heartless, intellectually bankrupt business practices they are supposed to be supplanting.

Köppen and Meinel agree that there exists a lack of methods and techniques for implementing empathy in companies, but their next, and last, articulation of it in practice reveals another error plaguing the entire design thinking industry. They say, "contrary to the traditional image of the rational, tactical, controlled employee, Design Thinking pursues the strategy of actively letting go to be able to even better place oneself in another person's position. These methods for the optimization of personal empathy are based on intuition as well as on the uncontrolled and emotional engaging with the other."[12]

Here they return to problematic ground. They began by arguing that empathy is about placing yourself in someone else's position, so you can know as they do (what they designate as external empathy), only to end with a position where intuition and emotion are the core of its pair, personal empathy. Most people in the design thinking world do not make this fine a distinction—between external and personal empathy—but with this new sleight-of-hand perspectival empathy suddenly becomes emotional empathy.

It is here that the call to be more empathetic loses its clarity and its usefulness. Empathy in research cannot be about emotion, at least not alone. Design thinking work is not about creating a disposition, it is about using that headspace to get something done—to learn something and then create something. All of these turns to psychological states, to mindsets, and emotion are problematic because they may in fact be distracting us from what needs to happen in research when the goal is to create something new. Yes, they are important elements, but there is no way we can turn this emotional understanding into a productive act. It is simply table stakes for being a good researcher. Ethnographic work of any kind cannot happen if the researcher is not emotionally receptive to others. So, instead of empathy being a goal in human-centered research, it is something that has to be there in the beginning. Working without it is a nonstarter.

One of the reasons for the need for this kind of empathy is to mitigate the effects of an overly rationalized, objective view—one which could so separate the research from the subject, or subjects, of the study. And this is the reason why design thinking provided a needed addition to product development and research for corporations. Technologists of all kinds, market researchers, and businesspeople are trained, and indeed encouraged, to not get into the details of human life. Design thinking brought a perspective based on empathy that encouraged these objective thinkers to consider a different way of thinking about people. But this does not really lie in empathy. It lies in Roger's definition, "understanding the user's private world as if it were your own." It is not about empathy per se, it is about the magic that happens through a shift of perspective.

Ultimately, to call this process empathy, or empathetic, and leaving it at that, is to miss a lot of the detail and nuance that is necessary to actually make use of this shift in perspective. Operationalizing empathy is a lot harder than making the most of a shift in perspective. The first is needlessly vague, and the other is part of many decades of work in the social sciences and history. It is especially true given that the bulk of the serious literature on design thinking defines empathy as a shift in perspective anyway. So, the term is actually unnecessary at best and misleading at worst.

With this in mind, we can actually just drop it altogether—with the understanding that the positive aspects of empathy are always present from the beginning. To be a good researcher means being kind, open, and empathetic at a minimum anyway. The methods and practices then are built on this foundation. Nevertheless, we can drop empathy from good research practices and put discovering, building, and assuming a new perspective in its place. This is the intention anyway, so we do not lose anything by dropping this opaque term.

Looking Beyond Empathy

If we now assume that empathy is table stakes, and while useful, it does little to help us with the practical aspects of a relativistic, nonjudgemental, nonpositivistic research practice, we must look beyond it. We must now separate ourselves from the buzzwordy world of design thinking and HCD and enter into a radically human-centric perspective that is more concerned with the work of real research. Within a radically human-centric perspective, empathy is always present. However, we are now more concerned with the perspectival shift that all of the design thinking descriptions of empathy were hinting at but unable to articulate or fully realize.

Waiting for us beyond empathy are the weightier intellectual problems and methodological issues of perspective, phenomenology, cultural formation, and meaning. Because to "know" or "understand" someone else, it is not enough to merely be empathetic. We must learn about how they see the world, how they navigate through it, make decisions, understand others, and reject the perspectives of others. Luckily, these are the very things social scientists have been doing for over 100 years. Anthropologists and sociologist work with the specific goal of getting closer and closer to a "native" cultural insider understanding, or at least a culturally appropriate one. The practice of ethnography was developed for this purpose. Consequently, we can rely on a preexisting set of perspectives, methods, and theories that will help us navigate past the boundaries of simple empathy.

Taking a radical human-centric perspective requires us to modify, update, or eliminate the research methods of design thinking and HCD because they are not rigorous enough to fulfill the goal of "knowing" or "understanding" someone else's perspective. Anthropologists know that this is a very large undertaking that usually requires years of devoted study and careful ethnography. It usually involves learning a new language, living with your research subjects, and obsessing over the details of someone else's daily life. Within an applied, or commercial, context this is usually impossible. The radically human-centric approach is a way of finding a way to engage deeply within a short period of time—to get as close to an insider view as possible within the constraints of the project. While we do not spend years in field, we do orient ourselves with the same specialist knowledge and make use of similar field practices typical in "real" ethnography.

What Lies Beyond Empathy?

The first step towards gaining "knowledge" about another person's perspective is to understand the difficulty of the task. Understanding how someone sees the world around them, makes sense of these things, and runs their own life involves an engagement with the social structure of their lives, their cultural milieu, and their idiosyncratic take on both. There are several entry points into this complex network of socio-cultural formations and personal action, but they collapse into three major categories: experience, language, and practice—or how they understand the world, how they talk about it, and what they do to create themselves and their social world. I have touched on several of these topics earlier, but now I want to put them in order so we can begin to understand what is involved in conducting a radially human-centric research project.

Phenomenologically "Seeing"

The study of experience does not begin with emotion, and it does not end with empathy. Rather it is a study of how someone—you, me, anyone—perceives the world around them and how they make meaning of what they experience. It is the study of everything through the eyes of a perceiver. Its proper name is phenomenology or the study of things (phenomena). The roots of phenomenology begin with Greek philosophy, most notably in the writings of Plato and Aristotle. In their work, phenomenology is so closely linked to epistemology, or the creation of knowledge, and ontology, the nature of being. Plato considered the problem of how things appear to us (phenomena) might be different from how they actually are (nomena). His point was that it may be possible for an object to exist in reality separate from the way we perceive it. The problem here is that its "being" might be different from how we see it.

In his famous example of the cave from *The Republic*, Plato created a thought experiment where people experience a world that does not truly represent what the world actually is. Plato explains that there may be people who have lived their entire lives chained in a cave where everything they know comes from watching reflections of things projected onto the wall of the cave.[13] They are unable to turn their heads and therefore cannot check the veracity of these reflections. Therefore, these shadows are their "reality." He makes the point that this is likely true for most people—we are all unable to know the true nature of the things we perceive. We understand the world only through what we experience and how we perceive it. The only escape is to learn about the true nature of things through other means, by which he meant philosophy.

There is a difference between the philosophy of phenomena and the discipline of phenomenology, the study of experience). The lines of division concern the potential impossibility of understanding the true nature of things (nomena). The philosophy of phenomena considers the connections between nomena and phenomena, whereas phenomenology seeks to understand and traces the structure of experience by studying perception, thought, memory, emotion, action, socio-cultural activity, language, and symbolism. All of these are the objects of study for the social sciences. While there are differences in the emphasis and methods dividing anthropology, sociology, archeology, linguistics, and behavioral economics, the ultimate goal is the same. Social scientists study how people perceive the world and make meaning out of it.

One of the most fundamental differences between social science researchers and design thinkers or design researchers is an explicit understanding of the impossibility of completing this task. The final outcome of understanding how someone else perceives the world is a receding goal; it is always out of reach.

The deeper you go, the more you realize how much farther you have to go. Knowing that this is ultimately an impossible task allows social scientists to focus on the comparative features which give this knowledge its form. We cannot become someone else, nor take on their insider knowledge entirely. So, we have to view them from our vantage point and take note of the differences and commonalties between how they understand the world and how we do. We study the structures that facilitate perception, meaning, and understanding like language, culture, social institutions, and rituals. We also examine the results of these perspectives like the performance of identity, the social production of meaning, processes of acculturation, and the social discourse that creates perceptual commonalities between individuals living in the same socio-cultural milieux.

You will immediately see that much of this is entirely missing in human-centric approaches and design thinking. Part of this results from the fact that design thinking and HCD are still on step one—empathizing—and have not advanced beyond the starting point into the hard work of coming to terms with how to study the details of someone else's worldview. What makes the situation even more difficult is the fact that to understand someone's view of the world you have to focus on *conscious* experience, in addition to unconscious experience. But business research, user research, and even design research have all borrowed from social psychological models that study unconscious or universal experience through the lens of behaviors. Both of these issues have contributed to the mess that we have now where commercial and design research are unable to fulfill the promises and the roles set for them. Design researchers are taught to study the particular, but only to consider them as examples of universals. With this in mind, I will now turn to a description of many of the theories and practices social scientists and radically human-centric researchers use to study the details of other people's lives. It is not necessary to discuss the intellectual tradition of phenomenology and each of these various intellectual paradigms at this point. This would be a very long, and involved process. Instead, I will provide a useful synopsis of the major thinkers and theories that are immediately relevant to a radically human-centric approach to applied research.

Experience

The nature of experience is a difficult thing to study because it resists an attempt to fix it as permanent, singular truth. Physicists studying quantum mechanics share this problem as they must contend with variable, potential states, and with realities that do not operate in the same way as the world we can touch and feel. For one thing, it is unclear whether any of us share any experiences exactly. Rather every one of us have different perceptions of the world that surrounds us.

Expanding beyond Plato's point about the fragility perceptions' relationship to reality, many philosophers have tried to explain just how we perceive the world around us, and whether, or not, our perception provides an accurate representation of reality. John Locke, Rene Descartes, and Immanuel Kant all struggled with the relationship between the world as it is (i.e., independent of human perception) and our perception of it. They all had different variations on the relationship between an object and our sensory experience of it. The key problem they identify is the fact that humans perceived the world through unreliable sensory organs. There is nothing to guarantee that when you or I look at something, taste something, or hear something, we have a truthful, objective sensation. We might have some neurological damage, or there might be some external factor that changes the nature of our perception. If you have ever tried to look for socks that are the same color in near darkness can understand how easy it is to skew color perception.

This perceptual problem resonates throughout any study of perception or experience. Far from being an interesting, but insignificant, part of any explanation of experience, it is a problem that scales and takes different shapes depending on the experience you are studying. What is a problem for an individual becomes a massive issue for groups of people. There is just no guarantee that we can understand the world around us objectively. Consequently, we must always understand experience as something that is subjective, incomplete, and ineffable. And this is before we begin to consider how difficult it is to communicate the details of personal experience with any clarity or certainty.

Now, we can get into the joining of phenomenology to psychology and meaning in the work of phenomenologists Franz Brentano, Bernard, Bolzano, and Edmund Husserl, but I think that will take us closer to the actual nature of perception and understanding—which is too close to the unanswerable part of the problem of experience. Because we are trying to focus on how to "understand" someone else's experience, now knowing that it might be impossible at a fundamental level, we have to look to the communicative aspect of this. How do two people come to share an experience of something in the world?

If two people experience the same thing, they hold a rock, see the same sunlight, hear the same bird song, they share the same experience entirely, right? Not necessarily. There are many mitigating factors that could alter that experience. One could be preoccupied and not attend to the experience with their conscious mind. The other could be sick and not able to hear the bird. One could have perfect pitch and hear the musical pitches C, E, G, while the other hears the notes but does not know what the pitches are. One could be color blind and not see the green flecks in the rock. Or they could both have the same experience but interpret it differently—that is the meaning of that weight, light, or sound, could be different. Here, what we encounter is the effect of perspective. Two people can "share" an experience but not interpret it the same way. Their experiences are linked by the same objective source but quite different in their outcome and their meaning. There is a kind of parallax effect, where although the basic event is the same, it shifts in the perceiving of it. If our two perceivers differ in the way they interpreted the experience, then the gap between its meaning can be very large indeed. And this is just for simple things. It becomes even more complicated when we add aesthetic or symbolic constructs into the mix.

In practical terms, there is always a difference. The difference between two people's experiences can be caused by individual, cultural, social, psychological, neurological, and physical differences. The difference in interpretation will always be there. But it does not mean that one person is wrong in their interpretation and understanding and the other is correct. We have to be ready for the fact that although their experiences may be united by a single event, that is, they saw the same thing, held the same rock, or heard the same bird, they are both right in their interpretations. This can be true even if their interpretations are quite different. When we are studying someone else's experience of the world, empathy serves us only to be prepared for this problem. It gives us nothing to resolve the issue or to come to a closer understanding of it.

To resolve this difference, we must be ready to accept that both experiences, interpretations, or meanings are correct. As the researcher, we may even be one of the two people with differing perspectives. Our job is to explain the difference and resolve it. To do this we must embrace a relativistic position that can accept and accommodate the validity of both sides.

A relativistic position is necessary for human-centric research. It is essential in a radically human-centric study. At a minimum, it is the route to a greater degree of objectivity than one would have in an extremely subjective study. A relativistic position allows the researcher to differ, even disagree, with the perspectives and beliefs they encounter but to allow for the possibility that both are correct. In fact, the most illuminating insights about human behavior and thought demonstrate how two oppositional beliefs can be resolved into a single, more universal way of seeing the world.

A relativistic position also provides space for the researcher to reflect on how their own perspective differs from that of the people they are studying. Anthropologists consider this reflection essential for the work we do, because no matter how hard you try, you cannot entirely remove yourself. You have to take account of the perspective you bring to your conversations and observations. And this goes far beyond the simplistic problem of bias because if we are trying to learn to inhabit someone else's perspective and experience the world as they would—so we can design for them—we have to be aware of how we experience them and their behavior. Thus, we must be reflexive of our own in order to more clearly "see" theirs. This reflexivity demands a relativistic position from which to operate—one that is at once somewhat separated and yet also invested in the truth and validity of the perspectives the researcher encounters. The implications of this are that a radically human-centric researcher needs to learn to accept different knowledge, ways of knowing, and understanding of the world they share with the people they observe.

Here, we can begin to see what awaits beyond the limits of empathy. Yes, you need empathy to get to this point, but now we are presented with several of the constituent elements of an "understanding" or "knowledge" of someone else's experience. We have to examine the nature and quality of their perception, the direction of their interpretation, the meaning they derive from these experiences, and the distance between their experience and our own, or that of others in the same context. This is already a lot of management. But if we are to "truly grasp the context and complexities of their lives" we have to first start with the context and complexities of how they experience the world.

Once we have begun this process, we then have to consider how language, signs, and the vagaries of linguistic and nonlinguistic representation impact how we communicate the content and flavor of our experiences. We are confronted with a double difficulty; we cannot share the truth or exactness of experiences with others and we cannot fully convey the content and meaning of these experiences to others. We cannot even be certain how we make meaning out of something for ourselves, how are we able to communicate the intimate details of an experience that does not fit into words or symbols that well? We have to answer this question because this is the next challenge lying beyond empathy. How do we learn about someone else's experience when the mechanisms they use to communicate it to us are so profoundly inadequate to the task?

The Meaning made from Experiences

Meaning and experience present us with some complications about how all of us understand the world around us. As we can see, any phenomenological study of human understanding and behavior is troubled by a lack of shared experiences. At best, we share most of our experience with others. This means we can at least depend on some overlap to help us understand each other.

But how do we actually know anything about someone else's experience? We are not able to literally see the world through their eyes. Instead, we have to communicate. We have to talk about it together. This puts language at the center of any study of experience, and with language comes the problem of meaning.

Language is an incomplete tool. It helps us communicate, but it does not carry the exact nature of our experience. It is not even very precise. Each of us struggle every day to put our thoughts and the content of our experiences into words. What makes this even harder is once we have managed to do this, there is no guarantee that the person we are speaking to will understand what we have said in the same way. They may not think about the world in the same way your words have captured what you are trying to say. They may not understand those words in the same way. They may even hear the words but interpret the meaning differently. As a consequence, they will not be able to understand your experience in the same way you do. So here we are presented with a new problem: language cannot convey the true nature of what is already an incomplete, idiosyncratic experience of phenomena. What each of us says about the world is a shadow of what we experience, and what we experience is a shadow of what is actually there. Instead of making things easier, our dependence on language pushes us farther away from a solid understanding of how we, and others, understand the world.

At this point, we can get caught in a close study of language itself. This is what linguistics is for. It is the field of study that examines how language uses a large, but finite, set of sounds, letters, words, and phrases to convey a nearly infinite number of ideas, thoughts, experiences, and pieces of information. And while this is extremely important, in a commercial setting, a linguistic study of the utterances of someone else is not going to yield the kind of phenomenological information we need to understand and know the world as they do. We must look past language for now and move on to what language does in social settings, it conveys information and meaning through representation.

Here we see that past the first step of empathy, there are three new issues we must tackle: experience, language, and meaning. Realistically, there are many more to discuss, but for now, we have to consider these three as windows into the nature of experience itself, then how people represent this world in language, and finally how they convey what they mean in what they say. This is a long way from the simplistic tool kit in design thinking and human-centered design. In fact, few design thinkers even get this far because design thinking and human-centered design protocols skip over most of this and rush straight to needs, problems, and designed solutions. The closest that most design researchers and consultancies get to acknowledging the need for a research format capable of examining experience, language, and meaning—at a minimum—on the way to understanding someone's problems, appears in suggestions to hire an anthropologist. Within a commercial context, this is part of what an anthropological researcher brings to the table. They have an awareness of these problems and are trained to build solutions to them into any piece of exploratory fieldwork.

Studying meaning is almost as difficult as developing an empirical, objective understanding of experience. However, because meaning is developed through conversation and trial-and-error in real life, it means any human being is already equipped to study meaning through representation in language. The only major difference is remembering to take careful notes and ask more questions while engaged in conversation with someone else. But before we get to how to study meaning in applied research, it is important to understand the basics of how it is forged in the use of language and nonlinguistic signs.

One of the first substantial thinkers to try to link a modern conception of experience to meaning was the American Charles Sanders Peirce (1839–1914). He was a creative and careful thinker and clearly a prodigious talent with a unique mind. A polymath with a very wide range of skills and interests, he founded a new branch of philosophy, developed a new thread of inquiry in logic, was a founder of modern meteorology, and developed one of the most rigorous and complete explanations of how we make meaning out of experience. He also apparently had a party trick where we would write two letters simultaneously, with one handwriting in English and the other in German. This is not evidence of his scholarly merit, but just a great way to demonstrate this man's brain worked in ways ours do not. He was able to do all of this while having a day job as a geologist, and later professor of mathematics. A lover of strange new-neologisms, Peirce called his approach to experience phaneroscopy, but couched it under a philosophical approach to understanding meaning called either pragmatism or pragmaticism. His major expression of this new line of philosophical thought was the theory of signs which he called semiotics. I'll leave the details of these various theories, methods, and philosophies to others to explain.[14] For our purposes here, it is semiotics that is the most important because Peirce's semiotic theory is a foundational piece of some anthropological inquiries. Peirce's model provides us with a way to understand how a thing in the world (phenomenon) is understood by a perceiver (has intentionality). It does this by being associated with a sign.

Peirce believed meaning in the world was fixed through real experiences and constant verification. He rejected the importance of an ideal object (nomena, or Kant's *Ding an sich*), existing independently of human experience, and wanted to stick to what was available to our senses. With his semiotics, he was concerned with how we understood the meaning of various signs. How do we understand what a pointing finger, the word "tree," or a statue of blind justice means? How do we make sense of objects that have no defined connection to culture like a rock or a pool of water? The task he set himself was to create a theory with an almost mechanistic explanation of how all of these things are experienced by an observer and how they become meaningful and communicable.

What he created was a set of triads and dyads explaining what the sign was, how it made meaning, and how this meaning entered into someone's experience. The first triad, *icon, index, and symbol*, is the most famous and useful. If a sign is an icon, then there is something about the sign that resembles what it is referring to. A picture of a tree is an icon of a tree. An index is a sign that makes meaning through an association. A dark cloud is an index of rain. It is not raining itself, but its association with rain means it can stand-in for the idea of rain. A symbol is a sign that makes meaning through an abstract connection alone. The word "tree" does not resemble a tree in any way, but we use it to refer to a tree by associating the word and its sounds with the idea of a tree. It is a symbol for a tree because it is learned and reinforced through use.

However, this theory is a theory of signs, not of the things themselves. Here we see how signs are actually modifiers of the experience of something. A dark cloud signifying rain can be anything from an actual cloud, to a photograph, to a drawing of a dark cloud. All of them mean the same thing—they are indexes of rain—despite being different things themselves. Now, to understand the difficulty of communicating an experience of rain, we have to consider how this association is made for two people with different experiences. Can a dark cloud mean rain for someone who has never seen a dark cloud? Is a dark cloud an index of rain then? Can a dark cloud index rain for two people who understand the association but have a different idea of rain? Peirce had an answer for each of these questions. But instead of getting into the details of the difference between a *rhematic indexical sinsign* and a *dicent indexical legisign*,[15] I want to focus us away from the minutia of Peirce's theory towards what his system of signs tells us about the nature of experience, meaning, and communication.

First of all, as Peirce made it clear, we understand the world around us through signs, not just through the things themselves. For all of us, a cloud is never just a cloud, and a tree, is not just a tree. They are both a cloud and a tree *and* signs for other things. This means to understand someone else's experience, we have to understand the signs they see and interpret them the same way, in addition to seeing the same objects. We will never share the same sensory apparatus so a strictly phenomenological approach to understanding another's perspective will not work. But we can share the same signs. So, to understand someone else's worldview, we have to learn to share the sign system they use to make meaning out of it. It means we must understand the nature of the associations that make an indexical sign work or understand the arbitrary cultural information behind how the written or auditory symbol "tree" can signify a tall plant with bark and leaves.

Empathy provides us no tools for learning the semiotic system another person uses to understand the world around them. We have to go past empathy to even begin to mine the complexities of signs and the way they mediate experience. Here we encounter a major argument for using an ethnographic approach in all kinds of human-centered research. There is no other methodology or tool capable of providing the researcher with opportunities to learn the social and cultural information necessary to share a sign system with another person—especially someone who is from a culture different from the researchers' own. Participant observation and other ethnographic practices are the way we engage with experience, meaning, and communication. But this is ethnography in its fullest sense, not in the simplistic one-on-one interview formats found in design thinking and human-centered design research. This kind of ethnography requires the researcher to put themselves in a position akin to Wittgenstein's child.

In his *Philosophical Investigations*, Ludwig Wittgenstein critiques older models of how we learn language as children.[16] In his strongest critique, Wittgenstein counters the model for learning the meaning of things that Augustine outlined in his *Confessions*, saying, "When they (my elders) named some object, and accordingly moved towards something, I saw this and I grasped that the thing was called by the sound they uttered when they meant to point it out. [...] Thus, as I heard words repeatedly used in their proper places in various sentences, I gradually learnt to understand what objects they signified [...]."[17] This view of learning language and the meaning behind it is about receiving the sign, as Peirce would have it, and learning the association that allows it, the signifier (the sign), to stand for the signified (the object). Wittgenstein refuted this because we do not learn solely in this manner—and also because not every word denotes an object. Instead, Wittgenstein shows how a child learns the meaning of the word through its use and through adult's edits and corrections. This is essentially a kind of trial-and-error. But if we think about this process with an ethnographic lens, while this helps the child fix the meaning of each word, it is also a way of learning about the world. It is even a social encounter. And this is the point that we must now deal with. Meaning is not developed through a phenomenological encounter. It is not dependent on experience alone. It is not even entirely related to language. Meaning is socially created in dialogue with others and the world we all share. This means we have to push even further past empathy to understand the social production of meaning.

The meaning of something has a direct impact on how we experience it. It is actually possible to see the meaning of something as more important than the direct experience of it. This is especially true of the kind of work we need to do in an applied context. To use one of Peirce's famous examples, we will consider "redness." The experience of "redness" is difficult to articulate. What is redness? What is the color red? How does something signal redness? How do we communicate redness? Does it even matter? But if we see red as the color of a particular team, then all of a sudden, redness has a meaning beyond simply being the experience of light in a particular wavelength.

One way of answering these questions is to see the production and transmission as a social act and not as an individual act. Yes, a person sitting alone in a room can make meaning of an experience. But this is totally idiosyncratic and is only valid in their experience. It has no meaning for anyone else. However, when meaning is communicated it expands the limits of that experience to others. But they will play a role in the determination of that meaning too. This means that meaning is produced together and shared as a social construct.

The implications of this for our goal of understanding someone else's experience are profound. First, experience is unique to an individual, whereas meaning is created together with others. This means the meaning of an experience—the only communicable element of that experience—is not theirs alone. Second, it means they do not get to have the final say in what their experience means. Experience and meaning are always created together in what anthropologists and cultural theorists call a productive dialogue or discourse. Thinking past these issues, we are now confronted with the problem of what happens when two individuals with different experiences and ways of seeing the world enter into a dialogue about what one, or both of them are seeing, thinking, feeling, or knowing. It is important to consider this now because this is exactly what happens in a research encounter. What happens to the individual experiences of the interlocutors? It is only possible for the two people to come to a consensus about a few things in any dialog, which means this conversation actually creates a third meaning, shared between them yet separate from their own in a few respects. However, it shows that in creating this third set of meanings, one person cannot transfer the details and meaning of their experience to the other without resorting to this "averaging" dialogue. This means it is actually impossible for one speaker to "understand" the other's experience in a real way. It also means that what we are taking about is the true problem of bias in qualitative work. The fundamental structures of the discursive production of meaning blend two or more perspectives to create a common, shared meaning. That means the researcher helps to build this. They cannot avoid it because it is impossible to even have a conversation without engaging in a social discourse.[18]

The social production of meaning has been a topic of discussion in the social sciences for a very long time. However, anthropologists and sociolinguists have only gotten further along recently using the work of a few major thinkers, Charles S. Peirce, J.L. Austin, Erving Goffman, Michel Foucault, Kenneth Pike, Pierre Bourdieu, Michel de Certeau, and I would add Janet Wolff and Maurice Halbwachs to this list as a way to help outline the very social nature of the development of meaning for signs and experiences. We will discuss some of their work in turn, but I leave it to you to explore the rest. First, we will examine how we can reach the common ground necessary for the most basic transfer of meaning between two individuals.

Peirce gave us language to talk about what happens in this encounter. I will spare you the details of the *intentional interpretant, effectual interpretant, and the cominterpretiant,* and give you the *commind* and *commens*. These are the terms that help us identify the need for common ground between two speakers. When two speakers are able to communicate meaning they share in the commind, the common ground between them. Perice described the commens as the shared meaning that is shareable because of the common ground between the speakers, or as he put it, "now an item of information has been conveyed, because it has been stated relatively to a well-understood common experience. Thus the form conveyed is always a determination of the dynamical object of the commind," whereas the commens itself "consists of all that is, and must be, well understood between utterer and interpreter, at the outset, in order that the sign in question should fulfill its function."[19] Thus what we need to learn from him are that for meaning to be transferable there needs to be a process where our two conversationalists speak their common ground into being. This is a form of reciprocal dialogue where experiences are shared, discussed, and averaged. Once the commens has been developed, then the real work of communication can begin.

This should feel overwhelming, because it is. I offer it here partially to demonstrate why the promises of design thinking and design research in human-centered design unable to handle the reality of the situation. As we can see in this very quick description, the common ground between speakers necessary to communicate even the most basic piece of information, let alone the details and emotional weight of someone's experiences, must be robust and complete. You have to come to a consensus on the meaning of a number of things before new information can be transferred. And that new information must be "averaged" and agreed upon through the same process. This is the issue at the core of the incompleteness of design thinking.

This communicative work is exactly what is meant when design thinkers suggest that designers empathize with their customers/users. They have to share common ground. But the appeal to empathy says nothing about *how* to establish this common ground. And we have not even discussed the complexities of this common ground and how to build knowledge and understanding once you have a basic communicative pathway. This process is difficult enough when the two speakers share a common language, culture, social class, identity formation, religion, political perspective, and upbringing. When they do not, all of these factors become barriers to communication. They must all be attended to in the development of the commens and commind. This is the work of an anthropologist. We study these very things in order to aid in the development of a human commind and commens. We study differences in order to highlight the essential commonalities we all share. Our training and experience help us provide productive descriptions of how these differences actually contribute to a single, shared experience. It also means we are able to remove ourselves from this process and work to mitigate our biasing of it. These are not common traits or skills of design researchers or design thinkers.

One example of what a radically human-centric approach needs to bring to design research is an understanding of the problems of observing and creating knowledge about someone else's experience. Here I am not talking about the nature of their experience. My focus is on the problems confronting a researcher when you want to learn about how someone else sees the world. This can be summed up in Kenneth Pike's illuminating distinction between *emic* and *etic* information.[20] Imagine an alien coming to earth to study humans. This alien is given a ticket to a hockey game and decides to go because it is a good opportunity to study human behavior up close. However, the alien has bad hosts, and no one provides it with any context. It just shows up, sitting it in its seat trying to make sense of what is happening.

The alien notices that the building is very large and different from every other human building. Instead of a lot of floors delineating smaller and smaller spaces, it has a single open area. There are 25,000 people sitting in colored seats all facing an open area that has a large rectangle of frozen water on it. This frozen water has a lot of different colored lines on it and is serving as the floor for a group of 12 humans wearing differently colored clothes and carrying sticks. Everyone is clearly labeled by name and number, although this seems to have little do to with the activity on the ice. The crowd watches them move back and forth while they eat a meal and drink a lot of a bubbly, golden-colored liquid. When the 12 humans stop moving on the frozen water there is a lot of loud noise pushed through an amplification system. When that noise stops the 12 humans return to their efforts, moving around the frozen water chasing a small disc and hitting it with their sticks. Occasionally one of the two things can happen. Two of the 12 humans stop to hit each other with their hands while everyone else watches, or the disc is hit into a structure intended to stop its movement. When either of these things happens many lights go off and all of the seated humans stop eating and stand up to make a lot of noise. Eventually, all of this stops and everyone leaves the building, putting all of their meal waste on the floor.

This is an incomplete, yet totally accurate observation of what is going on when humans attend a hockey game. While it is detailed, it totally misses the point of what a hockey game is, why it is played, what the rules are (both on and off the ice) and what is actually going on. It makes connections between things that are actually not causally related—the music is not a factor in the action on the ice, it is a symptom of the change of the state of play on the ice. All of this is *etic* information or something that is readily observable. The alien has observed a hockey game, but has not managed to get to the *emic* information, what one needs to know to understand the rules of hockey, and all of the background information that is needed to participate in this event either as a player or a spectator. Emic information is the knowledge of insiders. It constitutes the unspoken elements of what is going on. It contains the *why, and as such* is the goal of any human-centered research. But like our alien, you have to get through a lot of etic information first and make a lot of mistakes. Once again, empathy cannot help it, or us, here.

Pike's distinction between etic and emic information reveals the problems inherent in phenomenological research and the need for a common ground. If the alien was able to get closer to being a cultural insider, the etic details would be less necessary, and it would have been able to examine the emic details of the moment. Issues of why ritualized violence enhance the spectator experience or why music is used to manage the focal awareness of the crowd become easier to see. And it is these that provide the opportunities for altering the experience. The alien would only be able to suggest that the net be walled up to prevent the puck from getting in, or that maybe if one team had all of its players on the ice, instead of having most of them sitting on the bench the whole time, they might have a better chance at winning the game. Design thinking and design research do not get this far in their consideration of human behavior. They are usually stuck in the etic details, and therefore can never build something engage in the emic experience. Because their approaches have no mechanisms for developing a real common ground with their research subjects, they are doomed to solve the wrong problems. They are unable to even understand the nature of what is going on, let alone what it means or how experience is expressed.

These problems are even more acute when we move beyond a person's experience of the physical world around them and consider the socio-cultural constructs governing most of our lives. Humans do not live in a direct, unmediated relationship with our environment. Instead, we live in a web of social and cultural formations that give our lives meaning and provide the communicative common ground necessary to do more complicated things than the content of our experiences. So, to push even further past empathy and get closer to understanding how someone else experiences the world, we need to be able to examine the socio-cultural web that structures their thinking, their relationships, their work, and their material world. It is here that we leave the world of design behind completely and enter the realm of culture. Design is an expression of culture, and therefore it is a sub-set of larger domains of human activity. To understand design more fully, we have to contextualize it by placing it within a larger cultural perspective.

Structuring Shared Experience

Ask five social scientists to provide definitions for "social" and "cultural" and you will get over 20 answers and a lot of humming and hawing. The reason is because these terms are extremely difficult concepts, despite being in the names of our disciplines—social anthropology, cultural anthropology, sociology, and cultural studies. There are many excellent overviews of this definitional problem, so I will leave that aside for now.[21] What I want to highlight is the role of culture in our lives. Many in the business world see culture as solely the domain of the arts, literature, and what one client once called "the things that don't really matter." This is not surprising. Many business schools have taught a form of neo-liberal chauvinism for some time now, where anything not directly related to the exchange of money and economic power is seen as nonessential, or even morally questionable. It is this belief that has led some business-forward individuals to call for the elimination of the humanities from university curricula.[22] This small definition of culture, where cultural activity or artifacts are all that is left over after you set science and economics on their pedestals, is not new. It is a mistaken belief that some disciplines, ways of thinking, and mechanisms for generating knowledge, such as economics, engineering, computer science, and the hard sciences, are entirely objective and therefore not affected by the subjectivities of culture. In *the Order of Things*, Michel Foucault describes a devolution thinking where ancient and medieval areas of study once connected and part of a larger total, were systematically divided and separated in order to create a modern way of thinking.[23] In this way, music, once part of astronomy, mathematic disciplines, and artistic expression, became something entirely separated from pure mathematics, and was lumped in with literature, an endeavor it shares less with.

This process made the initial disciplinary boundaries between areas of knowledge that we use today. Now mathematics, engineering, physics, astronomy, and chemistry are separated from aesthetics, literature, art, music, and dance. Over time, we came to believe that those in the first cluster were more important because of their connection to a technologized approach to generating capital. We relegated the second cluster to museums and to the humanities' half of campus— usually housing them in the older buildings on campus which are untouched by donor money, unlike their counterparts at the business school or science centers. This relegation created the circumstances in business that required intervention from design and design thinking in the first place. The pseudo-science approach used in late twentieth-century business was problematic because it made a mistake common in liberal economic thinking: that economic activity was a sufficient area of study in order to understand humans in general. This was not any more true then, than it is now. And while nineteenth-century economists like Thorsten Veblen created this problem, they did so without critique. Design thinking was a way to introduce some of the "softer" side of human knowledge and activity back into business and engineering thinkers shaped by decades of over-emphasis on STEM education.

Design thinkers, and even designers, also have an underdetermined idea of what culture actually is. They have not been disabused of this small-scale belief themselves. They have not yet benefited from the perspective of those who study culture and society, the sociologists, anthropologist, philosophers, and cultural critics. The result of this problem is the lack of solid socio-cultural analytical methods in design thinking, design research, and human-centered design. These disciplines are almost as culturally blind as the business and engineering cultures they were brought in to enhance.

Given the fact that design thinkers, design researchers, UX researchers, and human-centered design practitioners have set themselves the goal of understanding the customer/user's experience and done so without a solid understanding of perhaps the most important component of that experience, we must make alterations to existing practices. To fulfill the promise of design thinking and human-centered design, we must study experience and design in, and as, culture. We need to understand how culture provides the common ground for communication, the development and transmission of meaning, and structures how we come to know the world. The goal of empathy in design thinking is to understand someone else's experience and to see the world through their eyes. To do this you must learn about the culture that helps them make sense of their experiences and structures the way they "know" anything at all.

A radical approach to human-centricity uses a fully developed understanding of culture. It does not relegate some knowledge to the purgatory of "out of scope" or "unnecessary for a business study." A researcher using a radical approach to human-centricity begins with culture and ends with culture, finding the relevant answers on the journey. Moreover, a researcher applying radical human-centricity has the tools to track and trace how culture shapes experience and helps our research subjects express it. In this way, radical human-centricity offers a way to get closer to the status of cultural-insider needed to record and make use of the emic details of a research encounter. In this way, a radical human-centricity is actually human-centric. It studies people as they are in the context that they participate in as cultural and social insiders.

With this in mind, we have to settle on a suitable working definition of culture for our needs. This is not easy. It could be said that once a final definition of culture has been established it would be time to shutter all of the anthropology departments in the world. This is essentially the final purpose of the social sciences, which means it may never happen. So, it is best for us to particularize our definition for use in an applied context. That means we must look at how culture shapes experience, understanding, and knowledge.

We have already looked beyond the limits of empathy to individual experience. We now know we also need to track meaning, communication, and types of knowledge to do so. But all of this has been within the limits of individual experience. Culture then is what provides the scaffolding for the experience of a group of people in addition to that individual. This means culture is about collective experience, perhaps before it defines and shapes individual experience. At any rate, in applied and commercial research we have to find the definitional connections between individual and socio-cultural experience, so we are obliged to see them as connected.[24] So, how do we do this?

We must adopt a radically human-centric model of experience, which is to say, we must borrow from well-established anthropological and sociological models to correct the omissions of design thinking, design research, and human-centered design. The first step is to acknowledge that idiosyncratic, individual experience cannot explain how people behave or even understand the world. The second step is to also acknowledge that the received cultural formations and social constructs do not define how people think, act, or believe either. We are in fact, trapped in between two explanations. This problem is best articulated by philosopher Roy Bhaskar in *The Possibility of Naturalism*, where he lays out the problem facing social scientists.[25] We cannot explain how people live, think, and believe through models of society that say social things are the sum of the parts, or that individuals are defined by society.

We must instead, find a way to bridge the gap and demonstrate how everything in human experience is at once idiosyncratic and individual while also being social. We have to be satisfied with this tension. In fact, in a radical approach to human-centricity, we expect it and use it to our advantage. This means we have to acknowledge the key feature of experience not covered in most phenomenological models, the individual shapes social and cultural experiences through their actions, and societal and cultural constructs shape how individuals understand everything, even themselves. We must then study them in tandem. The implication of this is clear. The kinds of insights capable of driving real understanding—thereby fulfilling the promise and role of empathy—are ones that highlight the work done through these connections. It also means insights allowing us to see the world through someone else's eyes must be grounded in a deep knowledge of the socio-cultural world shaping that person's experience and the way they communicate. Those that do not are mostly superficial observations and cannot get at the emic information we need to create transformative designs and strategies.

Anthropologists and sociologists have seen culture in action in many different ways. Consequently, we have a number of definitions of what it is, how it works, and where it is found. The one I want to highlight now is how culture structures experience. This is best found in the seminal work of Pierre Bourdieu and in his book *Distinction* and in his point that culture is the result of the actions of people and a structure that governs those actions, in his words "a structuring structure structuring structure."[26] As such, it is an ever-changing construct that provides us with the scaffolding to understand the world, ourselves, and each other.

Bourdieu calls this structuring structure *habitus*, which is still as ambiguous a concept as the day he coined the term. However, we do not need a straight definition, because there are elements of habitus that help us understand how we need to tackle the concept of culture and its relationship to experience in applied and commercial work. Habitus is unconscious. It is something we have and do without thinking. Bourdieu uses two terms for this having and doing: *hexis* and *praxis*. Hexis is a Greek word with roots in Aristotle's early phenomenology, it essentially means to have, or to possess the disposition of. Bourdieu's example of the *hexis* part of *habitus* is body language. And because his book is concerned with the concept of social class and how we make decisions and act to maintain our social class, his example is about the different in the way people of different social classes hold their body. The *praxis* part is about what people do (his theory is commonly called practice theory). The part that governs our actions is what holds the logic of *hexis* and *praxis* together. The ways of thinking, epistemologies, categories, ways of seeing, and everything we've talked about above structure these two.

An eagle-eyed reader will notice *habitus* shares a root with *habit*. This is important. Like a habit, *habitus* is learned, largely unconscious, and governs our actions. The part where it is different from a habit is that it is also restructured through our actions. These features are important to us because they show us how a culture connects a set of individuals, structures their experiences, but gives them space to restructure the culture itself.

We learn our habitus from someone else. It would be silly to think that we are able to create a culture out of thin air. No, we learn all of this from our social and physical environment. We will not get into the complexities of this here. Suffice it to say, we learn our culture from the people around us when we grow up. Any they are teaching us much more than we realize. Beyond just teaching us to speak and what to talk about, they are also teaching us things that we might otherwise believe are universal. Habitus involves more than the obvious things. So, for instance, part of our habitus is how and when to smile. If you think back to when you learned to smile, you cannot remember. What was an instinct as a child was slowly turned into a social sign. You have to learn when to smile, how big to smile, and for how long. These are not innate traits like the instinct to smile itself. In some cultures, people learn to not smile that much, whereas for others smiling is an important social cue. In either case, the learning of these culturally coded habits is called acculturation.

When someone is acculturated into a culture, they are "brought up" in it. They can do more than simply interpret these signs. We can go as far as to say they are only able to see these signs. They see the world through the lens of what they have learned. Other's sign systems might be far enough away that they are not understood in the same way that another's language might sound like just sounds if you do not speak it.[27] Being acculturated is learning to be in a culture, not just learning to read it, and this does mean to the exclusion of alternatives.

Once we are acculturated, we simply exude the details of this culture. We do not think about it because the culture is us and we are the culture. What we have learned becomes our operating system from which we make decisions, interact with others, and understand new and old phenomena as they come into our experience. Everyone who shares this habitus will recognize us as part of their world. Our actions, our words, our thoughts, and our beliefs all have their place in the world that is shared between us but embedded in each and every one of us.

The next part is where habitus structures what we do. Because we embody this cultural way of being, and we share it with others. We act in a way that is appropriate within this framework. There are many things we *could* do, and even more things we *should* do. But to say we choose how to behave is largely forgetting that we are acculturated into a habitus. We are not even totally aware of the large options because our habitus focuses on us in one way or another. What this means is that the schema we use—and social psychologists believe are innate—are learned structuring structures. We learned them, and they govern how we think. They provide the limits which allow us to make distinctions between things; what is good/bad, valuable/not valuable, pure/dirty, and many other things are all part of our habitus. The colloquial way to refer to this is to "share values," but that misses so much. All of these are actions in thought and belief. Habitus structures our physical actions and our behavior too in just the same way.

So far, this is fairly easy. Where it becomes difficult for people unused to the vagaries of culture, is that this changes. Culture is not pinned down. It shifts, changes, and evolves. And this is true for our programming and our habitus. When we act, we put things into practice, we inevitably make alterations. Our habitus-guided actions alter our habitus as we go through the act of doing them. We make errors, modifications, and learn new things and constantly rewrite the programming of habitus. If we did not do this, then most of what we have built in the last 200,000 years would not have happened.

The upshot of all of this is that culture is the world we live in, but it is constantly changing because of our actions. As researchers we must then understand that what we study is in constant flux and change. People change themselves as they behave, and what we write down in a report is not entirely true the moment we write it down. The only way to understand someone's perspective, or to see the world through their eyes, is to participate in rebuilding their world with them and to step into their cultural world as completely as possible given the constraints. If we cannot do that, we are doomed to have a partial or mistaken understanding. It also means we must be satisfied with change as a fundamental feature of experience, self, identity, meaning, and communications.

While culture structures individual thought and action, it also structures what is commonly held between individuals. In this way, culture provides the common ground we discussed earlier. Culture exists everywhere. It is not a "thing" or an "artifact" it is part of these things. It is found in the sound of music, from what instruments are used, to how songs are built, to what kind of songs it is possible to write. It is found in business, where it provides the logic behind why business thinking can be separated from history, physical, and literature. It also exists in providing the grounding for the way we go out to eat, how we behave in bars, and why hockey games are a good idea.

If we extend this further, culture helps us define who "we" or "us" are delineate ourselves from "them." "We" are people who share the same background, values, history, language, and view of what the world should be like. All of these are culturally defined. "They" are people who are different. While these boundary lines are often arbitrary—a lot of cultural things exist that way just because they exist that way—they feel like they are essential and important. In fact, they feel so important people are willing to go to great lengths to assert their validity. Just think about the way people get heated about politics. Most of the content of that conversation centers on a difference in cultural or sub-cultural perception. Everyone in that conversation could very easily change sides and argue with similar vehemence. These are cultural debates and are not really about reality, but about how we understand reality through our cultural lenses. Consequently, the argument concerns what should be common and shared, not what is real.

Here we are beginning to see how cultural phenomena do not "exist" like objects exist. They only exist through human action, which means they must be continually enacted and maintained through behavior. An identity, for instance, is a manifestation of a cultural structure. It outlines belonging, membership, and establishes a particular take on a habitus. But it does not mean anything until it is put into action. We have to *perform* an identity through thought, speech, and action.

Anthropologists study performance as the act of creating and recreating these social and cultural constructs. How do people perform membership in a particular society? How do others perform belonging in a particular economic class? How do others perform a particular sexual or gender identity? And finally, now to we perform ourselves? All of these actions are guided by habitus and help shape the individual, but they also create a performance meant to be read by others in our larger socio-cultural milieu so they can understand who we are, or want to be.

Like many of the concepts I've discussed here, this is a very large topic with a lot of very interesting and contentious findings. What I want to take away from performance, is that it is the way in which individuals participate in the larger cultural constructs. It is a way in which we communicate the meaning of our experience and our personal understanding in a socially and culturally legible way. And once we understand this, we have to deal with the fact that this further complicates the task of learning to see the world through other people's eyes or walking a mile in their shoes. We have to be able to read the performances of the social actors in their environment. We have to understand how much of what they say during an interview is actually performative. If we can't read the signs, then we miss what they mean. Being able to look for, catch, and decipher the social and cultural performances of our respondents is an essential part of getting closer to understanding their experience. We cannot even understand the basics of the interview, let alone their epistemological and phenomenological perspectives without attending to the performance of a cultural and social role and its impact on the individual and the group.

The emic details of culture provide constraints in addition to facilitating action. In a book called *Fame Analysis*, sociologist Erving Goffman outlined the details of frame theory and demonstrated how even something as basic as speech in a social encounter is actually governed by a large number of rules and we have less choice in these moments than we otherwise believe we do. The broad strokes are as follows. First, social action, including speech is not open to entirely free expression—to be totally free would prevent understanding. We need to build and maintain a temporary set of rules for most of what we say and do to make sense. This should remind you of Peirce's commens and commind. The example Goffman uses is the difference between formal speech and informal speech.[28] There is a big difference between conversations that begin with "Good morning, ma'am. How are you today?" and "Hey, what's up?."

Both of these conversations, indeed, every conversation, has a frame that makes it easier to understand. The frame is the emic instructions of how we should interact because it is an acculturated, unconscious structure that allows us to communicate or perform socio-cultural constructs more easily. We use speech structures—phrases, words, tone of voice—to "cue" the frame, thus indicating what frame we will be using. If I say, "good morning ma'am" and "s'up?" I am cuing to very different encounters, each with have different vocabularies and limits on the kinds of topics we can discuss and how we can discuss them. These phrases also "key" the frame. Here Goffman is using a musical metaphor. The "key" is like a musical key, setting the terms of what kinds of actions and speech is appropriate and what is not.

Once we are in the frame, we have to obey the rules that it lays out. This is an example of a social and cultural structure that exists independently of the speakers, but controls and shapes how they behave, what they say, how they say it, and dictates how these structures are set up and ended. This means people do not have that much free choice in how they express themselves. The way they express themselves is governed by the rules of the frame, structured by their acculturated habitus, and limited by the need to perform a social role or identity that they themselves did not invent. If we're being very honest, there is actually not a lot of individual choices left in this set of constraints.

Schema and Cultural Models

What I have been trying to do so far is connect individual, private, untransferable experience with shared cultural and social experience. I have been doing this through the theories and methods most commonly used in anthropology and sociology. However, there is a different way to view all of this, one that shares more with the systems of knowledge found in social psychology and business. This is the connection between schema and cultural models, or mental and cultural models.

I must admit, I have great misgivings about this because I dislike the concept of a mental model. In my opinion it is a concept that is better explained in a different way. It has also become troubled because it has entered the buzzword dictionary and has strayed a bit from its theoretical roots. As an anthropologist working in the design and strategy consulting worlds for some time, I have heard the term "mental model" used for so many different purposes—often with wildly different meanings. I've heard people use mental model to mean the object that we are supposed to study in qualitative research, that is, "discover their mental model so we can change it." Many of the designers prefer the idea of a mental model as the preconceived notions that someone has that allow them to problem solve in the way that they have done. Both of these are troubling to me because they are trying to locate the cause of a person's perspective on, and experience of, the world in a single place.

Properly understood, a schema (mental model) is just an organizational principle that allows someone to interpret something. This means all of us do not just have one, we have many. It is a heuristic for interpreting the data that we perceive, and as such is part of the mechanisms social scientists study when we use phenomenological, semiotic, communications, practice theory, frame theory, or other approaches to understanding people and their ways of experiencing the world.

I prefer to couch these heuristic mechanisms in the terms we have described above. The "mental model" known better as Piaget's schemata is meant to be a categorization of knowledge and a way of obtaining knowledge. As such, it duplicates much of what I have discussed here. Cognitive anthropology has introduced cultural models as the social counterpart to schema or mental models.[29] But I find it just as easy to explain these issues within phenomenology and semiotics. I also find them more useful given the fact that they study things commercial clients are more interested in. The nature of individual's neurological and psychological dispositions, Jean Piaget's true focus, are a bit far away from a study of how to properly design a hospital entrance experience for everyone who will walk through the doors.

However, radical human-centric approaches always have room for other theories and other ways of looking at the world. If you needed to study people in a way that requires you to isolate someone's schemata for interpreting visual information, then using a mental model/cultural model format would work well.

Reflexivity – Difference – Perspective – And Bias!

Now that we are starting to understand the complications of studying another person's experience, we now have to account for our own. As we discussed earlier, the difference in perspective and the problem of bias is present in any human-centered research project, qualitative or quantitative. However, now that we see that to move past empathy, researchers have to learn to become part of the process. It is absolutely impossible to be "objective" in this kind of work, particularly because we are products of our own cultural formations, and even our understanding of data is guided, structured, and governed by everything we just discussed. Writing a client deliverable is a particular genre of writing sitting within a frame governing its tone, vocabulary, length, etc. Through it a researcher performs a kind of "knowledge" and expertise necessary to express the information in the right way so it will be understood by a set of individuals who need to see the researcher prove their membership in the same social and cultural unit that they are from. Objectivity went out the door before the researcher even began setting up the project.

Consequently, we need to mitigate the socio-cultural bias and difference in perspective caused by research simply being a researcher in the field. We need to blunt the impact the imposition of our own way of seeing the circumstances has on how we understand what we are seeing, hearing, and learning. This is not accomplished by removing the researcher from the study, but by including them and their perspective. Since the early 1980s anthropologists have practiced what we call *reflexivity*, which roughly means being explicit about what we have brought to the field and how this affects our understanding of what we learn. This reflexivity is the reason why anthropologists always hedge what they are saying. Instead of asserting the truth of something, like "customers always want to see themselves reflected in your designs," we would be more likely to say "what we found in field suggest that customers like finding something familiar in new designs, but this was only apparent after we discussed design more closely."

Methodologically, reflexivity allows us to acknowledge the weaknesses of our study up front. It allows the readers to assess our thinking. But perhaps more importantly, it allows us to place a perspective that is more familiar to the audience into the insights. This familiar jumping-off-point provides the opportunity for comparison, which means we can now start to discuss the commonalities and differences in the habitus, culture, approach to performance, meaning, and experience between the researcher and the research subject—the human(s) we wanted to study.

By stating that the purpose of human-centered design research is about learning to see the world "through someone else's eyes" design thinkers are suggested they are more interested in understanding the differences they found in field and designing against them as provocations. This is what "needs" based research is all about. Find things that are different and design around them. But this misses half of what you need to do to understand someone's experience. The commonalities are just as, if not more, important than what is divergent or surprising. We have to approach experience research through pathways of commonality anyway, since if we do not share anything with our research subjects, we have no basis for empathy or anything else. The route to emic information goes through the shared etic details, and we need to acknowledge this as we create our insights.

By collecting both commonalities and differences we are well-positioned to demonstrate how their different experiences of our commonly shared environment provide us with a shift in perspective. And this is essential because this perspectival shift is the very thing we came to find. It is the lens through which we can design for others. There are several articulations of the role of experience (as empathy) in design research that focus on 3rd person and 1st person experience.[30] This can also be external or internal, or otherwise. All of these divisions demonstrate that there are at least two perspectives in any research program. But this is true with any interaction with two people. In fact, in a face-to-face interaction, there are four perspectives: the two internal perspectives and the external perspectives that both individuals carry around with them as representatives of different cultures or sub-cultures. Understanding the dynamics of all of these competing perspectives provides us with opportunities for design. If we see the world one way, and our intended customers/users see it slightly differently, how can we use design to create a project that satisfies both of us? How can design become a conduit between us and provide a new commonality, a new shared space, upon which to build a relationship?

Finding Possibilities Past "Empathy"

The rest of this book is really a statement of what we should do with these theories in a more practical way. I hope that by now you can see that the statement that "empathy," however wonderful it is, can do anything to help us understand another person or group of people is incomplete.

Instead, we need to acknowledge all of these issues and constructs and work to study them and find how they are shaping the experience of the person we want to know more about. If we do this, we will be able to get much closer to the promise of human-centric research and design thinking.

It is important to note this is not an exhaustive overview of the social science theories and methods relating to understanding someone else's experience. We have only discussed what I believe to be the most relevant concepts for how to frame the task that we are actually facing when we want to "walk a mile in someone else's shoes." Next, we have to put all of this into practice. We must understand the methods to take a researcher from an outsider to an insider with the ability to translate this way of being into a book, a film, or PowerPoint slides. To get closer to this, we must understand how a radically human-centric perspective does the *"graphy"* half of ethnography. We should understand how to use storytelling to help others understand.

Notes

1 Battarbee, Katja, Jane Fulton Suri, and Suzanne Gibbs Howard. "Empathy On the Edge: Scaling and Sustaining a Human-Centered Approach In the Evolving Practice Of Design." IDEO, 1. https://new-ideo-com.s3.amazonaws.com/assets/files/pdfs/news/Empathy_on_the_Edge.pdf.
  I have selected this article because Ideo and its researchers have worked very hard to define design thinking and have been the major promoters of empathy as a key feature of DIY design research.
2 Battarbee, Katja, Jane Fulton Suri, and Suzanne Gibbs Howard. "Empathy On the Edge: Scaling and Sustaining a Human-Centered Approach In the Evolving Practice Of Design." IDEO, 1. https://new-ideo-com.s3.amazonaws.com/assets/files/pdfs/news/Empathy_on_the_Edge.pdf.
3 Gasparini, A., 2015, February. Perspective and use of empathy in design thinking. In *ACHI, the eight international conference on advances in computer-human interactions* (pp. 49–54). ; Kouprie, M. and Visser, F.S., 2009. A framework for empathy in design: stepping into and out of the user's life. *Journal of Engineering Design, 20*(5), pp. 437–448; McDonagh, D. and Thomas, J., 2011. Design+ empathy= intuitive design outcomes.
4 Again, while this toolkit is used to train HCD and design thinking practices, it is really nothing more than a business development asset for Ideo. There is a lot of practical advice in the booklet, but the description of empathy is not part of its step-by-step processes—for those are just about design innovation—but part of the justification for the design intervention. As such, there is very little reason to actually define and operationalize empathy. Its evocation and the virtue this brings are sufficient.
5 Ideo.org. 2015. *The Field Guide to Human-Centered Design.* San Francisco, CA, Ideo. org. https://www.designkit.org/resources/1?utm_medium=ApproachPage&utm_source=www.ideo.org&utm_campaign=FGButton.
6 Ibid., 10.
7 Solutionism is the dominant philosophy in the technology and the design or innovation worlds. It is a statement of belief that the world is filled with problems that can be addressed with designed solutions, often those involving technological fixes.

8 Ideo.org. 2015. *The Field Guide to Human-Centered Design*. San Francisco, CA, Ideo. org, 6. https://www.designkit.org/resources/1?utm_medium=ApproachPage&utm_source=www.ideo.org&utm_campaign=FGButton.

9 Köppen, Eva, and Christoph Meinel. "Empathy via design thinking: creation of sense and knowledge." In *Design thinking research*, pp. 15-28. Springer, Cham, 2015, 16.

10 Greenson, R.R., 1960. Empathy and its vicissitudes. *International Journal of Psycho-Analysis, 41,*. 418–424.

11 Rogers, C.R., 1989. *The carl rogers reader*. Houghton Mifflin Harcourt, 16–17.

12 Köppen, Eva, and Christoph Meinel. "Empathy via design thinking: creation of sense and knowledge." In *Design thinking research*, pp. 15-28. Springer, Cham, 2015, 17.

13 There is a famous counterfactual in phenomenological philosophy that holds reality might be entire artificial and we are all brains floating in jars being fed the stimuli needed to believe we are living in the world we understand to be 'real.'

14 Misak, C. ed., 2004. *The Cambridge Companion to Peirce*. Cambridge University Press. Short, T.L., 2007. *Peirce's theory of signs*. Cambridge University Press.

15 Just don't worry about it. If you're interested read Short's excellent introduction. But you will be forgiven for not reading it.

16 Wittgenstein, Ludwig. 1991. *Philosophical Investigations: The German Text, with a Revised English Translation* 3rd Ed. Wiley-Blackwell.

17 Augustine. 2009. *Confessions*. Oxford Classics, 10.

18 It is important to note here that this is where expertise comes into play. Untrained researchers, or design researchers who lack a solid grounding in the ethnographic process will be unable to mitigate the impact of this fundamental phenomenon. It is also important to note that this *bias* is distinct from the bias more commonly identified as a problem in commercial research. That bias is really nothing more than the imposition of opinion through weak question design practices. What we are talking about here is the fact that it is impossible to engage in phenomenological research without participating in the discursive production of meaning. You create meaning together with your participants just by talking to them. It is *that* meaning you take home. Rarely is their unique understanding recorded.

19 Piece, Charles Sanders. 1992. The Essential Peirce, Volume 2: Selected Philosophical Writings, 1897–1913. Indiana University Press, 478.

20 Pike, K. L. (1967). *Etic and emic standpoints for the description of behavior*, In K. L. Pike, *Language in relation to a unified theory of the structure of human behavior*, Mouton & Co.: 37–72.

21 Engelke, M., 2019. *How to think like an anthropologist*. Princeton University Press, 25–55.

22 Knochel, Aaron D. 2017. https://theconversation.com/why-do-conservatives-want-the-government-to-defund-the-arts-71866.

23 Foucault, M., 1970. The order of things: An archeology of knowledge. *AM Sheridan-Smith*.

24 Incidentally, this is one of the reasons why I find the application of methods and theories from social psychology in applied and commercial research settings so completely baffling. Their methods and their approach require the removal of the socio-cultural background. They cannot find universal, in-built behaviors without doing this. So the fact that businesses and tech companies the world over rely on research practices and insights from a field that methodologically and methodically removes the very thing we should be researching must make no sense to me. There is, of course, a place for psychological research in applied and commercial research.

But the processes and methods found in psychological research and social psychology should not be the core of our research approaches. I would actually go as far as to say unless we make a radical reset, and remove psychology from customer/user research, we will never attain the goals set by the ideal of human-centricity. The radical approach will be to balance our research practices with fields, ideas, and methods more capable of connecting individual experience and the difficulties of communal and group experience.

25 Bhaskar, R., 2013. *The possibility of naturalism: A philosophical critique of the contemporary human sciences*. Routledge.

26 Bourdieu, P., 1984. *Distinction: A Social Critique of the Judgement of Taste*. Routledge, 72–95).

27 Yes, I have going a bit far to make a point here. Many cultural things are perfectly intelligible to individuals outside of that culture. However, if we are trying to set ourselves the goal of "seeing the world through another's eyes," or "stepping into someone else's shoes" then we must understand the complexities of doing this.

28 Goffman, E., 1974. *Frame analysis: An essay on the organization of experience*. Harvard University Press.

29 Bennardo, G. and Munck, V.C.D., 2014. *Cultural models: Genesis, methods, and experiences*. Oxford: Oxford University Press.

30 Kim, J. and Ryu, H., 2014. A design thinking rationality framework: Framing and solving design problems in early concept generation. *Human–Computer Interaction*, *29*(5–6), 516–553.

Chapter 5

THE WORLD AS IT IS

Making the commitment to work in a radically human-centric manner is brave. It involves taking a step away from what does not work very well, towards something that is difficult but more rewarding. While this involves doing away with many of the moribund, out-of-date practices still used in the world of commercial applied research, doing so leaves a large hole in a conventional research practice. These older ways of working have been so entrenched, that they leave a big hole when they are gone. But once this is accomplished what do you do now that you cannot rely on easy methods like personas, gamified synthesis, focus group settings, and quick, tactical customer/user engagements? You fill the void with detail, stories, experiences, and careful, methodical analysis. To do this, you must learn to meet the world and your respondents on their own terms and study their thoughts, behaviors, and contexts without resorting to the kind of abstraction, reductionism, and simplicity of the older format. This means instead of adapting market research or design research tools to fit circumstances they are not suited for; it is better to approach researching people in innovation contexts armed with the new tools a radical human-centric approach provides. These come from anthropology, foresight, and new forms of design research methods like transition design and design anthropology. All of these are intended to study, analyze, and make sense of the world as it is, not the simplified version we might want it to be.

This will not be an easy task. Once you leave behind the ideologies and methods of market research you are immediately confronted with how complicated researching real life can be. People are not easy to understand, rational, decision makers who have "needs," market research makes them out to be. A radically human-centric researcher is confronted with a messy, multiplicitious world filled with people who inhabit many social roles simultaneously, lie, and act in ways that are not clear to themselves. It is not possible to find a generative grammar of behavior, this was tried in the 1950s and 1960s and the project did not go very well. You cannot control the situation to focus on mythical phenomena like the "naïve response" or simply collect observations to identify an "unmet need." And you certainly cannot identify, describe, or explain a "mindset" with a quick survey of 1000 suitable respondents. A radically human-centric study has to handle a world of contradictions, gaps, and idiosyncrasies. It is—to use the word that strikes fear in every businessperson's mind—complex.

With this in mind, we are now going to explore many of the shifts in thinking and approaches needed to fulfill the commitment to a radically human-centric approach to real research. But we cannot do this without first understanding that at its core the commitment to a radical human-centric approach is a commitment to evidence-based, empirical work.

Being Radically Human-Centric Means Avoiding Abstraction

This begins with a radical statement: market research is not empirical, or truly evidence-based. Market research can be objective at times, maybe even rational, but it is not empirical. As I have already shown, most of what market research does in producing its NPS scores, demographic and psychographic profiles, active user assessments, and in the development of its personas and segments is studying humans in an abstracted form, under closely controlled laboratory-like conditions. Yes, this yields a large amount of "data" about people,[1] but it studies them as something that they are not: uniform groups with identifiable and definitional characteristics. Market research is a way to create "simple" models of people suitable to fit into operationalized frameworks to organize decision making and action in business contexts. This, unfortunately, applies to data science as well. It is all about rushing to a normative model of the world, eliminating the real detail of life in favor of idealized proxies standing in for real humans.

Market research practices are poorly adapted to innovation research. They are meant to deductively explore a set of hypotheses or findings in greater, statistically relevant detail. And they are very good at that, but they are the wrong tool for the job in any exploratory research program. Because design processes must begin with an exploratory phase, it means market research approaches should have no place in design thinking or human-centered design. This is because market research relies on quantitative practices, which are objective in their structure. They work within the limits of the data they have, and do not stray from this pool of information, be it sufficient or not. The objectivism and process-driven nature of these practices tend to reduce the world to only what can be obtained through quantitative surveys and analysis. Anything else is left out. This also contributes to the incorrect belief that market research quant is unbiased. While the procedures come from "pure" practices like statistics, the research is only as empirical as the initial data collection and interpretation. However, in most cases commercially applied quantitative studies are preconditioned by the assumptions of the researchers. The recruitment practices where respondents are either overly screened or under-screened, introduces bias immediately. Making matters worse, when the survey questions are built without a grounding in a strong empirically based ethnographic study, they introduce more bias into the system by solidifying the assumptions of the author. What you end up with is a survey of what researchers assume they will find. There will be no surprises. The respondents are able to answer the questions they are given. But because they cannot break the structure of the encounter long since established—they must answer within the limits set by the researchers— the empiricism of the study is lost immediately. You will get data, but it will not be contextualized or tested against the reality of their lives. They simply respond to what they are given. The bias inherent in how the questions are written, the language that is used, and the ideologies that underpin them is baked into the process from step one. This is a long way from scientific quantitative methods where questions are developed through observations, explanations are suggested, everything is tested, and respondents are given a way to opt-out of the ideology of the survey designers in their responses.

What compounds this problem is the fact that the data is always immediately abstracted by categorizing them within a demographic or psychographic model that is untested in the survey. This demographic categorization enters the system in the screener, before anyone has answered the first question. This means that the people are preorganized. If these demographic categories are not viable, then the study is nothing more than an assessment of fake people.

The abstraction issue creates further limitations. Because the underlying categorizations are not tested, and the entire research instrument is designed to create another set of categories that build on them, market research quant results are not comparable across studies. One company's segmentation cannot be rigorously tested against another company's findings. In fact, there is little likelihood that two similar studies within the same company would yield the same results. Each study is telling a story about people in a way that cannot be retested through a repetition of the study with a different set of people or tested and/or verified by alternative methods like an ethnographic study. If a market research quant study was set up to be truly empirical, then they would identify things that could be immediately tested by other researchers. It would be grounded in direct evidence of the world of the customer/user/ patient and would have points of comparability throughout.

This makes each study a one-off, which means it cannot contribute to one of the major goals of empirical, scientific studies, the slow accruing of knowledge. Real empirical research is accretive. It builds on what is "known," then validates or invalidates this knowledge, and creates more knowledge. Few businesses have any sense of an ongoing engagement with the world, which means they do not build knowledge over time. Most of the studies they run, or have a consultant run on their behalf, simply gather data that is immediately and tactically relevant for what they are doing now. This is a real shame. Businesses could, and should, be using their research arms, or their research vendors, to contribute to an ongoing engagement with their customers. They should, over time, become true experts in the people they are trying to innovate for. Instead, they are relying on fleeting snapshots and *productive fictions*, most of which are not that productive and are simply fictions.

The idea of a productive fiction is well-known in anthropology.[2] It is a concept built on the knowledge that every study, every ethnographic insight, is only a partial telling of what was found in field. Since the purpose of an insight is to help those who did not meet the respondents know them, or understand a key aspect of their lives, it will always be partially fictional. Its incompleteness guarantees this. The trick—where the real expertise comes in— is to mitigate the fictional aspect as much as possible by remaining grounded in the details of real life. What this means is that an anthropologically inflected study is aware of the problems of the productive fiction and yet is grounded in what empirical truths are available to the researcher. To conduct empirical research, you have to get stuck into the world of the people you want to know. A radically human-centric researcher recognizes this and does everything to be truly empirical and not merely objective.

What This Requires

Studying the world as you find it, or the people as you find them, requires the researcher to be a rigorous researcher and open to a world that is not their own. The correct technique for this is to construct a study that uses an examination of experience, language, meaning, and action firsthand, according to a careful plan and well-executed strategy. This means setting up the study precisely, with full knowledge of the problems inherent in doing human-centric research. It means having the experience to make careful records of what you experience and to test everything you believe you know in a collaborative way with the people you are studying. It requires a form of associative analysis that connects and contextualizes observations—something which is a world away from the data management typical in commercial research. And finally, it involves testing your own understanding to mitigate the losses of perspective, fidelity, and detail that are part of creating a well-grounded productive fiction, like a well-constructed design persona.

An example of this came in a study where I explored the experience of chronic lymphocytic leukemia (CLL), a cancer of the blood and bone marrow. We were asked by our client, a large pharmaceutical company to provide an extremely detailed perspective of how patients experience this disease and how they interact with doctors, hospitals, and insurers. I and my collaborator, another anthropologist, conducted this work in three countries (U.S., U.K., and Germany) and in two languages, (English and German). Our preparatory research told us that the clinical understanding of CLL involved three distinct phases of the disease: diagnosis, watch and wait, and treatment. CLL is often a slow-moving disease and there are no therapies available to treat it in its early stages. After diagnosis, patients often go years—even a decade—before their blood counts cross the threshold where treatment can begin. What this means is doctors and oncologists diagnose a patient, and then test them periodically until they pass this threshold. Someone can live with the diagnosis for years with little clinical support, and no action—which is often very distressing.

The previous studies we reviewed from our client followed the same format of description and patients were categorized into recently diagnosed, living in the watch and wait period, and undergoing treatment. This was the format that we were expected to follow in reporting our experiential findings. However, because they wanted to dig into the experience of the disease, we put these aside at the beginning and instead build a research program where we engaged people in completely open-ended conversations. We recruited individuals using a very small set of criteria, basically selecting people from a large sample who had been diagnosed but were at many different stages of life (ranging from 20 to 70 years of age) and were distinct from each other in socio-economic status and educational achievement. We then sat at their dining room tables, on their couches, and in hospital waiting rooms and talked. We followed them into their first chemotherapy sessions. We talked to them and their doctors. We took tours of hospitals, and in one case, attended a funeral, having lost someone during the study. We took it all in as it came, resisting the temptation to let the clinical definitions guide how we understood what they said.

What we found was that in these details there were in fact five phases. The first phase was a new phase and involved the experiences of discomfort and fear preceding diagnosis—and therefore out of view of clinicians. This experiential phase involved noticing that something may not be right, learning to listen to one's body, and then finally realizing that there is a need to see a doctor. It also involves trying to explain a set of feelings that while symptoms of CLL are also symptoms of many other things. The frustration of misdiagnosis was a problem in this stage of the disease experience.

The long watch and wait phase that followed in the clinical definition was actually two stages, each defined by distinct experiences. The first, the real watch and wait, was a period after diagnosis. Provided they were diagnosed early, this watch and wait phase began immediately after diagnosis and usually mean living with minor discomforts that did not make a huge difference in people's lives. There was a sense of relief for those who were chasing a diagnosis. But there was a sense of dread for those who were otherwise healthy and just handed a cancer diagnosis out of the blue.

The second half of the watch and wait phase was largely invisible within the clinical definitions. Rather than just watching and waiting—which itself is a description seen from the point of view of a clinician—it was a period of steady, inexorable decline. People described increasing fatigue, difficulty living their life normally, and new pains and fears that make the whole experience harder. They also felt a lack of support from a doctor who only saw them every few months according to the rules of clinical practice. What was notable was the fact that everyone in this phase felt underserved, which is a clear indication of a service opportunity. It was the only instance in my career as a researcher in which there was a true gap in the system. We had to give this new phase a name, and we used a direct quote from several of our conversations: "the steady decline."

Had we stuck to the clinical definitions and used them as easy categories, we might have enriched the prevailing perspective with some new experiential insights. But because we build our program around staying agnostic and building the story from the details of our new friends' lives, we were able to test something which was unchallenged within our client's organization. The addition of the two extra phases allowed us to provide our client with a clear set of opportunity spaces where a service around their drug might make many people's lives better. We found these because we studied the world as it is and restrained ourselves from using old abstractions and categories to neatly package our data. The chaos of the fieldwork allowed us to push the understanding of CLL from an experiential perspective forward for everyone. This was a clear win for true empiricism.

What Are the Benefits of the Examining the World as It Is?

There are many benefits to taking the radically human-centric path. The first is that there is simply more to learn when you engage people on their own terms rather than your own. You are able to grow as a researcher and as an organization if you are honest about letting your participants change your mind rather than simply fitting them into a model of how you would like the world to work. This has the happy effect of ensuring a research project is less biased than it otherwise would be.

Understanding the world as it is in an empirical way also means you are better prepared for change. Real research helps you learn over time and gain the expertise needed to know, rather than have "data on" something. You will be able to contextualize change more easily because your knowledge of the world will be data rich, flexible, and longitudinal. This also means you will capture the detail that will help you make better decisions and design better products, services, and experiences for the people. Now what could be better than that?

Understanding the World As You Find It: Problems and Solutions

Why does truly human-centric research require bravery? The reason for this is simple: to do this kind of work you have to be ready to change yourself and how you think. If you do not, you will not be flexible enough to manage what you find. Understanding human experience is not about examining something from the outside as an impartial observer. It is a visceral experience where you must try to feel how it feels to think about the world in a new way. I showed that empathy is only the leaping-off spot for this process, but what allows you to do it is the willingness to leave your own prejudices, thoughts, and feelings behind for a while. Only after you realize that your way of looking at the world is only one of many possible options will you be able to truly understand what your respondents are saying. You learn that the major obstacle to understanding them is yourself. You learn that what you might consider mistakes in their thinking may actually be reasonable ways of looking at the world, despite being contrary to your own. In response, you must learn to inhabit other ways of thinking for a short time. In some projects this is very easy because the gulf between your "way of knowing"[3] and yours are not that different—although this presents its own set of problems too.[4] In others, the effort is considerable.

With this in mind, I want to turn to a set of issues that everyone encounters in the field. These represent some of the biggest obstacles to good research and the points where, until now, commercial research formats from market research to the style of ethnography practiced by human-centric designers run into major trouble. Importantly, these are the issues that you must overcome to understand the world from a perspective that is not your own and explain it to others.

First amongst these issues is the problem of practicalities of studying complexity—the term that strikes fear into most in the world of commercial research. Next comes the problems you encounter when you try to study something, or someone, exactly as you find it. After that we will explore what happens when you force your worldview onto a field encounter too much. Here we will examine the issues of over-designed research and the problematic legacy of laboratory conditions in market research. Following this, we will explore the technology problem that is lurking in most contemporary customer/user studies. We will examine how the dominant concepts of technology are mostly mythological and are hiding the reality of the lives we all lead with the technologies in our hands, homes, and bodies. After this I will touch how the fear of bias leads to the improper design of most traditional commercial research. With bias comes the belief in the naïve response—a concept abandoned by most serious social sciences decades ago. We will examine how the pairing of bias and the naïve response has stretched many stakeholder's expectations out of proportion. Finally, we will examine why the stalwarts of traditional commercial research—the "unmet need," "drivers," "customers," "users,"—are mythological constructs that do not appear in real research. We will then consider how personas and segmentation are ways of carving these concepts out of real life and examine the damage necessary to accomplish this task.

The World Is Not Simple: The Problems

What is complexity really? In commercial research even the term complexity itself is, well, complicated. It is used as an insult, as in, "I don't want to get into the weeds with this one. I find all of this complexity too academic."[5] In business, complexity is something to be feared. It is often feared to the degree that an entire marketing campaigns can be built around is antonym "simple."[6] I have already raised the simple versus complex relationship in Chapter 3. There I focused on the tendency to oversimply and reduce everything in business thinking. I now want to return to this issue and discuss some of the implications of this preference for reductionism.

Very often complexity is seen as a barrier to success, and entire work-streams are developed around simplifying something perceived to be complicated. In one case, I heard a client say, "We do not really understand our customers now. But we need to figure out how to develop a simpler way to understand our customers in the future. This simple model is key to solving some of the complex problems we have right now."[7] What this comment exemplifies is a very real tendency within commercial research contexts to create a false opposition between complexity and simplicity. If you believe that simplicity is good and complexity is bad, and the two are direct opposites of each other, then you operate in a way of thinking where reducing complexity is the fundamental reason to do any kind of research. This immediately means most rigorous research practices are suspect because instead of reducing complexity they strive to describe, explain, and predict what happens in a complicated world.[8] They expose the complexity and expect people to address it. The general fear of complexity and this dangerous belief contributes to the kind of reductionist applied research that is not human-centric at all.

However, the distance between real life and the specific questions businesses need to be answered to do their work can be narrowed. First, we have to abandon some old, problematic thinking and reset our expectations of what comes out of a research study and what the appropriate inputs into a design or strategy effort needs to be. This begins by leaving behind the belief that there is a simple, causal explanation for why something happens. A belief in direct, singular causality begins with our understanding of progress and change, two related phenomena (you cannot have progress without change) that are too simply explained. Most of us are still working with an old understanding of change, often called the "Great Man Theory" first put forward by Scottish philosopher Thomas Carlyle in 1840. His claim that, "the history of the world is but the biography of great men," is flush with a view that is of its time.[9] The 1840s was the time when the idea of the great genius began to take old, immediately following the time of Napoleon, who was often hailed as a transformative genius. Carlyle claimed that progress was the work of great men who pushed the rest of the world forward. Their character, being suited to this leadership role, allowed them to be a catalyst for change. And without them, we would not have advanced as we did. Given that this was also the time when industrialists were changing the world of business through the application of technology, it is no surprise that this theory was quickly adapted to show how the advancement of technology was also due to the work of its great men, the inventors, and that they were solely responsible for the advancements they provided. They vainly saw themselves reflected in these ideas—a tendency that has not left us.

While this theory has long since been abandoned in the social sciences and historiography, it is still lurking in the world of business, providing a foundation for the elevation of great business leaders like Steve Jobs to near mythological status. The theory itself is not important. Instead, I believe the fact that it is still around in the world of business is an indication of a preference for a simple answer over a more complicated one. Outside of the academic circles in business schools, the vast majority of business leaders are much more interested in a story that accounts for Apple's, Amazon's, or Facebook's success as the work of the great CEOs who built and run the companies, or a killer app that wholly guided their fortunes. This is much simpler and cleaner than seeing this success as the work of tens of thousands of people putting widely shared ideas to work in a more successful way than many of the lesser-known companies that fail for reasons not related to the idea itself. The simple, direct answer that takes us from x, to y, to z in a linear, causal way is much easier than the one that suggests a great person is simply the top of a pyramid of people just like themselves who are all doing the same thing with greater or lesser success.

This belief has always been always problematic. It clouds our ability to see the other inputs that enable a new idea, a new invention, or a new way of thinking to take hold. For instance, the great man theory helps us understand the towering achievement of the development of calculus or the formulation of a theory of natural selection as the mechanism behind evolution—both essential pieces of the world that we all now live in. But it struggles to explain how, in both cases, two people were able to come up with the same idea at the same time. Issac Newton and G. W. Liebnitz both developed calculus, independently of each other, simultaneously. Charles Darwin and Alfred Russel Wallace did the same thing with their theories of natural selection, developing almost the same basic principles in independent efforts. The ideas were clearly germinating everywhere, but credit was given to one "great man." This is a problem studied in archeology, where researchers routinely struggle with the diffusionist perspective stating technologies like metal tools started in one place and were then spread through contact, trade, or invasion. Its alternative, evolutionism, suggests ideas can be born in multiple places and this single source theory need not apply. The archeological record is usually unable to provide an answer either way. Given that this debate has been raging in the social sciences for almost 200 years, it is odd that the world outside has devoted itself to a firm belief in diffusionism.

Understanding the world without single causality—to see it as it is, means examining more than the efforts of these men. To understand the development of calculus or a theory of natural selection, we need to understand the intellectual context of the time. We have to understand what ideas these scholars were responding to and what came before them. We have to understand the way science was performed at the time. We must understand the entire socio-cultural context surrounding them to see why it was them and not someone else who developed the idea. This is because, in all cases, many people were working on similar or identical ideas at the same time. We could say the idea was already developed in the larger community and all it required was someone to articulate it. Properly understood, it was not the man that drove society (here the intellectual network surrounding their work), it was the society that drove the person, or at least impacted their thinking in a profound way. What this means is that we have to leave these kinds of simple models behind. Once you begin working with scepticism for causal explanations, it is impossible to believe in simple answers.

The search for drivers and gaps we examined earlier is also an expression of the desire for simple models of change and human behavior. While this is understandable, it is wrong. We must try to understand the "world as it is," which means the messy, chaotic place that we all live in. Simple is not really an adjective that belongs anywhere near "the world," "humans," or "behaviour." Instead, we need to set ourselves up as researchers, designers, and leaders to understand the world as a context giving rise to the development of new things. We have to study history, change, notable failures or near misses, and the action of individuals within this context. We must become comfortable with the beautiful complexity of ecosystems, ecologies, networks, and systems thinking of all kinds.

The World Is Not Simple: The Solution in Practice

Anthropology has often struggled with systems thinking for the same reason that commercial researcher and business thinkers have. It is very difficult and time-consuming to study things around the object of your attention. There have been many attempts to incorporate systems thinking into the work of anthropological studies. Gregory Bateson and the group associated with Bruno Latour have provided examples ranging from cybernetic anthropology to Actor Network Theory.[10] Their work has demonstrated the interconnectedness of human life and the fact that it is impossible to see humans as individuated actors living their lives according to their own intuition and desires. Incidentally, this is also why we should prefer to use perspectives and methods from anthropology and sociology rather than social psychology. The latter tends to individuate people and eliminates the information about how humans work within a web of understanding to live their lives. But to understand the way a system works, you must understand enough of it to describe, explain, and predict how it works.[11] Doing this is difficult because it requires the researcher to scale the project appropriately. If you spend too little time in field, ask limited questions, talk to too few people, or constrain the project scope too much, you cannot gain access to answers to larger questions.

Very often commercial research is out synch with itself, scoped too large but executed in too limited a manner. What I mean is that the research brief is asking for answers to large-scale questions like, "what do people need out of technology," "how do people listen to music," or "how do customers experience the designed environment in our retail space." To address these questions, a project is built with a two-week timeframe, with a discussion guide that is thematically incomplete, and only includes 20 people engaged in one-on-one interviews and then a second, larger group, through a survey. These questions need to be addressed with a much larger study, incorporating more people, and using different tools. But the convention dictates that this is what fits in a client's budget, and therefore this is sufficient to answer these relatively thorny issues. Instead of a research project, most companies really need a research department that never stops doing real research and a strategy and design team to make sense of it all. They usually opt for a consultant who is willing to make these mistakes and execute the project without question.

Conceptually, the fact that the scale (the conceptual size of the ask) and the scope (the approach the researchers use to study the situation) are out of step with each other leads to another problem. This forces the researchers to stay at the level of "the ask," the research question and goals, and not dig into the messy details sufficiently. This comes from a desire to address the majority of people requires understanding them at the macro-level only. If you were asked to study how young people are bending the idea of gender in the way they purchase make-up (as is the case in the rise of make-up for men) and only given three weeks to go to field in two or more markets, then every single encounter with a real person turns into an exercise in having them speak for their "segment" or "persona." The details for their lives have to stand as examples with enough universality that you can say, "young people believe that [...] " in the insights report.

To do this, you must eliminate quite a bit of who they actually are. You have to immediately generalize their statements—often at the moment that you are hearing them say what they have to say. A detailed conversation becomes a single "proof point" of a small finding. The problem here is that the process forces you to eliminate quite a bit to fit what you find into the categories that make logical sense at this level. This is actually a violent act, because you have to "fit" people into boxes and reduce who they are to just the details you need for your purpose.

The radically human-centric alternative is to painstakingly build a categorical description after talking to everyone, rather than prefiguring a "simple" model in your head and working towards that. You cannot work from the top down, from "model" to "learning" without first having developed the model from insights found in field. You must always work from the details of real life at the micro-level and build from there. The benefit is that ultimately your hard work is repaid because your model is more "real" than anything you could have built without this slow, details-up approach.

Ultimately, it is necessary to describe the situation exactly as you find it and then build a model of how it fits into the greater ecosystem of connections that surrounds them. The analysis emerges from the reality, not as a way to constrain it. To do this, you must stay within the boundaries set by the scope of the work and scale the project. This requires you to not attempt to universalize what people say too quickly. You must prevent yourself from looking for the answer to the big questions in their statements, but to leave that for analysis. It is also necessary to build the project at the right scale and to realize that larger questions take longer to answer, with considerably more effort. To answer questions about how young people are bending the idea of gender in the way they purchase make-up, you must first study conceptions of gender to understand departures from it. Then you must see how different people approach this in order to find commonalities between their idiosyncratic approaches. Next, you should test the validity of these commonalities with the people that you are working with. Finally, you have to place these commonalities within the context that you originally outlined and detail how it fits into other socially understood normative behaviors. All of this takes time, and could require two fieldtrips, or more, to accomplish. To believe that you can do it in a single trip of a few days is folly. Managing complexity requires a researcher to balance the scope of the question with the scale of the research response. Doing this in a radically human-centric way involves ensuring that the people you are studying do not get crushed between them.

The Parallax View: The Problem of Perspective

While managing complexity involves preparing to study belief, thought, and action more deeply, and in context, an RHC researcher must also prepare to manage what we bring to fieldwork in a more deliberate way. To be radically human-centric, a researcher must be prepared to mitigate the impact their presence has on the field site and on what insights come out of it. This is not only about bias but also about working to understand ourselves as a filter on what is seen, heard, felt, and understood. Making sense of the complexity of the situation requires a researcher to be aware of the perspective they bring into field and how their own perspective on the world—itself acquired through acculturation—changes what they find.

Anthropologists are particularly sensitive to the vagaries of perspective. We know it is an issue that goes well beyond "bias," but shares some of the same concerns. The idea of bias is an old one in applied research, particularly in commercial settings. It stems from a worry that the results of a study will be subtly corrupted because of the activities of the researcher. This is a relatively contained problem because bias is only a concern in the confines of the research encounter and in the analysis of the data. The idea being that a researcher looking to make their own argument will see something in the data that is not there. The problem really appears when you push the language into action, as in the "biasing" of the study. It is a skewing of the data by the actions of the researcher, either by contaminating the responses in the field setting (usually a laboratory) or in the analysis. This is a genuine concern, and all properly trained researchers are able to manage this well.

However, the issue of perspective is a deeper problem because it is not contained within the limits of simple bias—which is just bad research practice. Rather, it is one that appears when you consider how your own cultural background affects what you think is real, logical, rational, and self-evident. Your cultural background, the very basis of your knowledge of the world, is based more on agreement and repetition than on fact or laws. Many of the "truths" that all of us hold to be self-evident, are actually the result of our upbringing. The way we experience the world is guided by the acculturated knowledge we receive as we grow up and live in any socio-cultural context. Fundamental concepts like gender, identity, right and wrong, honour, what is shameful, how one should behave in public and private, are some of the received, culturally coded "truths" that can be quite different in other socio-cultural contexts. For some a smile is the friendliest way to present yourself to others. In some cultures, notably in a few in Indonesia, one tries not to smile too much to be sociable. In the U.S. the lack of a smile is what signals trouble. These differences exist at all levels of experience and even impact things that commercial research is supposed to study, from customer expectations when shopping, to what we expect from digital devices. The principal work of an anthropologist is to understand what these other truths are and help others to understand what it means to believe them. But they are, for lack of a better term, arbitrary. They appear in subtly or even profoundly different ways in other cultures. What one person living in the USA might think is shameful is nothing of the sort for someone in China or Belgium. The opposite may also be true.

The Parallax View: Problems of Perspective – Theory

If some of these "truths" can be so radically different depending on who you are talking to, then many of the truths behind our experience of the world may be also. The problem is easily revealed in this example. Colour perception is often held as an interesting battle ground to understand cultural difference and variations in an area where one might expect there to be some objective reality. Colors are just light at different wavelengths within a narrow range of electromagnetic radiation. The human sensory apparatus, that is, eyes, have evolved to perceive light. Our eyes are, within a relatively narrow range of variation, basically the same and are biologically organized to perceive light in the same way. However, across all of the languages in the world, there is a dizzying array of variation in how color is described. The work of scholars like Brent Berlin and Paul Kay (1969) and Harold Conklin (1955) clearly demonstrated that color terminology was so varied, that many cultures have as few as four terms for the whole spectrum that English describes with eight, and often use nonlight specific references to describe the colors.[12] The color that we call orange, for example, was referred to as red until the citrus fruits came to Europe, and we associated the color with a fruit called an orange.

How then, can some cultures have only a few words for colors like the Hanunóo Conklin describes, and others, like English, have many? Are people with only a few words unable to perceive the colors that the others can? Is their experience different or just their terminology? The answer is that the names associated with the colors are dependent on a huge set of linguistic, historical, environmental, and socio-cultural conditions and that these, and not an assessment of objective realities like the wavelengths of light. The reality is not different, but our cultural experience of it is. This is not limited to color categories. This situation is part of every aspect of the way we perceive the world, from how we understand the categories of knowledge (science vs. art) and how we understand our role as a consumer. What this reveals is that this problem will be there waiting for every researcher in any field encounter. Are these differences in experience or are these cultural, or sub-cultural, differences? Should this be studied through the lenses of phenomenology or semiotics? Where does the explanation for these differences lie?

Unless you share the same socio-cultural background with the people you meet, you will encounter what is often called the "parallax effect." A parallax effect is the same effect where if you put your finger up in front of your face. Close one eye and look, then close it and open the other and you will see your finger jump. The effect is one that once plagues astronomers where the location of objects will change depending on the position from which they are observed. They later learned to tame it and use the effect to measure distances more accurately. The example is apt, and I will explain why. In anthropology, the parallax effect is a metaphor used to indicate the distance between to perspectives. This term is often attributed to visual anthropologist Faye Ginsburg where she called for "juxtaposing these different but related kinds of cinematic perspectives on culture, one can create a kind of parallax effect; if harnessed analytically, these "slightly different angles of vision" can offer a fuller comprehension of the complexity of the social phenomenon we call culture and those media representations that self-consciously engage with it."[13] Her purpose was to show how ethnographic films made by anthropologists or other filmmakers could be productively compared with films made by indigenous peoples about themselves. The difference in perspectives would allow for everyone to come to a more complete understanding.

But there is no guarantee that this juxtaposition will be productive. Philosopher and intellectual gadfly Slavoj Žižek expanded on the parallax problem by identifying a *"parallax gap"* occurring between "confrontation of two closely linked perspectives between which no neutral common ground is possible."[14] His point was to highlight the very real possibility that there is may be no way to bridge the gap between two perspectives. He goes further and says that the problem of looking—like the work of a researcher—actually creates the conditions where "the subject's gaze is always-already inscribed into the perceived object itself, in the guise of its 'blind spot'."[15] This is a Žižekian way of saying that our understanding of what we study is made more difficult by a parallax effect that is not only dependent on our perspective, but that it also makes us unable to see something important because the act of researching actually changes the conditions so that we are blind to what counts.

The Parallax View: Problems of Perspective – In Practice

The issues with shifts and gaps in perspective one encounters in field and in analysis can be overcome by taking a reflexive position. It is essential for a researcher to understand how they fit into the puzzle. Only by "placing" themselves into the story, and being open and transparent about this, can they hope to mitigate the parallax effect and overcome bias. This reflexive positioning allows us to understand the depth of the differences and commonalities we have with our subjects. These differences and commonalities are the basis of any insight we might find. They are only legible if we are able to understand ourselves in relation to what we are trying to study. If we assume that the people we study are the same as we are, then we will miss the transformative aspects of what we learn. We will miss the key indicators of their perspective, potentially dismissing them as mistakes or misstatements.

Taking a reflexive position begins with an acknowledgment of the effect we had on the field encounter. To do this work well, and to truly engage our respondents and their world as we find them, we must declare our own biases and perspectives before we enter the field and afterward. Only then can we being to see what is truly part of the context, and what is not. Within a commercial setting, this means declaring the reasons for going to field beforehand and developing a set of hypotheses about what we might find in order to see how they are challenged by what we experience.

Then, we must write ourselves into the field narrative in order to understand how we fit. The researcher must appear as one of the characters described. This one can be a bit tricky. Overcoming the parallax effect involves laying out the details of our own perspective next to our construction of our respondents. In many cases, this means beginning the process in the development of double-sided fieldnotes that not only detail the flow of interviews or observations but also taking careful note of the thoughts of the researchers conducting the study. In this way, we can see how our own thinking directed the progress of the encounter. We can also understand the depth of the gulf between the two perspectives.

Finally, overcoming the parallax effect requires writing yourself out of the insights eventually. If the gap between you and your respondents is large, and you do not share a great deal in common, this can be quite difficult. A radically human-centric study is intended to explain the details and implications of another person's view of the world so that action can be taken, this means that some commonalities must be found. But when there are few, it is the researcher's job to develop a set of insights that educate the audience on the differences in the perspective so that they may learn to leave their own way of thinking behind and "inhabit" another's experience for a while. This requires the researcher to be in the descriptions. This is really what "empathy" means in conventional articulations of design research. It is not really about empathizing but inhabiting this different way of seeing the world or finding a way to make it clearer to others.

Resisting the Urge to Control Things

Understanding the world as it is means being out in the world where real people live. To ensure you are doing good research, you have to actually *be* in the world of your participants. This is very simple to understand, and surprisingly easy to do. We do it every day after all. However, it is still necessary to point this out and make the point that good research depends on actually *"being there."*[16] Conventional business research still relies on old and outdated ways of contextualizing human-centric research. It seems that even in the most human-centric versions of market research and user research, the idea that researchers have to be out in the world to understand it is resisted. This is partially because of a too-narrow focus and the inertia of the comfortable way to do things. Commercial researchers try to understand "behaviour" or "mindsets," but often do so in a way where the context is eliminated as being too "noisy" or "irrelevant." Consequently, research is still done in facilities with mirrors on the walls, or in office meeting rooms where conditions are easier to control. The focus group is still the dominant format for research in these environments. It is widely used in the world of market research and far too often in design research. Moreover, consultancies of many kinds conduct their research in these labs and sell it to their clients as ethnography.

This is really puzzling, because the focus group setting is not really the appropriate format for human-centered research. While we cannot expect market research practices to be human-centric—they are not by design. We need to address the problem of design research or even research for strategic design and commercial researcher's, frankly, dangerous addiction to the focus group and its facilities. This is because a focus group in a facility is a laboratory environment that was developed over a period of many years in the middle twentieth century to eliminate the very contextualizing details that we have to include to be human-centric or even radically human-centric. To understand the world of your customer/users as it is, and to contextualize their beliefs, actions, and desires within it, you need to be out in their world. Shutting it out in a sterile room and conducting research using the stultifying, structured approaches of the focus group is the best way to be decidedly nonhuman-centric. Good research is not convenient and often lacks air conditioning and a snack tray.

Death to Focus Groups! – In Theory

No contemporary social scientists use focus groups.[17] If they do, they are greatly modified from the format commonly used in conventional commercial research. The reason for this is because of the damage they do to the study, and the fact that this setting is better suited to validatory research rather than exploration and discovery. The structure and mechanics of a focus group are actually control structures that actively change the terms of the encounter so that the moderator, and the people behind the glass, are in charge. The space, the mirror, the formality of the conversation, the structure of the discussion guides, the exercises, and the mercenary nature of using paid respondents are features that are not found in real life. They alter the frame of the conversation, and in doing so change how the respondents behave in the session. This is important, and we need to explore how a "frame" works to understand why.

I have already discussed Erving Goffman's frame theory earlier. Here, I want to focus on two key concepts. Let us return to the two phrases I discussed there. As we saw, the best way to understand a frame is to examine the differences between the kinds of conversations that start with "Hey, what's up?" and "Good morning. It is nice to see you." A conversation beginning with "Hey, what's up?" is informal and usually only happens between people who already know each other. The informality of the words of the first statement indicates the speakers' desire to have an informal conversation. These words are, in Geoffman's terms, "keying" and "cuing" what kind of conversation the speaker wants to have. Keying indicates the rules of the conversation by showing what the limits are.[18] By keying, Goffman means to use a musical metaphor and refer to how a musical key, like F major, sets the terms of what notes can be used. The key signature of F major has one flat and shows that only F,G,A,B flat,D, and E can be used (and not the six other options). In conversation, the key shows that the informal pattern of conversation must be followed.

"Hey, how are you?" is also a "cue," or an indication that this kind of informal conversation is preferred over other possibilities. Cuing a frame involves making it clear that the conversation is beginning now under the set of rules indicated by the "key."

The frame is the rules-based moment that follows. If people stick to the rules, then no one feels that the other speaker(s) have said anything that is wrong. But if someone says something too formal in response, they break the frame and it feels jarring to everyone involved.

Frames, however, are not limited to conversation. A frame exists, and structures people's behaviors and experiences, by providing the ruleset for many human encounters. A concert performance is a particular frame that allows everyone to understand how they should behave. The structures of the experience, the spaces, the difference between a stage and the seats in the hall, the ticket buying, the playbill, all "key" and "cue" the frame. In this frame, audience members understand what they have to do and how they should be, just as the performers on stage do. This is true for business meetings, social events, and even public spaces like pavements and parks. There are multiple frames governing behavior in each one. So, we now understand that how we speak and how we behave is not entirely free to any of the actors in the frames. Both are tightly controlled by the rules of the frame.

A focus group setting and the way moderators speak in a focus group session are "keys" and "cues" for a particular kind of conversation—one that is fraught with many ethical, epistemological, and methodological problems. They indicate a frame that requires people to behave a certain way. People must participate on the terms set by the moderator, answer questions in a particular way, use a somewhat foreign vocabulary, and sing for their supper or risk being labeled a "dud." This kind of conversation is outside of their real lives. Perhaps more importantly, they are unable to change it. The terms are set by removing them entirely from their world. They are wholly encompassed by an alien environment and do not have the power to change the circumstances. Consequently, the focus group is a controlling, disassociating frame. It structures people's experience so they speak and behave differently than they otherwise would in their normal lives. It is, therefore, biased in the extreme, just not in the way commercial researchers conventionally understand bias.

The use of the mirror, translators, and moderators, only makes things worse. All of these characteristics of a focus group setting push the two groups of people who should be speaking directly to one another further apart. All of these features of a focus group are actually barriers to understanding. Their continual use only serves to create a frame that is alienating, dislocating, and ultimately useless in any substantive study of what people do and how they think. Simply put, focus groups study artificial behavior in an artificial setting. It's no wonder that studies relying on them produce insights about artificial people.

Death to Focus Groups! – In Practice

A radically human-centric approach abandons focus groups entirely. It does not try to control the conditions for our benefit. It also incorporates our knowledge of how behavior is structured by frames to understand them as part of the context inhabited by our research participants. This is because frames are essential organizers of human experience, and as such are the very things a good research study should be capturing.

This critique is needed because an understanding of context is almost entirely lacking in the majority of commercial research. Qualitative and quantitative Insight and foresight researchers are still not revealing the relationship between lived experience and the context in which it occurs. Digital content platforms still study only consumption behaviors. Retailers only examine the purchasing behavior and the "mental models" of their customers. Banks only seek to understand attitudes to money and wealth management. But the only credible way to understand humans and to engage with them is by understanding actions and beliefs in context. This means the frame of a particular behavior is actually what researchers should be studying, along with the behavior itself.

Commercial research, including more common human-centric approaches do not yet engage with the world—the combination of thought, action, and context. Understanding the world as it is means studying the entire package. Avoiding one side because it is easier is just foolish and doomed to fail. This means building practices that are able to manage complexity and explain the richness of lived experience to everyone who wants to know.

"Understanding the world as it is" cannot be a choice. It must be the guiding principle behind any study. That this is not the typical state of affairs in commercial research is perhaps the major contributing factor behind why most companies, NGOs, and policymakers still struggle to understand their audiences. As they stand now, Human-centric practices are not sufficient for this task. A radically human-centric approach uses the rigor and intention behind ethnographic methods to engage people without trying to prefigure the study. This includes eliminating any possibility that the lack of time, the need to be tactical, or the *lessez-faire* attitude to research common in business thinking can negatively impact the work. It is the job of a skilled, well-trained research to be a bulwark against the pressures that damage good research. Owning the "radical" aspect of radical human-centricity means always thinking about the ethics and rigor of the work, no matter what the application.

Notes

1 Even the idea of collecting "data" from people is antithetical to a human-centric approach, let alone a radically human-centric approach. The belief that we need data from people to run a business is entirely business-centric. People are not data, they are people. And to extract data from a context, without understanding how it fits into that context, is just reproducing the problem of the blind men and the elephant over and over again. You can explain something this way, but you cannot understand the whole well enough to easily see what is actually going on. Data is a key to a kind of understanding, but truly knowing requires you to see how the data you have fits into the whole picture.

2 Stover, L.E., 1973. Anthropology and science fiction. *Current Anthropology, 14*(4), pp. 471–474. Tinius, J., 2018. Capacity for character: fiction, ethics and the anthropology of conduct. *Social Anthropology, 26*(3), pp. 345–360.; Hannerz, U., 2016. *Writing future worlds: An anthropologist explores global scenarios.* Springer.; Geertz, C., 1988. *Works and lives: The anthropologist as author.* Stanford University Press.

3 Brentano, F., 1995, Psychology from an Empirical Standpoint, Trans. Antos C. Rancurello, D. B. Terrell, and Linda L. McAlister, London and New York: Routledge. From the German original of 1874. Husserl, E., 2001, Logical Investigations. Vols. One and Two, Trans. J. N. Findlay. Ed. with translation corrections and with a new Introduction by Dermot Moran. With a new Preface by Michael Dummett. London and New York: Routledge. A new and revised edition of the original English translation by J. N. Findlay. London: Routledge & Kegan Paul, 1970. From the Second Edition of the German. First edition, 1900–01; second edition, 1913, 1920.

4 Hayano, D.M., 1979. Auto-ethnography: Paradigms, problems, and prospects. *Human organization, 38*(1), pp. 99–104.; Anderson, L., 2006. Analytic autoethnography. *Journal of Contemporary Ethnography, 35*(4), pp. 373–395.

5 This is something every ethnographic researcher has heard in one form or another. This version came from an executive at a large technology company.

6 SAP "simple" campaign.

7 This quote came from the VP or marketing at a web company who needed to identify new a new customer base for software that was basically free. I do not mean to pick on people, because in this case they were genuinely struggling with a problem.

8 As I have written elsewhere, this three-part effort is the marker of good insights in any kind of research.

9 Carlyle, Thomas. 1840. "The Hero as Divinity" In *Heroes and Hero-Worship.*

10 Bateson, G., 2000. *Steps to an ecology of mind: Collected essays in anthropology, psychiatry, evolution, and epistemology.* University of Chicago Press.

11 The three-part model of describe, explain, and predict is what I advocate should be used to build good insights, whether they are intended for an academic ethnography or in a PowerPoint deck aimed at C-suite executives. A good insight can describe the context and everything in it, explain what is going on and why this is important to know, and predict (within practical limits) how it will change in the near-term future. Any articulation of human behaviour that does not do this, is not an insight, but is an observation. It cannot be used for the same purpose. It is the job of an applied researcher to do these three things.

12 Berlin B, Kay P. "Basic color terms: their universality and evolution." (1969)., Conklin, Harold C. "Hanunoo color categories." *Southwestern Journal of Anthropology* 11, no. 4 (1955), pp. 339–344.

13 Ginsburg, Faye. "The parallax effect: The impact of aboriginal media on ethnographic film." *Visual Anthropology Review* 11, no. 2 (1995), p. 65.

14 Žižek, Slavoj. *The parallax view.* MIT Press, 2009, 4.

15 Žižek, Slavoj. *The parallax view.* mit Press, 2009, 17.

16 Borneman, J. and Hammoudi, A. eds., 2009. *Being there: the fieldwork encounter and the making of truth.* University of California Press.

17 There have been some attempts to rehabilitate the format and use it within social science research, but these have been rare and not widely implemented. You can read more about this attempt in this journal article. Lunt, P. and Livingstone, S., 1996. Rethinking the focus group in media and communications research. *Journal of Communication, 46*(2), pp. 79–98.

18 Goffman, 42–44.

Chapter 6

RADICAL STORYTELLING

An innovation consultant's life is often filled with little absurdities. The very idea of selling innovative ideas is, when you really think about it, rather strange. But there are even more fantastical moments and absurdities lurking in the very center of how the industry works. In part, this is because those of us in the innovation industry—research and design consulting in particular—work in a business where almost everyone is unaware that all they do is tell stories. Storytelling is so central to the process, that the entire industry is just an organized chain of storytellers fueled by newer and newer stories. Customer/user/patients tell researchers stories about their lives. The researchers tell these stories to designers and strategists to activate possible changes. These designers and strategists tell stories about how these changes will help people live better and companies make more money. The designers also tell stories to engineers who build things. Then the companies use marketing departments to tell stories about the benefits of the new products to the customers who initiated the whole process. Journalists then review the products and tell more stories about whether or not the marketing claims are true. Finally, the customers decide for themselves and tell stories about how these products work or do not work to the next bunch of design researchers who come knocking. So, you can see, storytelling is everything. Now I want to explore what it means to push ourselves further toward a radical human-centric way of doing research by exploring what radical storytelling looks like in contrast to older formats.

Practical Storytelling

One of my early realizations about storytelling and its place in commercial research came in an unlikely situation. It started with a problem. My colleagues and I were halfway through a project before we finally learned what the project was actually about. We were sitting with our clients around a table in our offices in San Francisco. Two of them had flown a long way from Asia to be at this meeting, and the other two were quite agitated to have them there. We were working on the sensemaking stage together after finishing a series of ethnographies in the US, UK, and Germany. We were taking them through the early set of explanations for what we saw that I and my team had developed. We were starting to group these proto insights in preparation for a longer conversation about what their company needs to know to develop the product line they were hoping to build. The most senior member of their team, a VP of product from their headquarters, left the room to take a phone call. At this point, the remaining three team members began to open up.

"Yes," one said, "we can see that all of this happened, and we get it. But we need to focus on what this project is about."

"Oh?" I said, hoping that this was not going to be a problem. "What do you mean?"

The woman who had flown all that way with the VP looked at her shoes and then at her notes. She said, "well, he believes we can just put cameras in everything and use that data to build a better security system. He's a little annoyed that we learned people don't like cameras in their home." Then she went quiet. After an uncomfortable pause, she continued, "we initiated this project with your team to try to convince him to give up this cameras-in-everything approach."

"Oh." My colleague said. "Is that really it?"

"Yes, I'm afraid so. We will need insights that make it impossible to continue down this direction at least. It would be best if we can also offer an alternative—something that will help us keep this product line going in the same direction, just without the cameras."

As she finished, the VP came back into the room and we resumed our review of the insights. But because we had not prepared the most detailed PowerPoint decks, my colleagues and I immediately changed what we were doing. We began to highlight the preinsights that outlined a fear of cameras in the private spaces in the home but offered alternatives to the kind of context-gathering sensors needed to develop a truly smart security system. By the end of our presentation, everyone but the VP was happy with the result, and he was unhappy because we had shown him the problems he faced.

For those of us who have worked in commercial research, this situation is not that surprising. Many millions of dollars are spent convincing senior executives of one thing or another. So that is not really the core of this story. What I want to focus on is the adaptation my team and I made on the fly to tailor the work we were doing for the needs of the client. This is because this moment was actually a key event in the development of the work we were doing. Even though we had already conducted our research, the storytelling we were doing was not connected to the purpose of the project. Yet, we were able to adapt to this new information without compromising what we found, and consequently, we turned a body of information into a story with a purpose and a goal. We were able to unlock the potential of what we had learned because while we had already gathered what we needed to tell the story of what we saw, we now had a thread that would help us bring it together for a particular audience. The adaptation was part of the second phase of ethnography. We were beginning to translate to the audience and making adjustments in how we did the "graphy" work.

One of the differences between pure ethnography, of the kind, found in an academic setting, and applied ethnography is a conceptual one. The former creates new knowledge and disseminates it to a specialist audience. The latter is organized to turn knowledge into action. To do this, you need to have an audience in mind and a direction to push them in. There needs to be a focus, something like a "vanishing point" to point all of the information toward. And in this example, this conversation provided us with the constraints and clear audience we needed to focus the work. What this means, however, is that from this point on we began to favor some angles and pieces of information over others. To return to a concept I discussed earlier, we began to develop the productive fiction needed to provide a design direction for our client. In this case, this first involved building an argument about why an emphasis on visuality and visual sensors (cameras) were wrong for in-home security systems. We began the process of organizing the information we discovered to show our client what the friends we made in field would prefer and what they would look for in a smarter security system for their home.

Insights are not pieces of data. They are not information about "needs." They are not even necessarily objective "truth." They are carefully constructed interpretive statements grounded in the truth of someone else's life that make an argument. They are part of a rhetorical construct designed to influence the actions of someone else, usually a designer or business strategist. They are arguments. They are translations of one way of looking at the world into another way of seeing that same situation. Most importantly, they are stories about the world that help galvanize the thinking and action of the people who were not able to meet the customers/users themselves.

This may seem to be in direct opposition to a belief in commercial research that insights are empirical, entirely objective observations of the world. This belief crept in with the scientism of the psychological models business research depended on for so long, and with the belief that business is also a science. But with the inevitable erosion of this edifice of truth in psychological research and models this belief is harder to hold. The reproducibility project has transformed our understanding of the validity, empiricism, and "truth" of many of psychology's and social psychology's famous findings.[1] It is no longer possible to believe there can be an entirely objective study of human behavior. To believe this is to be stuck in the past. It is time for commercial research, and applied research in the technology sector especially, to embrace a different way to understand humans. It is also necessary to make the best use of a different way of talking about human beings, their lives, their actions, and their beliefs.

Storytelling is a human action. It is one of the core tools we use to make sense of the world around us. It is a key part of what it is to be human. It allows us to create knowledge, to assign meaning, to educate, and to argue. It makes absolutely no sense that storytelling has been largely eradicated from "objective" studies of human behavior in most research contexts. Only anthropologists still actively practice storytelling as part of their work in academic research. Others, such as journalists and artists of all kinds still do as well, but their work is wrongly considered outside of the boundaries of serious research.

I want to argue that in order to be radically human-centric in applied and commercial research, we must develop a radical approach to storytelling. This approach is at once rigorous, rich, and collaborative—just like the storytelling that humans have used for millennia to create a sense of community. A radical human-centricity needs to connect people and create lasting knowledge based on the sharing of knowledge, thought, belief, and action. It must be dialogical, dialectical, and argumentative. It must provide the context needed to understand an action if it was found in the field. In the current commercial context, only a radical shift in storytelling practice can do this. To design the next level of technologies, products, services, and experiences we must set the PowerPoint slides filled with statistics and "learning" pulled from focus group studies aside. We have to embrace an approach to storytelling that is descriptive, explanatory, and predictive at least, and collaborative and defining too. Human-centric storytelling must become more anthropological in its approach and purpose. What does this mean? An anthropological model for storytelling is about activating the analytical elements in ethnographic processes I described in Chapter 3, but connecting to an audience so they may understand as well. Storytelling is a way of deciding what to include, what to leave out, how to order the story, and what you are trying to accomplish. Storytelling is where rhetoric comes into the ethnographic practice and where the "graphy" half of ethnography comes into its own.

Context at Work: Thick Description

Anthropologists have long understood the power of storytelling. The stories other people tell have been a major focus of our work for over 150 years. More importantly, anthropologists have long accepted our role as storytellers ourselves. Our work is expected to have literary merit. It is expected to "hook" readers in and to highlight key cultural and social details through stories about other people and what they have said.

One of the key works in the anthropological literature is Clifford Geertz's "Thick Description: Toward an Interpretive Theory of Culture," the first chapter in his book *Interpretation of Cultures*.[2] In this article, Geertz asserts the power of contextualized storytelling as an essential feature of the ethnographic process and its ultimate goal, making other cultures clearer to those who are not insiders. He advocates for a kind of storytelling that is rich with detail and contextualizes the interpretation of what happens within a telling of what actually did happen. He clearly states, "if anthropological interpretation is constructing a reading of what happens, then to divorce it from what happens—from what, in this time or that place, specific people say, what they do, what is done to them, from the whole vast business of the world—is to divorce it from its applications and render it vacant."[3] But he couches this idea within a clear statement of the incompleteness of our attempts to do this. He continues, "cultural analysis is intrinsically incomplete. And, worse than that, the more deeply it goes, the less complete it is. It is a strange science whose most telling assertions are its most tremulously based, in which to get somewhere with the matter at hand is to intensify the suspicion, both your own and that of others, that you are not quite getting it right."[4]

This means human-centric researchers must come to terms with two defining problems. We can only make others' lives clear through storytelling, but this story will always be fiction of some sort. This is as true for qualitative stories as it is for quantitative studies replete with lots of numerical detail. The solutions for this partiality and the fictive nature of these accounts lie in the "thickness" of the description, in collaborative approaches to fixing the meaning of the details, and in the location of the researcher(s) in the story so others can assess their approach. With these in mind, we can see that quantitative studies struggle with this fictionalizing problem more because they are not thick descriptions, they are not collaborative, and they are not reflexively constructed. So, to understand others in an empathetic, rigorous, and detailed manner, we have to work on building rich stories built using thick description.

Insights

What is thick description in a commercial context where people are obsessed with simplicity and brevity? They must be direct statements of analytical truth written in a way to provide a description of what happened, an explanation as to why this phenomenon is the case, and a prediction of how designed change will make a difference to this person in this context now and in the future. These statements must be thick with supporting detail and constructed in such a way that any reader can understand what is going on and why it matters no matter how much background they may have. They should be self-sufficient stories capable of relaying the necessary details of a particular context and the socio-cultural framing needed to see how while this is true for the person in the story, it is also true for most of the people in the story. In addition to this, these "insights" must be filled with opportunities for design and action, either additive or subtractive—this is the actionability so prized in the commercial research world.

What people call an "insight" in commercial research is really just an observation of something that was said or seen in field. While these tidbits are certainly important and interested, they do not satisfy the level of detail or thoughtfulness for what I call an "insight." I reserve the label "insight" for thick descriptions with descriptive, explanatory, and predictive power partially because I see a major problem lurking at the very core of commercial, applied research. This problem arises because of an industry-wide tendency to conflate, or confuse the terms "learning," "observation," and "insight." This the lack of a clear hierarchy or difference between these terms allows some to assume all three are developed by simply asking someone a question about their life and receiving an answer. This allows people to believe whatever a person says in an interview, or whatever they do in a shop along or user testing lab is an insight, or a learning, or an observation. This reveals a belief that insights about human behavior are derived directly from people and what they tell us in the brief encounters we are able to have with them.

A radically human-centric perspective rejects this simple, one-to-one relationship between utterance and insight. Rigorous research demands that we allow for a variety of data in qualitative encounters, and as a consequence, I prefer to use "learning," "observation," and "insight" to identify different classes of information. In this new hierarchy, a learning has the only one-to-one relationship between what people say and what we learn. A learning is something we gather from an interview or observation that teaches us something about the person or the situation. It is a simple fact, and there should be hundreds, or more, in an interview, and thousands in a project. What is important about a learning is that it does not get you very far. It is just a fact. An observation, on the other hand, is something that is true for many people in the study that they may or may not know themselves. The term "observation" suggests some degree of separation and objectivity, meaning we can use it for facts gathered from ethnographic encounters that are true but take a bit of thinking to see clearly. Finally, an "insight" is the rarified form of information about a behavioral phenomenon capable of doing what I just outlined; it describes, explains, and predicts. To do this, it must be the product of the analysis alone, and consequently, it incorporates the perspective of the researcher and the audience at which it is aimed.

This is all best explained through an example. This insight comes from a now years-old project for a major global technology company. They came to use with the hope of making inroads in-home appliance market, where they are already dominant, but doing this by expanding the capacities of these appliances with technologies from their other divisions. In practical terms, this meant adding touch screens and making the user experience more data rich. They engaged us to explore the domestic world and the current, and future, role for smart devices, while placing an emphasis on smart home opportunities for appliances like refrigerators, washers, and the like.

After several weeks of in-home ethnographies and several different formats of customer/user interviews, we developed a set of insights and opportunity areas for our client. Two of the insights proved to be of major importance because they provided the client with the information they needed to reason through the viability of their strategy and potential designs in different contexts and in different countries. Although I have made some modifications and deletions to protect the client's intellectual property, the insights go as follows:

Difference between a "House" and a "Home"

Throughout our time in field we noticed that no one lived in their spaces in the same way. Everyone had a different way of filling the space with their possessions and their appliances. Many wanted to hide things away and only fill their space with items of personal meaning. Others, on the other hand, seemed to not mind the look of their appliances and put them in conspicuous places without a second thought.

While our participants' home spaces were very different in the way they were organized, there was an important unifying structural principle. All of the objects in the house were divided according to a simple principle, some were part of the house, and others were part of the home.

Now, it is important to see that throughout this project we have assumed that the terms "house" and "home" are synonyms of each other. This is not the case. In English this is possible, but it is different in French, German, Spanish and Korean, so we should not expect them to mean the same thing even in English.

What we found was that when people said "house" the were referring to the physical container of their lives. When they said the term "home" they were referring to what the house contained, and the softer, more conceptual side of live with the family.

Interestingly, once we noticed this distinction, we realized the objects in this context were divided between these two concepts (house and home). Objects that had some permanence, especially ones that came with the house when it was rented or purchased, were part of the "house." These included the refrigerator, washer, dishwasher, freezer, boiler, stove, and oven. Whereas other kinds of devices, mostly those with some portability or a temporary nature, were seen as part of the home.

Importantly, the line of demarcation between the "house" and "home" is culturally dependent. In contexts like Korea and France, where when a house is purchased or rented the new tenant needs to bring all of the appliances, there are more allowances made for these devices because they are more a part of the "home" than the "house," which is dumb indeed.

It is essential to respect understand and respect the dividing line between the "house" and the "home," as this will indicate how devices and home appliances are organized conceptually. This will likely have an impact on what people expect from these devices.

Between "Smart" and "Dumb"

After we understood the categorical division between "house" and "home," we realized this had a direct impact on which devices could be "smart," that is technologically-enabled, and which could only be "dumb," i.e. not acting like a smart device.

As people told us about the way they used their devices and what they expect from them, they indicated that devices of the home had more permission to interact with the family. The devices that are part of the house, have less permission. One woman told us, "I don't mind my TV trying to get my attention, but the refrigerator needs to be quiet," and she was expressing a majority opinion.

What this means is that devices that are part of the "house" are expected to be dumb and are not expected to interact with the family in any meaningful way. They are "just machines," one person said while gesturing dismissively towards the older LG washer in the corner of his bathroom. However, those objects that are part of the "home" are afforded a place in the home and in family life. They can be as smart, interactive, and data rich as it is possible to make them.

In my opinion, these two insights exemplify what a good insight can be. They manage to split the difference between short and pithy, and thick and data rich. They cover a great deal of ground in a short space and do so by narrativizing the data—that is, together they tell a story that pushes directly toward a set of design dos and don'ts. They are able to also delineate different customer types—not only those in the study but also any customer/user who makes a distinction. And they are able to do this while also indicating how different cultures will demarcate different market types. It is easy to infer that some will allow a smart refrigerator more than others, and it is easy to see how this can be tested in market, or even corroborated through quant.

I want to call your attention to how the voice of the customer/user was couched in the text and not called out in the simplistic "verbatims" littering market research delivery decks. There are also some hints of the spaces we visited, aspects of my position in this story, and smaller details like body language and the chaotic nature of family life in the boxes we call houses. All of these details were used to push the central point forward, that these two lines of demarcation create a hierarchy of devices where only some may attain "smart" status, and that this has a big impact on the product portfolio of any tech device company. But the relative "thickness" of this description allows for the veracity of the insight to shine through. Also, there is a preamble that describes, a critical section that explains, and a statement that provides a prediction about how our client should understand this insight to play out in different markets and in different contexts. As a consequence, these insights have every element I have described so far.

Problematically, the majority of human-centered research executed in today's innovation and design industry does not reach the level of these insights. If it did, there would be fewer failures in the development of products, services, and experiences. The lack of true insights contributes to the high rate of failure in many projects and the gaps in many strategic plans. While this may seem like an over-generalization, the evidence for this lack is everywhere. The large majority of businesses and consultancies do not engage in customer research capable of developing this kind of detail. Without a robust ethnographic process, it is not possible to develop insights of this kind. Quantitative studies cannot identify the directions for design that are captured in these insights. Market researchers who are not well versed in socio-cultural linguistics will miss the productive aspect of categorical divisions that led to the development of these findings. And finally, without a willingness to explore the storytelling aspect of insights delivery, it is impossible to connect much of the information captured in these insights. We need insights that push past the over-simplifications of learnings and observations, and we need to learn to tell stories that are able to provide enough detail for someone else to get a glimpse of what it means to "be there."

Process Changes: Notes Toward a Radical Approach to Storytelling

Expertise in Storytelling

Storytelling is the art of crafting a clear statement about the world that has a narrative arc holding the information together. To do this well, a researcher must be attuned to the nuances of the context in which they are immersed. They must know what is real, what is not, what is a dead-end, and what will be surprising to a client. This means they must know this context well and have already made many of the mistakes that are typical of the kind of quick in and out work of commercial research. As a storyteller, they must also know what to include and what to leave out or even omit. This means there are a few key characteristics of a successful research we need to be attuned to. A good researcher is as close to an insider as it is possible to get. A good researcher is an expert in their subject area and in adjacent areas and has worked all of the superficial nonsense out of their system before the study has begun. A good researcher is able to tell stories about this world, and this way of living, in such a way that the people who live it will agree with what they say and recognize the story. And finally, a good researcher is someone who is able to explain this world to someone who is not an expert.

One of the major problems in design research, and indeed in human-centric research in general, is the lack of appreciation for expertise in all areas. Few research studies in commercial design begin with a period of discovery where the existing ethnographic literature is scoured for information in any meaningful way. However, the denigration of expertise does not just come at the beginning of a study, where specialists are excluded from the work. It comes later, after fieldwork has been completed and everyone sits down to groupthink their way through the rest of the process. What I mean is that the sensemaking process, while well-intentioned, is actually one of the more problematic aspects of the design thinking process because it does not allow for the inclusion of the nuances an expert voice could bring.

Sensemaking in design research, usually called "design synthesis" is a murky, often superficial affair. While every researcher is different, there are few hard and fast rules for how this is practiced in design consultancies. I am going to avoid an engagement with the academic literature about sensemaking and design synthesis because I have noticed that practice rarely follows this ideal. Jon Kolko rightly identifies this process as an abductive one, but I do not consider this to be a ground-breaking observation. Technically jumping to conclusions is also an abductive method, so there is little to celebrate in this fact.

In practice, sensemaking in design research usually involves four steps. First the team individuates "data" onto post-it notes. Then they prioritize those post-its into "interesting" or "not interesting" categories. Next they "cluster" these post-its into groupings that indicate some degree of similarity. Finally, they try to justify this organization with some description and call it an insight.

This process is troubled for several reasons. For one thing, the individuation of information onto post-it notes is a process where many over-simplifications and assumptions are forged and immediately forgotten. The prioritization processes are never human-centric because there is very little way for the respondents to impose their perspectives onto the hierarchy. Consequently, this process is entirely designer centric. The clustering approach adds a second layer of untested and unquestioned assumptions to the system. And finally, the insight development process effaces the fact that the clusters are a set of designer-centric perspectives based on overly simplified views of what was said and observed in field. Despite all of these problems, the issue I want to focus on is the fact that this process eliminates any opportunity for expertise to enter the system, and by individuating and reassembling the details found in field, it precludes the kind of storytelling that can be "of" the context and not just about it.

Being "of" the Context

One of the distinctive features of a well-crafted ethnographic narrative, whether it is an insight, a foresight scenario, or an anthropological analysis, is that it is part of the world from which it came. In design, and business research, there is a tendency for the insights to be couched in the designer or business researcher's cultural frame. The story uses the language of the technology or business world of its audience. It is often laden with buzzwords and assumes the audience and the research subjects share a similar cultural frame. The worst versions of this assume everyone involved are worldly, middle class, moneyed individuals who have the same aesthetic sensibilities and value system. This is understandable because it makes design easy; as long as everyone involved sees the world in the same way, there is less to consider when creating something for that context. This is problematic because it is rare for both research subjects and the highly paid consulting designers to share the same view of the world. More often than not, there are enough differences to make these assumptions deeply problematic, if not the ultimate cause for some degree of failure in the design process.

The alternative is to create a narrative of what was discovered during research using the logic and cultural norms of that world to tell the story.

Crafting a narrative that forces the reader to encounter a different way of seeing the world partly because it manages the information as the inhabitants of that context would allow the reader to experience the difference in perspective. Practically speaking, this often means resisting the desire to retell the story in a more "natural" way and allowing the messiness of the stories heard in field to shine through. Resisting this urge to edit and sanitize allows the reader to encounter different ways of prioritizing information, differing value judgments, and surprising ways of reassembling the truth of the world. Given that these are the very things we need to know in order to "see the world through someone else's eyes," we should work very hard to ensure the stories we tell as researchers are "of" the world we encountered and not "about it."

Practically, this can mean something as simple as using only the terms for things people used in your encounters with them. This, naturally, also means avoiding the use of buzzwords, technical jargon, and business terms to describe the situation. Beyond ensuring that your descriptions of people's lives are literally in their terms, it also helps innovators, designers, and strategists to see these stories outside of their own comfortable perspective. They then can see past their own biases and perspectives. It solves the parallax problem somewhat, and it is engaged in the framing exercise that allows us to understand what people are up to. But making sure that a research report is "of" the context from which it came is also an act of multi-media storytelling. Providing the audience with visual, auditory, and other cues to what it was like to be there, helps them imagine what the experience of living there might be.

Locating the "Other"

What this helps us do is maintain the context as we tell the story and to manifest the last chapters' tasks and issues in narrative form. We must do this because sanitizing our stories and couching them in our own words effaces the context that allows us to locate the people we studied in their own milieu. If we tell stories constructed along the lines of our own way of seeing the world, with our own priorities and values, we eliminate the elements we need to demonstrate the naturalness and thoughtfulness of the people we are discussing.

One of the other key tasks in storytelling is to locate our research subjects and their behaviors in a contextual description capable of explaining why the differences in their perspective on the world make sense in their world. If we do not, it would be like examining the morphology of jellyfish outside of the water that supports their bodies and allows them to have a shape—an analysis, in this case, would conclude that jellyfish are flat.

By locating our subjects in their own context, we prevent ourselves from falling into another bad habit of business research, which is focusing too much on erasing differences. Commercial research often marginalizes opposing points of view in order to neutralize their impact on the design and strategy process. Commercial researchers and designers are pressured to work for the majority, which means over-simplifying and over-emphasizing commonalities and eliminating differences. The practice of persona development is predicated on this activity and is usually conducted with little consideration of the damage being done. This tendency has the effect of "othering" people who do not express the majority opinion and eliminating their voice from the study. The most egregious version of this appears in the overly common dismissal of "a bad respondent" who rejects some of the major tenets of the study by expressing a different way of seeing the problem.

The dark side of this tendency appears when we consider the implications of this removal of minority opinions and behaviors. When a researcher eliminates difference to construct a story of similarity, they are implicitly "othering" those in the study who did not fit the convenient narrative. They are creating a distinction between "us" and "them" which allows for a different opinion to be marginalized and eliminated for not fitting the narrative. However, if we contextualize the people we worked with in field and force ourselves to use the logic of their lives to explain how and why they act and believe as they do, we must create stories about why their minority position is as valid as the majority opinion, or at least why they conflict. These stories are extremely powerful for design development because they force the designer to design within the context that supports all of these different perspectives—incidentally, this creates a larger customer/user category to sell to. This approach is also more human-centric than any other process. It forces us as researchers to be responsible for reporting what we found, as we found it, and not crafting a narrative that effaces the validity of the humans we encountered in our work.

Double Translation: An Argumentative Approach to Actionability

Taking a radical approach to human-centricity requires us to attend to the needs of two groups of people, the people we study in field and the audience we are addressing. Thus, it is correct to see radically human-centric research as an act of double translation where we learn about people, their thoughts, beliefs, behaviors, and needs in order to understand them ourselves, and then work to communicate this knowledge to others in the form of insights and design briefs. We use stories featuring thick description, contextual information, and reflexive accounts to do this because it enables us to show our work and help our intended audience to understand how we arrived at our conclusions and then translated them into a format they can understand.

This means the stories we tell are not just descriptions of what we found in field or data for some design process. They are arguments to change the way a company works, sees itself, or builds relationships with its customers. This rhetorical importance should not be diminished, because if you cannot move people with the stories you tell, then they are ineffectual. When we speak about "actionability" in commercial insights, what we are really talking about is how they can be used as an argument to try something new, to design in a different way, or to realize the company itself needs to change to meet the needs of their customer/users. This means "actioning" on insight is really more about creating opportunities to change in response to what was learned in field.

Only rarely does a design process produce something entirely new. Most of the recent highly touted "disruptive innovations" like the iPhone, or Uber's platform, have been incremental processes combining older ideas with the technology capable of realizing them. The iPhone is the result of decades of science fiction, prototypes created at Xerox's PARC lab in the 1970s and 1980s, and even Apple's first handheld touch screen device the Newton. Uber's platform was just a direct replacement of older versions of taxi dispatch systems with a GPS-enabled app. If anything was disruptive about Uber it was their morally reprehensible business practices and use of hundreds of millions of investment funds to beat established players in a low-margin industry. The design of their system was merely keeping up with market norms and decades of UX best practices.

What this means is that actionability is rarely about pulling a data point out of a piece of research and designing around it. More often than not, the actionability of an insight lies in its ability to change the way the designers think. And for this we need to argue for change, support the reason to change, and point the way towards what will happen when the minds of everyone involved in developing this new product, service, or experience have changed to see the world more like their customer/users.

Researchers must be the facilitators of this change. We must be the conduits for information to pass from the customer to the design and strategy teams who have to do the actual "work" of developing and manifesting the incremental changes needed to design a new product. The thicker the description, the more pointed the argument, the easier the narrative is to follow, and the greater the impact on these teams.

This act of double translation highlights the role that the researcher plays in emphasizing topics and prioritizing information. The first act of translation is often hidden under the title of "analysis" or "sensemaking." No matter what you call it, what is actually going on in this moment is an assessment of what was learned in field and a decision-making process to determine what should make it into the final report, what is highlighted, what is left out, and how it should be organized. Going back to the project I described at the beginning will help me explain the implications of this in a radically human-centric setting.

Once my team and I had learned why the project had been initiated, we were free to highlight the reticence people expressed with in-home security system and smart home technologies, but because the VP was convinced this was a prudent way forward, and his team thought otherwise, we were in quite a bind. We found a solution that would provide his team with what they needed, help to convince the VP that there was value elsewhere, and stay true to the stories and desires of the people we met in field. Instead of providing a set of insights with all of the evidence pointing out why people did not want cameras in their homes, we decided to tell the stories from the field that pointed in a direction where security systems and IoT devices could be put to better use with other sensory devices. In a set of insights that were very similar to the "House and Home" insights from the appliance company project, we crafted an argument about the delicate balance between being protected and being under surveillance. We used a set of insights to establish this pair of concepts and showed how people were uncomfortable about falling too far to the side of surveillance. Then, in the next set of insights, we showed how people considered connected IoT devices to be acceptable provided they understood when they were recording data and when they were not—pointing to key UX design details. Finally, we showed how people would prefer to use data about their own home, and the fact that they did not want to be bombarded with updates, but rather for there to be a meaningful "null state," where having no information or notifications means that everything is working and the system is protecting them (provided they knew it was functioning properly).

In connecting all of these insights together, and ordering them in the right way, we created an argument for nonvisual devices to protect the home, but not spy on the occupants. We also showed how this network could use data properly and how our client could benefit from anonymized data. And we did this all while staying true to what we heard from the individuals in field. Our insights were always human-centric, but the order in which we revealed them, and in the way they connected quietly make it impossible for cameras to be in the home, all while making a positive statement about where the true opportunities lay. The story we told was one of the possibilities contextualized by fears of privacy and the desire to keep one's home safe. But we told it in a way that was a convincing argument for the audience receiving it. Ultimately, we developed a set of 15 insights for the project, but we used them to tell a complete story that was filled with the detail of the context we had studied. We used many of the familiar elements, descriptions, explanations, diagrams, direct quotes, and supportive quantitative data to tell this story. But because we considered the argumentative nature of what we were doing and found a solution where the participants spoke to the requirements of our client, we were able to close the loop. We translated what people told us into pieces suitable for our purpose and then structured the story, translating it for our client. Ultimately, we left a lot on the cutting room floor, which means our tale, like any other story of human action, was a productive fiction. But our role as translators and storytellers allowed us to be effective.

It is correct to see a radical human-centric approach to commercial research as one where researchers help designers see the world in a totally new way. By presenting them with as complete a picture as possible of the world they are designed for, they can inhabit it as their end-users do, and design within the logic of that system. They can productively lose themselves in this world. What this means is that commercial research and design research must stop being a tactical approach to mining people's lives for data points and "needs," and become a way to enter into a productive social relationship with the people who will ultimately use the product or service themselves. Storytelling is perhaps the most important way to achieve these goals and connect people productively.

Conclusion

Telling stories is a human act. It builds relationships, fixes meaning, and develops a sense of togetherness. The ultimate goal of any kind of human research is to add to our sense of common humanity. Any research that allows the researcher to stay at an arm's length from their subjects is not a human science, it is an exploitative, potentially violent process of appropriation. In order for us to fulfill the promises of human-centric design within the framework of a radical human-centric approach, we have to shift the emphasis back to building relationships and collaborating on defining the meaning of the phenomena in the world. We must harness the power of storytelling and do it together with our research subjects in order to arrive at the most productive argument for creating something new that we can all benefit from.

Notes

1 Open Science Collaboration. 2015. "Estimating the Reproducibility of Psychological Science." *Science*, 349(6251).
2 Geertz, Clifford. 1973. "Thick Description: Toward and Interpretive Theory of Culture." In *Interpretation of Cultures*. Basic Books, p. 4–30.
3 Ibid., 18.
4 Ibid., 29.

Part III

THE RHC APPROACH

Researching in a radically human-centric way requires a focus beyond mere process. Sadly, commercial research practitioners—particularly in innovation and design—are enthralled by process and the promises made in their name. One of my biggest critiques of how so-called human-centric research is employed in design thinking is the tendency to over-emphasize process overthinking. True, this is a bad habit in business thinking to begin with. But as I have described several times, adherents to the tenets of design thinking and market researchers tend to believe process guarantees success. This is certainly how design thinking is sold to customers and to potential practitioners. However, process does not provide anything other than structure. Process simply provides a framework for all of the small actions needed to succeed. Plodding through the steps will not give you good results. Only good observation and analysis provide solid insights. So, accept no substitutes.

My hope is that many people will begin to use the alterations to commercial research practice captured in my concept of Radical Human Centricity. Since it is essential to have some sort of outline of practice showing how these alterations work in a real-world setting, I will present one. The purpose of this section of the book is to help everyone collaborate, coordinate, and commit to the rigors of a radical human-centric approach. However, I cannot emphasize this enough: the process is only a way to organize the order of operations. Without the right people, skills, knowledge, and analytical procedures, the process is nothing.

With this in mind, this chapter is a detailed description of the actions central to a radical human-centric research program paired with an outline of the kinds of people you will need to involve, the skills you will need to have, and the things you must do at each step in order to ensure you fulfill the promises you make to yourselves and your audience. It is a set of alterations to existing commercial research patterns and to the design thinking approach itself.

Feel free to read this section all the way through. But this section is also divided into a number of sub-sections and key topics and can serve as a reference manual of sorts. The purpose of this format is to allow it to serve as a companion for setting up a research project of your own, or for collaborating with a researcher who will work on your behalf.

DISCOVER	DEFINE	DEVELOP	DELIVER
Research	Synthesis	Ideation	Development
Observe	Understand	Generate	Activate

AN OUTLINE OF THE RHC PROCESS

Broadly speaking, there are five parts to a radically human-centric approach. They are dependent on each other and make no sense separately. Instead of being a modular process, where you can plug one phase into a design sprint, or conduct it individually as a workshop, they must all be present for it to be any kind of research at all. So, while you must go through each step, there is no set timeframe, minimum or maximum, or proscription on when they must be applied. Rather, this is the set of steps every good research program must have in order to be successful. They can be executed rapidly or stretched over a long period of time.

The five steps are:

1. Scoping – Establishing the purpose of the research and tuning the approach to the goals.
2. Observing – Studying the world as it is and digging deep into the lives of others.
3. Understanding – Making sense of what you found in your observations.
4. Generating – Developing statements of truth about what you found and think and extrapolating the next steps.
5. Activating – Preparing your insights for your audience and helping them understand what to do about it.

There should be nothing surprising here. Every one of the actions one undertakes in each phase of an RHC research program should be intuitive and solidly grounded in common sense. I argue the real shock lies in why few people talk about research in this way. Rather than being a branded process, or a framework for success, these are just the steps to executing good work. They can be applied in a number of different ways or spread across different kinds of research. The Radical Human Centricity is less a process than it is a set of alterations to thought and action in order to achieve the goal of really keeping people and the reality of their lives at the forefront as we research, ideate, and design for the betterment of everyone's lives. These five phases can even be mapped over a design thinking program, getting us from an idea to a product, service, or experience in market.

Few of the steps in these five categories are sufficient in themselves to earn the name Radical Human-Centricity. Here the devil is truly in the details. What follows is a close description of what one actually *does* under these category headings. I will go through each sub-step and explain what actions are essential, and which ones you can leave out if you are lacking the time, or just do not need them. Throughout this process description, I will also make note of the problems in existing practices and how to avoid the failures of gimmicks and outdated practices and disproven theories masquerading as best practices. As you read through this process outline, I will also explain why expertise and experts are necessary to guarantee the success of any research program. This becomes important in the last two phases when you see there are fewer steps, but more work to be done. This is because a well-trained researcher has already learned to manage these tricky steps and is successful because of their training and experience and not because they are following a handbook. This is why I argue it is inadvisable to rely on a DIY approach to research, there is so much that is learned in school and on the job that is impossible for this book to contain.

SCOPE

The first step is to work on your own practice to maximize what you will accomplish in field. It is important to begin by understanding why research is needed in the first place. Usually, innovation and commercial research projects are initiated for good reasons. Sometimes they do not. Knowing the difference is a key piece in planning a solid piece of customer/user research. Good reasons involve a genuine curiosity about the world and a desire to use the results of the research to make the world a better place. They can also include a clear need to fill a lack of information about a particular group of people, a specific behavior, or an unknown or emerging market that requires new approaches to address. Bad reasons are more numerous. From my experience, they include a desire to address a political situation in a company (which in the case I witnessed involved disproving a VP's opinion), testing a commonly held, but fictitious belief (that millennials and generation Z are drastically different from other consumer groups), or to conduct a research program that has already been conducted and well documented elsewhere. More egregious examples of bad reasons include conducting research just to "cover your butt," to develop reductionist perspectives on consumers (such as poorly constructed personas or segments) in order to avoid doing other kinds of research, or to run a cheaper research program to avoid doing it correctly. I am using these examples to make it clear that the first step in conducting a radically human-centric research program is to decide if the research is needed at all. If there are solid, honest reasons, then you should do research. If there are not, it is better to just leave people alone to live their lives in peace.

The second step is to scope the project properly. This means spending the time to carefully match the goals of the project with the approach and methods you will use to accomplish them. Scoping research is not about deciding how much money to spend, how much time to devote, or how many people to recruit. Scoping a research project, particularly a radically human-centric one is about making sure you do not bite off more than you can chew, research the right thing, and treat the people you study with respect, and care. Make sure you are able to study the topic you have set yourself within the scale of the project. This can also mean do not "boil the ocean."

A properly scoped research project is minimally invasive, nonviolent (we will cover this in a bit), and specific enough to not be a waste of everyone's time. This last point is very important. Research projects tend to change over time. Done well, researchers will uncover things they never expected to find, and the project will shift towards these new issues, problems, and discoveries. But if you do not scope for this shift, you risk eliminating what you were supposed to be looking for in the planning stages. If you leave things too much up to chance, you will study too much and become overwhelmed— this is usually described with the trite and overused "boiling the ocean" metaphor. Timing is an important part of this process. Make the project too short, and you miss out on the richness. Make it too long and you risk exploiting, even annoying, your research subjects by overstaying your welcome. Finding the right balance between these, and many other issues is the central skill in scoping a project.

Scoping a research project is the first opportunity to employ the reflexivity described in previous chapters. Understanding what you need to study, and how you will do it, is an exercise in knowing yourself and your organization. The more you understand the intellectual underpinnings of this research need, how to frame what you think you know, and how to plan for the research itself, the more radically human-centric your research will be. So, to build a radically human-centric research project, you need to understand the idea behind the research, how to frame your hypotheses, and how to plan for the research, all while matching your skills, time, and goals to the emerging program.

1.0 The Idea

Research always starts with an idea. Someone has to have an idea to initiate a research program, and this idea begins with a reason. The idea is the spark of a research program. It is the concept to be tested, an inkling of possibility, or a realization of impending failure. In any case, this idea is the impetus for research. It is a belief in something being true or false, such as the thought that different generations buy ice cream for different reasons. It is a feeling that there might be a gap in the market that can be filled by a new app or device. It is a hypothesis that if your company simply understood the hierarchy of genres in music you would be able to deliver a better user experience for your users. These may not be good ideas, but they are ideas. And more often than not, they are the forgotten part of research scope.

For many people, these would be business ideas, or problems to solve. Even opportunities to build new products, services, or experiences to offer a new cluster of customers/users/patients are also the ideas that launch research.

As such, they need to be interrogated before a reasonable research program can begin.

Reflexivity is the key to understanding the history of these ideas. And when I say history, I do not entirely mean the development of this idea. No. What I am referring to is acknowledging the source of this idea, its reason for being, and whether or not it is a reasonable thing to think. It is also about understanding why this idea grew within an organization and why it needs to be addressed with a research project. So, the first step in an RHC research program is to consider these questions:

1. Where did this idea come from?
2. Is it a reasonable idea, or are there other ways to think about it?
3. Why do you not already know the answer?
4. What changed that revealed a gap in your knowledge?
5. Does this research program come out of a need, simple curiosity, or just a work-flow reason?
6. Who/what in the organization requires this research?

1.1 The History of an Idea

As a consultant, I have often had to counsel clients to do this work in the initial meetings to discuss a potential project. Very often, they are not totally clear why they are commissioning a research project to begin with. They know they need to learn something about their users/customers/patients, but do not really know how that will help. I imagine most consultants and researchers have experienced this problem. They see that research is needed, but do not totally understand why their client wants it. This is because the clients themselves do not fully understand what they are asking. So, it is important to spend time with them to help them understand. Yes, it is possible the project might disappear during that conversation. But it might grow and develop into a rich and engaging research plan.

This means you must think about the people you will be studying before even settling the question of whether or not you need to meet them at all. They do not need to meet you. You are the ones who need them. So, before you even decide if research is necessary, decide why you are going to intrude into their lives. Is the idea that began this project worth barging into people's houses and asking them a bunch of questions?

The five questions are important because they lead you to settle different aspects of the process. The first, "where did this idea come from" establishes the origins of the need. It might be that it is the result of prior research or an unanswered question. If so, this means you need to understand the earlier research in detail to be clear about what was missed and why. The second, cuts the wheat from the chaff. For me, this is a go/no-go question. Is this idea something you can test or explore further, or is it just the product of faulty logic and can be solved simply by understanding the logic of the ask? The third is a key part of this. If the organization cannot explain why it does not already know the answer, then there is something broken in the knowledge chain. This means the research program needs to include some training and perhaps even some serious auto-ethnography to understand how the organization uses knowledge and data. The fourth, "What changed that revealed a gap in your knowledge?" places the organization into context. Is this an internal change that precipitated this research or did the world pass them by? In either case, this is an important question for triage purposes. The answer helps the researcher see what they do know and what they do not know. The fifth question is to test how frivolous the research ask is. Asking "Does this research program come out of a need, simple curiosity, or just a work-flow reason?" elicits an answer which reveals if this research is just to tick a box, or cover the bases, or if it emerges from an honest need to understand. If it is the former, it is unnecessary. Finally, "Who/what in the organization requires this research?" illuminates who the final audience is. This is an essential point. If you do not understand who is going to receive the insights, there is little possibility for them to be useful.

Once these questions are answered, you are ready to start interrogating the thinking about how you will turn this idea into a research project.

1.2 Assumptions behind a Need for Research

One sunny morning in Chicago in 2015, I was sitting in a hotel dining room having breakfast with several clients who worked at a global clothing retail company. I was particularly exhausted because for the previous four days I had been living out of another hotel working on a different project with another client. Such is the life of a consulting researcher. There were about five of us: four of them and myself. We were there, at that table, trying to gather our strength for the long day of fieldwork ahead. At first, the conversation was typical for a breakfast where everyone is tired, out of place, and relatively unsure who the other people are. Needless to say, the conversation was not great. But after the toast and juice, we moved to preparing for the day at hand. After getting the bulk of the work-related issues squared away, the conversation turned to possible work we could do together in the future. One of their team, "Bill," was talking about research the company desperately needed. He said, "I think we really need to study millennial's characteristics and behaviours."

"But Bill," said "Emma," "isn't that what we're doing right now? I mean, this project is about studying millennial omnichannel shopping habits."

Turning to her, Bill said, "true, but we really aren't getting to the essence of millennials. I mean, they're so different, and we don't understand them as a generation. If we can't get a handle on that, we can't get ahead of the generational change."

Everyone nodded, except me. "Sabrina," the youngest of the client team suggested we needed to build a project based on examining millennial attitudes towards fashion first before we got to the core of how they shop. She said, "As a millennial, I think it is necessary. We don't want the things our parents want, and if feels like our brand isn't talking to young people."

Her words made me wonder about this line of thinking, and while I kept these thoughts to myself, I asked myself if "millennials" are the same as "young people" and if a project of this kind was even feasible. I was uneasy about this conversation and kept silent notes in my project notebook, which is why I can examine it here. My misgivings about it rested on unease about the assumptions lurking behind this potential project.

First, this kind of problem was very fashionable at the time. Millennials were one of the hot topics in innovation consulting. And there were probably a lot of commercial projects and consulting hours spent on discovering the details of this difference. However, that was why I was uneasy. It seemed to be too easy, too trite, and somehow too thin of an idea to fully support a research program—let alone an entire innovation strategy. For there to be any substantive—not superficial—differences between so-called millennials and prior generations, there would at least be a clearly identified framework, mechanism, or previous generational work, suitable to fall back on. A theory of generational change would help, even if it was only partial. But none of this exists, and I was left wondering if the idea of millennial difference is really just a contextually dependent reading of the behavior typical of all young people, of youth itself. If that were the case, then there is no such thing as a millennial, but just a young person, who behaves as youths have for millennia, and will grow out of it eventually. It is possible that as the so-called millennials age, they would change, just as other generations have done before. This would mean there is more to be said for how young people behave than a single generation being that significantly different than another. Given that the industry quickly shifted to nervously worrying about Gen Z, suggest my thoughts were more correct than Bill's. I should have said something, because that millennial project was horrible and yielded nothing of value.

I am bringing this conversation up to highlight a key fact of research scoping. To ensure the quality of research, you have to interrogate the assumptions that lead to the central question being asked. In this brief example, there are several assumptions lurking behind the key points being discussed. First of all, the idea of the "millennial" itself is an assumption of the reality of many things. At the time of the conversation, it was a relatively established concept, but it was empty. No one at that table could define a millennial or even outline the date range that defined the generation. I myself have been defined as a member of the MTV generation, a millennial, and Gen X because I was born in the ambiguity of the late 1970s. To ask for an entire strategic and innovation program based on such a nebulous concept is certainly worthy of greater scrutiny.

Next is the idea that a generation has "characteristics and behaviours." Definitional characteristics are hard to find when something is so vague and mythical in its structure and heterogenous in its composition. It is likely Bill was just talking about kids in the USA, which would be one thing. But to say, "a generation" and expect some unity, is folly. Where is the global, macro-scale applicability? And this is before we get to the idea of understanding a "generation" as a whole. While this is something many consulting researchers have claimed to be able to do, it is actually an impossible task. The assumption that it can be done at all in context is laughable. Perhaps one can create some statements about a generation in a historical review of a period in time, but that kind of work benefits, at least, from some distance and an ability to reflect on a time that has come to a close.

Finally, we come to Sabrina's comments. When someone speaks for a group, it is always worth thinking about the assumptions and the perspective of the speaker. She could not really speak for millennials because she was just presenting an opinion based in her own individual experience. And what she said is true for most of us, regardless of our age. We do not "want the things our parents want." But that is not grounds to group everyone of a similar age together. It may be just true that sons and daughters do not want what their older family members want. There is no evidence to say this is because there is some sort of shared ethic or ethos that is unique to one group. Sociologically and anthropologically speaking, that makes little sense. Where is the evidence for cultural barriers demarcating one sub-culture from the other? How do people share a culture across a generation when they do not share a culture across social, economic, and geographical boundaries?

You are getting the point, so I will not continue. However, I do want to make it clear that this brief except is rife with booby traps and bad logic. In order to wrest a good project from this minefield, it is essential to test your basic assumptions and never consider any concept settled or sacred. This is where the scepticism I discussed in Chapter 2 becomes essentially important.

So, how do you do this? Begin by asking these questions.

Always start with "what do you already know about this idea?" Most research projects actually begin with a problem in thinking, or logic, like the one I highlighted above.[1] While there is no such thing as a millennial or millennial shopping habits, there was a reason Bill and Sabrina spoke about millennials with confidence. The idea came from somewhere. And like the idea of "Normcore" that also propelled many a clothing brand's innovation and marketing teams off a cliff (despite having been fabricated out of thin air, almost as a joke)[2] the idea of a millennial has a source, a history, and a set of explicit, and implicit assertions about the world. Using the term "millennial" Gen Z, or even Gen X, without understanding this past, is a dangerous thing to do. You might be agreeing with something you totally disagree with. So, before you based a research program on this idea, interrogate its assumptions and your own by asking what you know about it. You might find you do not need to think of this idea ever again, or you might tighten your thinking and hone your research question.

The next question to ask is "what do you think you're studying?" This is the time to be skeptical and precise. What is it you are thinking about when you articulate the idea behind your research need? In the case of Bill, Emma, and Sabrina, their idea was not those millennials exist, but that there is a large group of people, mostly young people, who they do not know well—and these people represent a new market with new challenges. If they had been able to get past the "millennial" issue, they would have seen the need for some simply scoped work. Instead, they bought into an idea they had heard from others and did not fully understand. Because they could not articulate what they thought they wanted to study, they could not ask for the appropriate piece of work. And they did not, in the end, get it right.

Finally, you need to ask, "how do you think it should be done?" This is more than a mere processual question. When each of us thinks about researching a particular topic, we always have a particular method or approach in mind. These thoughts are assumptions that require attention and reflection. The approach you select might be because of a personal preference, a desire to avoid the harder path, or even because of some failure to grasp the situation. After satisfying yourself that none of these are the case, the next questions to ask yourself are as follows. Is it possible to do this work in a reasonable amount of time? Is the topic the kind of thing we can do ourselves? Do we need specialist assistance? Is the kind of research report I am envisioning the right way to capture the details of this work? And finally, am I the right person to make this decision?

Commercial research warrants closer attention to detail than a lot of other kinds of human-centered research, because time and scale, and cost, are always problems. If you do not ask these hard questions and reveal the potentially fatal assumptions about a particular subject at the outset, it can doom the research entirely. It has always puzzled me why people do not do this more. It is likely a large number of commercial research projects should be about entirely different topics or accomplished in completely different ways. But they were executed poorly because of plain bad thinking. A true RHC project eliminates these problems right away so the rest of the project can start off without damaging flaws.

We have dealt with the thinking forming part of the initiation of a research program. Now we will consider the desired outcomes and expectations.

1.3 The Expectations

Research projects usually have a purpose, even if that purpose is understood or not. In an RHC research program, it is essential to make this purpose explicit and known to everyone. Mostly this is because there are too many research projects that accomplish very little or do not need to be run at all. Bad research is worse than no research at all because research influences the world. It impacts the people you meet. It changes minds for the better or not. It can obfuscate the truth that needs to be revealed, and it can intrench bad thinking or unfounded beliefs. So, it is important to consider several questions about what the research is for and what you expect to get out of it. Once you have these answers, it will be much clearer what kind of research is necessary—if it is needed at all.

1.3.1 Why Are You Doing It in the First Place?

This question may seem obvious, but it is not. I would expect most consulting researchers have participated in projects that only reveal why they are needed halfway through. I will give you an example.

In 2015, I conducted a close examination of the use of smart home security systems in San Francisco, NYC, and Seoul, for a Korean electronics company. I have already told you about one moment in this project's history. Now let me give you the full story. This project started off badly. During our first day of research, the man who hired us was fired by HQ. His replacement was someone who had some odd thoughts about the place of technology. He unironically thought the Facebook "like" was an improvement over face-to-face interaction. With the change, the reason we were in field shifted. We were no longer conducting a phenomenological study of potential invasive smart home technologies in order to redirect the development of new, humanize versions. Now we were conducting a user study of smart home products in order to feed the pipeline.

Like good consultants, my team switched gears, even though this new study was not what our original client, and his bosses in Seoul had told us they wanted. Not saying something at this juncture turned out to be a mistake. About halfway through the project, they asked us to change the second half of the project to do something else because the project sponsors in Korea were unhappy with the direction. If you remember, this was the moment where we were told that the project was initiated to convince the vice president that using cameras to obtain contextual information for use in services was a bad idea. We made the change.

Now, this trifling problem can easily be explained away as a simple corporate miscommunication or omission in the chain. And it was certainly that, but it was not the first time we had to change this project's direction. No. It was the second time. We had essentially been given three briefs to the following. The omission was their overall lack of consensus on what the project was actually about and what it was *for*. Collectively, they had no idea why they were doing this very expensive project. As a result, it was next to impossible to meet their needs or provide a perspective that would help them. Once we got our most clearly articulated brief, we addressed the objectives of the project. While I do not believe changing the mind of an SVP is a good reason to disturb over 75 people over two continents, it is at least a clear reason to commission, design, and execute a research project. Our other two handler's ideas were not good reasons to do research and needed some review.

What does this review look like? This is another exercise in reflexivity. This process must begin with an assessment of the context in which the need for research arose. Is this research needed to solve a pesky problem? Is this research to learn about an entirely new area? Is this research that someone desperately wants to do? Is it necessary for an internal process to continue? Is it simply needed to put more into a company mechanism that requires input—just more grist for the grindstone? Or, finally, does it come out of a genuine need to know cause by a gap in your understanding of people?

All of these reasons can initiate a research program, with some being more important than others. But being completely clear about why this research is necessary, and explicitly stating this fact in the brief, will help the researchers understand how much, or little, research is needed to fulfill the need. The reason that initiates this research says a lot about the client, the audience, and their needs. Without a clear statement, everyone gets to play another round of "guess what I'm thinking" until someone finally decides why the project was commissioned. Needless to say, this is inefficient, expensive, invasive, and requires a positive adjustment.

To make this change, an RHC-style project begins with an assessment of the commissioning party's internal organization, thinking, and knowledge culture. We call this a stakeholder analysis, but the name does not really matter. We interview everyone in the immediate team, the stakeholders of the project, the intended audience of the insights, and anyone else deemed important by our client. We also review all the prior research. With both tasks done, we generate a baseline report that frames the project and allows us to fully understand why it was commissioned in the first place. We usually do this work in the kick-off and in the first week of the engagement if the client has not done this already. But it is also an important question for the researchers.

1.3.2 What Do You Hope to Gain?

What does research do? Good research helps people learn something about the world around them they did not already know. Great research is able to uncover something no one knew until that moment. Bad research does neither of these things. But learning something is not a fantastic goal for commercial research, which needs to *do* something for the client beyond simply creating knowledge. Understanding what is gained in the execution of this research program goes a long way to scoping the project correctly.

This question is fundamental. You have to know what you hope to get out of a research project to know how it should end. While the first question helps an RHC researcher understand how a project should start, and what its shape should be, the answer to this question also allows them to understand how it should end.

To answer this question, the commissioner of the work should be reflexive, empathetic, and skeptical at the same time. They should consider the goal of the project and weigh it against what the company expects it to deliver, the impact the work will have on the participants, and whether or not these two can be resolved in a satisfying way. Answers like "actionable insights," or "personas" are not acceptable. The answer should come in the form of "we need this project to tell us 'x', because we do not understand 'y', and it must be delivered to us as format 'z'."

This format directly speaks to scoping. Knowing what "x" allows a researcher to understand what the actual lack is in the organization. This lends itself to developing a research plan to find whatever "x" is. Knowing what "y" is, helps them understand the context of "x" and what else they need to find in field in order to help their client digest the information. The final part, "z" is absolutely necessary because not every project can be delivered on a PowerPoint slide.[3] There are so many possible options for delivering insights in an engaging, and culturally sensitive way. RHC researchers use whichever is the appropriate bridge between the researched culture and the organizational culture of their client.

Often the answer to "what do you hope to gain" is less about the client's processes, goals, and what inputs they need to accomplish their goals, than it is about enacting an internal change, like introducing the value of new ways to work, or settling an internal debate. If this is the case, gaining knowledge or understanding is not the central goal. The results of the research can also be put to use to help the client achieve consensus on a particular topic or to solve a disagreement. It is important to understand these conditions too. When you understand what is gained outside of the knowledge and understanding, you will also understand how that knowledge should be packaged, and what you are arguing against as you state the case for why your perspective on your participants is correct.

As you can see here, the role of the researcher is again that of a translator. Much of what you learn after asking this particular question is about the people commissioning the research. Nevertheless, it is all essential to know. If you do not understand these things, you are not setting the stage for successful research, and you are potentially preventing yourself from having the right kind of in-field experience, developing the right insights, or crafting the report for the best reception.

1.3.3 *What Is It Supposed to Do?*

The next question is about the purpose of the research and its impact. Like the last one, this question is more about the client. But having a solid answer here helps researchers understand the role their work will play in the larger context. The purpose of the work is also a key factor in choosing what tools and methodologies should be used to conduct the principal research. Something that is part of a rigid "jobs to be done" framework generates vastly different results from a design ethnography, or a cultural exploration.

Here, it is important to understand who the recipients of the research will be, what they typically receive, what their level of subject expertise is, and what they need to do with the insights produced. If the receiving team is supposed to design something, then they require insights that create a world they can inhabit and worth within. They need to know a lot about the processes of the people living in this world and what kinds of inefficiencies there are in these habitual actions. They also need to know where the world and its inhabitants set the limits to what can be accomplished, added, or subtracted from this world. On the other hand, if they are used to briefs in the ridiculous jobs to be done framework, then all they need to know are a set of steps and the barriers that will prevent any attempt to alter these pathways.

This is for the audience. The other side of this question is the responsibility of the research. What do they need the insights to do? The client might need to learn something they are not prepared to receive before they can understand the underlying issues of the insights that were found in field. They might need to be convinced they are wrong about a particular detail of their customer/users. They might need to learn a large number of basic facts before you can move on to developing a perspective of what they should do. Each of these contains a very different research requirement. One genre or style of insights cannot accomplish more than one of these tasks. So the researcher(s) need to ask themselves what their job is. What is the work supposed to do for the client? And we always need to remember we are being thoughtful and careful here so that the client gets the best input possible, and we can maintain our empathetic thoughtful, and rigorous process throughout.

1.3.4 How Big Should It Be?

The last question in the initial assessment of the thinking behind any project brief is the first of the practical details about scoping a research project. However, asking "how big should it be?" is not just about the length of time it will take, how many people it should include, or how much it should cost. Usually these are decided by external considerations anyway with the possible exception of the number of participants. This question helps everyone determine what the scope and scale of the findings should be. These two factors identify the appropriate object of the research and the level of detail in which it is scrutinized. How big it should be is a question of how much you need to learn and how much of the world you must study to obtain this knowledge.

Consider this sentence: "this research project will examine the listening habits of users in Korea." This is a fair research statement. It identifies what is being studied and where. But it is lacking the detail needed to mount a successful research project. For that, we need to be more specific. Scoping a research project is about being very precise about the nouns in that sentence, "research project," "listening habits," "users," and "Korea." What kind of research project should it be? Is it qualitative or quantitative? Is it a combination of the two? Is it a foresight project or focused on the current state? Next, when we see "listening habits," what is meant here? Is this a study of the dominant cultural aesthetics that acculturate individuals into certain kinds of listenership, or are we studying the decisions made in private to listen to a particular song in a single moment? You can see the huge difference in the scope of a project studying the former versus the latter. Next, do we mean "users" of an app or "listeners" of music. Or do we mean to understand what happens when they are one in the same. All of these will yield different results because they will have to examine people from a different perspective. Finally, what is meant by "Korea," a country of many dialects, regions, cities, and 55 million individuals? Or is it just the urban population in Seoul that is of interest?

Scoping a project is the act of determining just what is going to be studied and what level of detail is needed to examine that object properly. Scaling the project, then is how you tune the research program to study the object at that level of detail.

Scaling a project, on the other hand, is about deciding how best to organize a project to meet the scope. This is where the thinking becomes action and is where we must rely on expertise and experience. Only someone who has done several projects of different sizes has the experiential understanding necessary to balance the research question and the research action. It is unfortunate that this is the case, but as in many areas of activity, there is no substitute for an expert. Scaling a project is an issue that can kill a good research question. The research has to decide what kind of research to do, how long they will need, how many people to include, how to challenge their findings, and what medium and genre they will use for their final report. All of these things take time. And in commercial research, where time is literally money, these considerations have cost implications as well. When scaling a project, a good researcher will also consider the impact the research itself will have on the environment and individuals who will fall under the lens. Too little time with them will result in superficial work, which is a waste of everyone's time. Too much time is an annoying imposition at best, and a damaging disruption at worst. Everything here has to be held in perfect balance for the success of the project. The best rule is to be in field just long enough for people to start to repeat themselves. Once you know what they will say, it is time to go. Beyond that, there is no easy way to teach this skill. The only option is to trust in the expertise of the researcher and make sure you pick one who knows what they are doing.

2.0 Framing the Research

Once you have your research questions, you have scoped how detailed the project needs to be to answer the research questions, and you have established the scale of the program needed to answer them, it is time to frame the project. This is a key step in setting up a piece of research. It is the time to start to make practical decisions about how you will execute the work. As such, it is the bridge between the idea guiding the research and the practical details of what needs to be done in field.

This phase begins when you generate a solid research brief. This brief can be a call for proposals or even just a sentence. But as we will see, it needs to make several points very clear. After that it is time to generate some hypotheses, examine what kind of work has already been done in this area, and finally make the final evaluation needed to ensure the research idea and the research plan are balanced. It is essential to spend the right amount of time on this process, which can take weeks, but it can also happen very quickly. Rushing through this process risks asking for a project that is ill-conceived and doomed to fail. There are too many projects in commercial research that fail at this stage. So spend the amount of time you need to get this step right.

2.1 Getting the Brief Right

A research brief is a statement to the people who will execute the project— whether they are yourself or someone else. The purpose of the brief is to completely, and comprehensively, outline a research program. This means capturing much of what was covered above and translating this into a statement of requirements. It needs to clearly state the purpose of the research, the reason why it is necessary, the scope of the questions that need to be asked, the scale of the research effort, and the details of how the report needs to be structured. It also needs to outline who needs the work, how they expect it to be executed, where they need it to be done, what they hope to find, and when it needs to be done. The brief needs to elaborate on the key idea behind the work. It needs to expose the gaps in knowledge and help the researcher understand what the key assumptions are and which of them are problematic.

This is not as easy as it sounds, because it is easy for problematic thinking to creep in at this stage. I was involved in a project for a North American pharmaceutical company. When they initially brought me and my team their research brief, they asked us for a result without fully thinking through what they were actually asking for. I say result, because what they wanted was clearly stated in the research brief. They asked for a research project to develop a global view of disease experiences across several different disease types so they could build a universal patient experience map. They meant well when they asked for this. They were trying to establish a baseline between several of the conditions they treated with their products, and use the commonalities to build a set of services that would improve patient care. This is a very good thing. However, they asked for a universal patient journey, which is a deliverable type. It is the result of a research project, not really the impetus for one. This meant there was no solid research question. They were essentially asking us to conduct research on the patient experience suitable to produce these experience journeys. However, they did not actually tell us what they wanted us to research, just that they needed it all captured in a journey map they can use later on. The brief said nothing about what they thought the patient experience was, what they knew about the conditions, or how they saw it fitting together. They were lacking the details we needed to build the research, despite being very detailed on how the project should end.

This reveals a major pitfall of the research brief. Even when it is detailed, well organized, and clear, it can still be opaque and functionally useless. What makes a research brief work is clarity on what should be studied and why it needs to be examined. With this in mind, it is important to make sure any research brief has these features, at minimum:

a. A single opening sentence on what is to be researched.
b. A single sentence explaining what the research is for.
c. A single sentence exposing why the research is necessary.
d. A statement about the assumptions behind the research ask.
e. A statement about the expectations and audience who will receive the work.
f. A statement about how the work should be delivered and the best format to do this.
g. A single sentence about the scope of the research program.
h. A single sentence about the scale of the research effort.

2.2 Hypotheses Are Created to Be Wrong

In my experience hypotheses are a good thing, but few people in the innovation industry really use them to their best advantage. I have found that most of my clients have always considered hypotheses to be true statements about their customer/user/patients that have yet to be fully proven. Even research consultants seem to see hypotheses as something other than they are. Very often they see them as something coming directly out of assumptions or beliefs about the world, or worse yet as simple statements of what the final result of the project will be. For example, the company InVision has this statement on their website, "Now you can combine the solution and question, and turn it into a hypothesis."[4] For them, a hypothesis is the result of a set of prioritized assumptions and an anticipated assumption. They suggest using the template of "we believe that x (solution) for y (persona) will z (outcome)" to develop a hypothesis. This is, of course, not the case, because it is a statement of purpose, not hypotheses that can be tested. This problem is common across the entire industry and is repeated by adherents to design research and design thinking.

First of all, it is too complicated; it has too many components that are themselves in need of research and testing. It contains a solution to a problem that may or may not exist, a persona does not exist, and an outcome that is a desire, not an end point. But this is not its major weakness. If this is the hypothesis for an entire project, it is missing one major component. It does not allow for the possibility it is wrong. Each of these elements assumes forward motion as the only option. If there is no problem, then the solution is unnecessary. But it does not talk about the potentiality of the problem, only about the solution. It talks about a group of people who cannot exist because none of us live the life of a two-dimensional persona, and the outcome cannot be in a hypothesis because that puts the end in the beginning.

Secondly, it is making the assumption that people can be studied under the conditions of a science experiment, which is developed to control all, or at least most, conditions in order to isolate the variable in question. This kind of hypothesis does not belong in human-centered research because there are always too many variables, and a researcher cannot control any of them with any hope of isolating a single one.

In human-centric research, it is necessary to take a different view of the humble, yet powerful hypothesis. Instead of these troubling statements about broad areas of human behavior, it is better to use simple hypotheses that can be tested in a system where the researcher cannot control anything. In radically human-centric research, it is necessary to see hypotheses as the bridge between the researcher's view of the world and the people they are researching. What this means is they must be simple, numerous, and sacrificial. Hypotheses about people should be built to be wrong and therefore should be research tools, not directly connected to the intentions of the business. When they are proven wrong or modified, something meaningful is learned.

Academic anthropologists and sociologists are not clear about how hypotheses should be articulated when setting up fieldwork. The emphasis is more on open learning. If a research project is to understand the use of gendered phrases in a dialect of Wolof, or understanding how violence amongst white nationalist football hooligans in the UK reveals class stressors and the formation of identities of victimhood, then having a single guiding hypothesis will not help. These research questions are too large for a method beginning with hypotheses generation. But in a commercial setting, it is important to limit the scale and scope of a project.

With this in mind, we need to think about the hypothesis as a statement of belief about what is true in the world we are entering. A single study must have many competing hypotheses outlining the breadth of the research. These help us enter the field and coordinate action once there. They must be designed to be wrong or right. Either way, they should live or die in a way that teaches us more than we knew before. For example, if we are conducting a research project on omni-channel shopping behaviors, a good set of hypotheses will include ones outlining how people navigate the differences between online and in-person shopping. There should be hypotheses predicting how people will use both to their best advantage but allowing for a wide variety of different approaches. There should also be hypotheses about the details of these individual approaches.

This adds up to a lot of hypotheses. So, to make matters easier, they should be very simple statements. They should be things like "people use online shopping environments to research potential purchases," "people struggle to shop online and, in the store, simultaneously," and "people prefer to do research first and then touch the clothing before buying." These are simple statements. They are intuitive and easily built before the research is done. They are easy to test. Most importantly, when they are wrong, they not only destroy assumptions, but they also rescale and scope the work. If we hypothesize that some people prefer to do online research first and then touch the clothing before buying, and later learn there are some people who do not need the tactile experience when doing their research and those that do, we immediately see we need to change how we are grouping people, what constitutes "research before buying" and that there is not a sequence of events but a constellation of possible "learning and trying" experiences. Here we not only deepen our understanding, but learn that we need to talk to more people with different approaches, and fill in what that constellation is, all while questioning our understanding of the boundaries between behaviors. Disproving "people prefer to do research first and then touch the clothing before buying" helps us go in multiple directions. We learn as our hypotheses fail, so making them as particular and specific as possible helps us to hone the project as we go.

This means we need to give up on the hypothesis as a limiting factor, as it is in the scientific method, and see it as the way to find avenues of learning suitable to help us learn more about the world of our customer/user/patients as we go. It also helps us remove the need for some ill-conceived framework, and eliminate the space for assumptions to creep in. By keeping the hypotheses simple, it is also possible to be more specific about what we expect to find, which makes them more testable. It also allows us to remove ourselves from the system and focus on what matters, the human qualities that are central to any RHC approach.

2.3 Understanding What Has Been Done Before

One of the weakest points in commercial research is its separation from other sources of research knowledge, most notably the academic literature on the social sciences, behavioral economics, and psychology. One reason for this is the lack of true experts in these areas taking part in applied and commercial research programs. But another reason lies in the cultural separation between those in business and the academic world we discussed before. This division is drawn along the lines of things that are "about the real world" and things that are "academic"—with the latter being considered problematic, not relevant, or too difficult to understand. This is of course nonsense, and it has a significant impact on the quality of commercial research of all kinds.

The impact of this is a lack of understanding of what has already been learned about a particular topic, culture, behavior, group of people, or phenomenon. Simply put, there is a tendency within organizations to reinvent the wheel with every research project. It has been my experience that most prior research is considered to be irrelevant when embarking on a new study. This can mean a team will largely ignore its prior research deliverables when creating the brief for a new one. They will certainly not refer to any ethnographic, anthropological, sociological, cultural studies, or behavioral economic reports to see what others have done in this area, even within their own company.

I do not know why this is the case, but I have noticed there is no sense of continuity in research. Most consultants and innovation groups are always looking forwards and do not consider the work done, even in the recent past, to be relevant. There is no sense that knowledge and expertise build over time, just that a research project fills an immediate gap It is then discarded once its usefulness has diminished. This is a real shame. There are so many good reasons to build some expertise on a particular subject before one begins new research. Certainly, to be human-centric, let alone radically human-centric, it is necessary to make the most of the work others did in the past. This is just common sense, and yet it is rare in commercial research, and nearly nonexistent in design research or design thinking circles.

The solution to this problem is simple. A radical human-centric approach demands the evolution of knowledge and expertise over time, and an aggregation of knowledge to push beyond the obvious. This means starting any research plan with an assessment of what happened before. This means good, old reference research and the development of a literature review in the grand tradition of graduate school. No, this is not a sexy step, but makes everything so much better, and even easier in field.

There are only two points to cover here. The first is doing the due diligence to prepare for the field. This does not have to mean exhaustively reading in the new area. But it can mean understanding what kind of work has been done by academics, journalists, and commercial researchers in the recent past (5–10 years), and developing an understanding of the topics they studied, where they went, and what they found.

The second point is to do everything you can to avoid reinventing the wheel. This means you have to trust in the expertise of other scholars and researchers and use their work—after evaluating its quality, of course—to develop an initial perspective on what you will be studying. This means reading ethnographies, research reports, and journalistic articles in a way to understand what worked, what did not, and how you can improve and grow what they learned in their study of the same, or similar, people. The result of this work will be a more robust research plan, better hypotheses, and the possibility of starting on step two, rather than having to do the entire study from the beginning.

2.4 Connecting the Need with Outcomes

The final step in framing the research is a balancing act. Once a researcher knows what they will be studying by reading (or creating) the brief, has developed some solid hypotheses, and has learned what others have found in similar studies, all that is left to do is to balance the outcomes with the stated needs of the commissioning entity.

By balancing, I mean to assess whether the desired outcomes of the project are attainable within the scale and scope of the research itself. To do this, it is important to ask yourself if the expectations for the outcomes are reasonable within all of the constraints (time, cost, required detail, geographical spread, etc.). If you do not, then the research project will fail as a piece of applied work. It is essential to ensure that everyone involved understands what to expect from the work. But there is a human-centric reason too. Balancing the result to the ask ensures the conclusions of the analysis do not outstrip what was discovered in field. If you have to rethink mobile phone experiences, but you are only able to talk to 20 people across two countries, you are not well balanced. It means you will waste your time, waste the time of the participants, and have to stretch too little butter over too much bread. Balancing the impetus for the work and the expected results helps you to set the frame for the intellectual work that happens in between.

3.0 Making a Space for Planning

Now we move on to the last conceptual considerations of building a proper research plan. After this, the practicalities will become of central concern and the thinking will be done. Planning a human-centered research project in a commercial setting should be an exercise in managing the practicalities of where you will be going, who you will be talking to, how long you will be there, and what you will do when you are in field. However, a radical human-centric protocol demands greater attention to these details. Often little attention is paid to the impact this work will have, what research methods, or tools, are needed, what the right team will be to conduct successful research, and how to mitigate the problems arising in doing all of this. For this reason, there are considerations every RHC researcher must attend to before the practical elements of building a research plan are decided.

It is important to note how the more practical elements do not appear in the framing stage of a project but show up in the observation phase. This is because recruitment, building assets like surveys and questionnaires are part of the engagement with the field. They are not preparation; they are research activities. Consequently, it is important to establish the terms of the engagement first. This will shape how those activities are accomplished.

At this point you might be asking yourself why there is so much conceptual work in the framing phase of an RHC project, and that this long list of activities is a bit beside the point. Thinking through all of these issues first ensures that the research will be robust, humane, and attuned to the nuances of what you are in field to study. Not doing this thinking leads to bad research, full stop. It need not take forever, and indeed, with practice it is easy to do quickly. This is one of the reasons why I recommend using skilled researchers with degrees in the social sciences, they have already learned to manage these issues correctly before the execution of the project starts. This is partly why RHC research requires experience and expertise. DIY formats of commercial research fail because the researchers are unaware of these tasks and complexities. Now, we will turn to five topics that need to be considered before the practicalities are begun.

3.1 The Ethics of Research

Academic, NGO, and governmental research is governed by strict ethical protocols set by review boards and a long list of "laws" that ensure noninvasive, well-managed research. Commercial work has no such governing body and most consultants and in-house innovation teams spend almost no time considering the ethics of research. This is a big problem, and it leads to abuses in field, unintentional though they may be. In my years of doing applied and commercial research, I have worked hard to apply the ethical standards I learned when doing my dissertation for my PhD, and in my academic work. I have refused clients, resisted their requests, and trained other researchers in a code of behavior that is well above what is typically followed in business research. But I have noticed I am one of the few worried about such things. Consequently, ethical problems are rife in the world of commercial research.

The most common abuses lie in a tendency to objectify the people who are participating in the study. As I discussed earlier in Chapter 4, the formats of market research, and even design research (despite its claims of empathy), are indented to objectify people—to reduce their humanity to a set of easily understood characteristics and patterns of action, which are referred to as "demographics" and "psychographics" or their "persona." As I described before, when these terms are flying about, the person does not matter. They are only important as a potential exemplar of a universal type. When research is intended to eliminate the particular and focus only on this universal, people become tokens of this type, and it is easier to break ethical boundaries to get to the object of the study, the list of general characteristics, or the problem to solve. This leads to clients asking for five hours of in-home interviews captured on videotape—sadly, an actual request from a global automotive manufacturer's innovation team. Requests like this are made from a perspective that considers only what is good for the company, not what is good for the people in the study. This is something a strong ethical review would eliminate.

For a research program to be ethical it must consider what is best for the people who are under the lens. If this means it is more difficult to complete the study, then that is the burden of the researcher. For a research program to be truly human-centric, to say little of radically human-centric, the researchers must consider these issues:

a. The degree of engagement with the participants
b. The truthfulness of what they are being told
c. The value of the information they are providing
d. The way their personal data and information will be handled
e. The way they are being represented
f. Everyone's safety (physical, mental, and medical wellbeing)

All of these are hard. Again, that is the burden of the radically human-centric researcher. Many of these are simply not followed in commercial research, and this negates any claim to being "human-centric." So let us quickly explore what is involved in each of them.

3.1.1 The Degree of Engagement with the Participants

What this means is how long you will be with them. How long they have to talk. Where they will be expected to be during the research. How they will be recorded, and what the content of the conversations will be. In-home ethnographies are not benign events. They are deeply invasive. The best course of action here is to be as minimalistic as possible. Ask yourself if you really need to sit on their couch and force them to host you just to talk about a feature on an app. You will also need to write everything down and allow them to edit the terms of engagement before you show up at their front door.

3.1.2 The Truthfulness of What They Are Being Told

In my experience, most consultants and innovation teams lie to research participants on a regular basis. This is simply wrong and should never happen. Sadly, it is common practice to bend the truth, or omit it altogether, in order to maintain a sense of "objectivity." These lies range from white lies about what the research is about and who a particular guest is who is observing the work, and go up to gross lies told to placate a troublesome participant. People participating in research deserve total honesty. Get them to sign an NDA (nondisclosure agreement) if you are worried about company secrets. You will find when you are honest you get better answers to your questions. People are not stupid. They know when researchers are lying, even if by omission.

3.1.3 The Value of the Information They Are Providing

What people say in field is often worth a great deal of money in the right context. Research participants should be respected on this basis alone. What we collect from people in field has real value, and the people you meet in field should understand this. This can, sometimes, lead to the price for this information going up. What this means is honoraria for their participation should also be balanced with the cost of the project and the value of what they say. Companies regularly make millions, if not hundreds of millions, on the details learned for $150 a person. This is exploitative and unethical. Pay for value.

3.1.4 The Way Their Personal Data and Information Will Be Handled

Everyone in a study has the right to know how the information they relay will be used, stored, managed, and developed into insights. They need to know this before they agree to participate and the researcher must stick to their promises. This means every researcher needs to have an established protocol for how they handle the intimate details and personal data of their research participants. I have seen too many people's likenesses live for years in an organization on powerpoint decks to believe that there are solid ethical protocols in place in most consultancies and companies. Also, do not claim their information for yourself and have them sign it all away. To be radically human-centric you have to acknowledge they own it and you are merely borrowing it. Do everything you can to protect them in every way. Anonymize data. Do not give out transcripts. Do not take photos you do not need. And destroy everything in a reasonable amount of time.

It is also important to follow any industry ethics protocols. Of all commercial clients, pharmaceutical companies have to have real ethics protocols. You might be obliged to keep all of the records of a research project for up to seven years when working for them. This means maintaining secure cold storage for all data and materials collected in field.

3.1.5 *The Way They Are Being Represented*

Representation is a problematic issue in the social sciences. What right do we have as researchers to speak for the people we work with in field? When they are vulnerable populations, like marginalized individuals, chronically ill people, or people who are not powerful enough to shape their own public representations, we have to be especially careful. We may even have to ask if we have any right to do it at all.

It might seem that a small piece of commercial research about listening habits or app usage does not require this kind of worrying. This is simply not true. Even bank customers and website visitors have the right to be represented to others in a way that is understandable and acceptable to them. This means we have to consider the terms they use to describe themselves as essential. We have to listen carefully to what they say they are and not just make up our own mind. And, most importantly, we need to give them an opportunity to edit what we think about them and what we say to others.

In practical terms, it means to be truly human-centric, researchers have to build in feedback sessions where the participants are told what the insights will be and give them an opportunity to provide comments and offer suggestions. I have found sessions like this to be some of the most profoundly useful activities I have ever done in field. But as you can see, it breaks the typical format of a commercial project from a standard agency or management consultant, which use a snatch-and-run approach to research. You have to spend more time in field, which is expensive. You also have to be told you are wrong. In either case, the benefits far outweigh the difficulties. Opening yourself and your thinking to scrutiny allows them to participate in how they are represented, which makes them partners in how their stories are told. This is a positive, ethical, and human-centric action.

3.1.6 Everyone's Safety

Done well, ethnographic research can be as revealing as therapy. In fact, I have sometimes been told that group interviews and individual explorations actually were therapeutic. This has been particularly true for people who participated in healthcare-related projects. But this means this work is potentially dangerous for their mental health and their place in their community and social circles. Researchers need to consider how their interviews provide a safe space for the participants and what impact their insights may have on the people involved. We must strive to keep people safe in many areas of their life. This goes beyond keeping the details of the study private. It also means we have to ensure we do not go too far in the sessions and do not expect too much of our participants.

When a good researcher is in field, they should be open and vulnerable. They need to absorb as much as possible. This also means we need to consider our own safety and health too. We sometimes become privy to life stories that are very difficult to hear. This means we need to have processes in place to allow researchers to decompress after the research is finished. I have had to seek the help of a therapist to manage the discoveries I made in a piece of research on the experience of certain cancers. One participant died from their cancer during the research process, which was particularly difficult. We also have to consider the bodily safety of the researchers. We go into people's homes, and for everyone involved, everything should be done to keep us safe too.

3.2 Choosing the Right Tool for the Job

I have already mentioned this section is something between an outline of things to consider and a how-to guide for the Radical Human-Centric approach. Not wanting to break that in-betweenness, I am not going to launch into a long, and detailed statement of methodologies here. Although, that is certainly something that needs doing later. Commercial research is overly dependent on tired, and patently silly practices and methodologies. But I will not. It would need to be a very lengthy statement, and it is not my intention to detail every methodological foible of commercial research and design thinking. To a very real degree, this book is the first step in that process. There is much more that needs saying. Here I will simply point out that selecting the right methodology and research approach is of central importance to any research program. It is, however, not something that can be easily detailed briefly. In fact, that is what graduate school is for. It takes years to understand the various merits and drawbacks of a number of different approaches to human-centric research. It is why any RHC research program relies heavily on the expertise of specialist researchers. Much of their expertise and experience is organized around selecting the right way to go about research humans, their lives, and their behaviors.

While it is unsatisfying, the best advice I can give here is to trust your specialist researcher. Beyond that, choosing the right tool for the job involves knowing your research tools and approaches. This begins with a strong theoretical and practical understanding of the difference between qualitative and quantitative research. Here I do not mean that one uses words (qual) while the other is focused on numbers (quant). On the contrary, it is about understanding what they are actually for. In the most general sense, qualitative research is inductive. It is best employed when you need to make inferences about the details of many lives in a more generally applicable way. Quantitative research, on the other hand, is deductive, and facilitates a way to take these general statements about people and find ways to test their validity across a larger, more general population, while also adding detail on this larger scale. Foresight research, which we have not discussed in detail yet, uses a different basic format to extrapolate a conclusion from a set of details, essentially skipping to the end and filling in the details afterward. This is a process called abduction. The differences in their basic structure make them well suited to one kind of logical process and relatively useless for others.

There are different logical structures in commercial research

Every form of research has a different purpose and order of operations. The underlying logical structures provide the basis for their use.

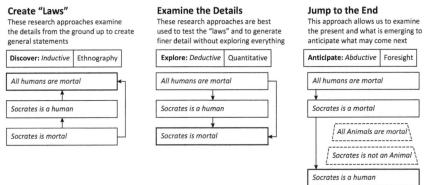

Create "Laws"
These research approaches examine the details from the ground up to create general statements

| Discover: *Inductive* | Ethnography |

All humans are mortal

Socrates is a human

Socrates is mortal

Examine the Details
These research approaches are best used to test the "laws" and to generate finer detail without exploring everything

| Explore: *Deductive* | Quantitative |

All humans are mortal

Socrates is a human

Socrates is mortal

Jump to the End
This approach allows us to examine the present and what is emerging to anticipate what may come next

| Anticipate: *Abductive* | Foresight |

All humans are mortal

Socrates is a mortal

All Animals are mortal

Socrates is not an Animal

Socrates is a human

This difference goes well beyond the dubious assertions I have heard from many of my mainstream commercial research colleagues that quantitative is more "objective" and "qualitative" is subjective. In fact, it is really the other way around. Nothing is more objective than being physically present in the details of someone else's live. What they are trying to say is that quantitative research is more rational, in the philosophical sense of the term, while qualitative research is more experiential. They mean empirical, not objective, and multi-valent not subjective. And they are wrong on both counts.

But if you need to study the experience of someone living their life in order to find opportunities for making interventions (read: products and/ or services), then you cannot use a research process that studies human action at scale and works through rational deduction, making stepwise moves from a general rule to a detailed conclusion. Thus, quantitative processes cannot help you. Instead, you need a research tool grounded in the details of this life that works by folding the experience of everyone involved into an understanding of how the entire chaotic mess works. This is what ethnography does.

You must understand your tools at this, and even a deeper level, to be able to make this decision. So often, there is a complete lack of interest in the theoretical underpinnings of method in commercial research circles. This is a real shame, because it means everyone is using a hammer to put a screw into the wall, or a screwdriver to hammer a nail into a board. Yes, it is technically possible, but there is a better way. Understanding the tool and the research topic allows you to use a screwdriver to drive the screw in and put the hammer to use on the nail.

3.3 The Right Team for the Job

Selecting the right team for the job is an often-overlooked step in a research program. And while it seems obvious that the right team will execute a project at a high level, I have witnessed many consultancies and innovation teams use the wrong people over and over again. For a five-month period, I worked with a consultancy in Finland that claimed to work in an anthropological mode. It was not until I briefly joined the team in Helsinki did I find that they had three anthropologists in the entire company, myself being the third. But instead of using these anthropologists for the majority of their research, only one of us was a consistent fieldworker. Instead, they pulled a bait and switch on almost every project, promising an anthropological perspective, but using team members with only a bachelor's degree intro to anthropology or no formal training at all. As a result, they claimed they had a cutting-edge practice, but conducted unimaginative and mediocre market research instead. This was a team that believed focus groups were a format for anthropological research.

The right team for the job has experience, deep expertise in process, method, and the subject at hand, and is willing to experiment and adapt to the situation. If you are conducting ethnographies or phenomenological studies, use an anthropologist. If you need to produce a close analysis of social structure, use a sociologist with qualitative and quantitative experience. If you need to create concepts for new designs for a novel product, use design research. Too often companies assume researchers are interchangeable. The technology industry is particularly guilty of this belief, which is evidenced by their preference to use social psychologists or HCI researchers for everything. The background, training, and subject expertise of different kinds of researchers prepare them to conduct very specific kinds of work. But their training allows them to set up these projects in more nuanced ways and avoid the pitfalls of that method. Anthropologists and sociologists understand how to mitigate the chaos of the ethnographic process. They also understand ethnography is not just interviewed. A social psychologist is not prepared for this kind of work, and while they can learn it, they will never have the subtly or nuance of someone who has prepared for this during their entire education. They should prepare different kinds of research intended to explore situations where an anthropologist or sociologist would be lost.

An RHC model requires that the team be matched to the research requirements. This not only saves time, but it also ensures that the team can approach the fieldwork with the kind of sensitivity and nuance only prior experience and expertise can provide.

3.4 Leaving Space for Failure

This is a small point, but it is as important as any other. It is essential to prepare yourself for failure in any research plan. There is an informal axiom amongst anthropologists that the field tells you what your project is about. And most experienced anthropologists have found that the result of an open-ended ethnography is seldom what you had intended it to be when you go into the field. Normally, you discover what you should be studying while you are in field; an off-handed comment from one participant becomes the title of the article or book after redirecting your attention totally. It is essential to allow yourself the space for transformative discovery. If you plan too much or adhere to the plan too tightly, you risk missing the very thing you went to look for.

Notes

1 I hesitate to call these "biases" mostly because I am trying to address a larger topic. The conventional meaning of "biases" in business is more akin to 'ingrained beliefs' than what it actually refers to in research. A bias causes you to knowingly or unknowingly put your finger on the scale when weighing the validity of a particular issue, fact, or belief. They are not innate, but neither are they always learned. Because of this, I am avoiding the term simply to prevent this passage from being initially misunderstood.

2 "Normcore" was a term created by the agency K-Hole on October 13, 2013. While they did not mean it seriously, it became a key feature of this particular company's way of seeing the world.

3 In fact, I would argue PowerPoint is perhaps the worst medium for educating anyone known to humankind. Research should always be delivered in a format that is 'of' the field where the information it conveys was found. The document, film, interpretive dance, or book, should be part of the culture being studied. There should be some experiential quality for the audience receiving the insights to help them enter the field and reach a greater understanding. Plonking something into PowerPoint destroys any chance for that to happen because PowerPoint is 'of' business culture. It is actually damaging to the very thing you should be doing in a research project.

4 https://www.invisionapp.com/inside-design/hypothesis-driven-design-process/ (Accessed January 2021).

It is likely the necessary actions in the Scoping phase of the Radical Human-Centricity approach seem new and nebulous. This is because close attention to these issues and this kind of conceptual problems are uncommon, if not entirely absent, in conventional commercial research. The thinking work of the scoping phase is not the kind of thing normally appreciated by clients or researchers who are focused on "innovation" for commercial gain. Neither the speed-obsessed world of technological innovation nor the efficiency-minded post-Taylorists in business strategy will not find the time spent on these efforts to be worthwhile. As we move into the RHC perspective on the more common, practical, and familiar research actions, it will become increasingly clear why all of this navel-gazing is necessary.

The Observe phase marks the beginning of principal research activities. What distinguishes an RHC approach from the alternatives—academic fieldwork, design research, commercial ethnography, market research, design thinking gimmicks—is the careful blend of approaches from all of them, and a practically minded ethic of improving each step wherever possible. It is possible to say that the RHC approach requires researchers to never do the same project twice. Each one must be matched to its circumstances and be altered to fix what went wrong in the past. If the Scoping phase was executed properly, then there is an established body of thinking which will help researchers to make decisions regarding what needs to be improved and how to do it. Each step of the Observe phase should be guided by knowledge gained in the Scoping phase.

OBSERVE

4.0 Set-Up

An RHC research program is different from almost all commercial research because it shifts the location of the fieldwork to encompass the very beginning of the project. Fieldwork should not be relegated to its own discrete area of activity. Fieldwork does not start when you enter someone's living room. No, it begins when you think about who you might encounter. Even conventional elements like a recruiting screener used to identify participants force researchers to project themselves into the field site and imagine who will be there. It is not "deskwork" done prior to fieldwork; it *is* fieldwork. This means the fieldwork for the project begins as the research plan is activated and the hard work of turning an outline of how to execute the research is turned into real actions involving real people. The set-up of the project is the time to manifest the ideals of an RHC approach.

4.1 Recruiting

There are three major considerations in an RHC recruitment process aimed at correcting the failures in recruiting. The first begins with an acknowledgment that recruitment in a commercial setting is actually the first opportunity to learn about the people you will be studying in field. It is not a separate action, but the moment you will begin generating insights. Second, it is essential to see recruitment as an inherent weak point in commercial research. In real ethnography, there is no recruitment, or rather, recruitment is part of the entry into the field site. An ethnographer spends a lot of time getting to know as many people as possible before understanding who is an informant, and who is not. In commercial research, recruitment is normally conducted by sub-contractors, recruitment partners, or research assistants. This means it is a practice of the distribution of responsibility and action. If the recruitment partners are not able to understand or fully participate in the human-centeredness of the work, then it is compromised. They need to be sensitive collectors of information, because you test your hypotheses from the first moment you pick up the phone to find participants. If you cannot benefit from what you can learn during this stage, you are missing a major part of the learning process. Third, it is essential to not fall victim to the conceptual sleight-of-hand that is all too common in the commercial research industry. This problem rests in a misunderstanding of the differences between research types and leads to a belief that what is a "best practice" in quantitative methods also applies to qualitative or ethnographic research. This is not true. Qualitative research does not need to follow the strictures of sample size, population representation, or psychographic or demographic deals because it does not study human activity in the same way as quantitative practices. It generates the hypotheses quantitative distributions are meant to test. So, to expect a qual recruit to be the same as a quant recruit is folly.

4.2 The First Respondent Problem

In Chapter 3, I discussed the implications of what anthropologists call the "village idiot" problem, which is better referred to as the "first respondent problem" instead. As I mentioned before, it refers to the problem that the first respondents you meet are not always the best sources of information describing the context because it is possible, they are outsiders themselves. What they have to say is not necessarily representative of what the full insiders would say about themselves.[1] As we saw earlier, this problem is amplified in commercial settings.

An RHC approach works to mitigate this issue at a minimum, if not to avoid it altogether by recruiting people in a different way. This typically means more work and more time, but what is lost is gained in the quality of the research. Options can come in the form of snowball recruitment where you find a few people who help you find more, or simply by calling people not on any list until you can find people willing to participate. In a commercial setting, this process is often not acceptable, given the time constraints. But effort spent here not only improves the quality of the project but it also helps to eliminate the amplified version of the "first respondent problem" and consequently can save the project from being fatally compromised from the beginning.

4.3 Pre-Research

In commercial research, there is a process called "desk research," which has no process or method behind it. It is, obviously, done at a desk, so we cannot argue with that aspect. However, its claim to be true research is dubious at best. While there are individual practitioners who still adhere to rigorous background research methods, the quality of desk research is determined by the individual doing it. This is a shame because it is a waste of an opportunity. One of the most important parts of the RHC approach is the development of the researcher as a participant in the research. The time doing desk research should really be time to get up to speed on an unfamiliar topic of field site. It should be a moment for the researcher to learn, transform their thinking, and to build on past knowledge. What this means is the background research one does before entering the fieldwork should be an almost sacred time—part preparation, part self-development. So, we should all work to take desk research very seriously.

This is important because the researcher needs to be aware of their own perspective and how their knowledge and experience will color what they see, feel, and learn in field. Pre-research should not just be about scraping some factoids for the deck, it should be a time to prepare the perspective the researcher will use in field. This means developing some expertise, processing the implications of the literature review work done during the scoping phase, and deciding how to present yourself in field.

This last point is a key outcome of pre-research. One of the ways an RHC researcher increases the speed and efficiency of commercial research is to know a great deal about what they will discover in field before getting there. By having a vast body of knowledge to draw upon, the researcher will be more immersed in the conversations, will ask better questions, and will be testing assumptions and hypotheses from word one. But with this expertise, it becomes important to decide how to present yourself and your knowledge in field. An amiable idiot might get further than a tiresome know-it-all whose questions are really just leading statements. During the pre-research, it is important to know what you need to be in field. It is always wrong to mislead people, but it is a good thing to know about the socio-cultural expectations and limits of your respondents. Pre-research is a good way to learn about how you will fit into their lives and how you can avoid being a problematic fool asking stupid questions.

4.4 Know Your Field Site

Another outcome of this pre-research is knowledge of the field site itself. This is also about building an understanding of what you will experience so you do not go off in the wrong direction right away. I will give you an example.

I worked on a set of commercial projects that was exploring the patient experience of a number of chronic conditions for a pharmaceutical company who was making what was essentially a miracle treatment for all of them. In my initial research and pre-research of the chronic conditions, I found pain was a commonality that brought them together into a coherent set. This became one of my hypotheses, and I committed to studying pain as part of the experience of living with these conditions. However, throughout my pre-research, I was bothered by the fact that we were going to visit patients with these conditions in nearly 12 countries, with almost as many languages. I knew from my training in socio-linguistics that there was no guarantee the term "pain" would cover the same conceptual and experiential space across these languages and socio-cultural contexts. So, I, together with my colleagues, decided to prepare ourselves to be receptive to the differences. Doing so would allow us to make comparisons later on. Our review of the client research in the scoping phase indicated this was not a topic of inquiry in any of their prior work. Our early encounters with the team demonstrated there was little, to no, understanding of the expansive meaning of the term "pain" within the company. So, we had to set ourselves up to study pain in context.

Now, when I say "know your field site" I am not just talking about a physical location. I am referring to the complete social/cultural/physical complex comprising the context. Working in an RHC manner means not reducing things but bringing yourself up to work at the needed level of complexity. In this case, it meant we had to prepare a background understanding of how pain is understood within the different social, cultural, and environmental circumstances each of the field sites represented. Some were hot climates, some were not. In some places, people blamed the weather for their pain. In others they did not discuss pain at all.

To access the commonalities and differences in the experience of pain, we had to define pain in all of these contexts. But we did not have the time to develop an understanding of the contexts in field. We had to do it during our pre-research.

What we found was that there was a huge socio-cultural impact on how pain is described and understood. It means the field sites were not as comparable without the context we developed prior to, and in, the field site. Ultimately, the experience of pain, depends on how individuals interpret internal, unsharable information through the terms and ideas they have learned by being a member of a particular socio-cultural context. This meant the type of pain they felt, the degree of its painfulness, and their ability to discuss it with doctors or loved ones, were different in each place. This, of course, means local culture impacts the experience of pain. Had we not understood our field sites enough to anticipate this, we would not have been able to locate these differences and find the few commonalities we needed to build a service halo around the drug. The project, in short, succeeded because we learned about our field sites before we even got there.

This work involves knowing how to manage sources of information and reading between the lines. The second skill is perhaps the most important. Knowing how to make inferences and educated guesses based on information that may seem ancillary to the topic, or beside the point, is important. We even read travel guides to see how people talk about medical care in each of the countries to understand what the local vocabulary is, and what outsiders can expect to experience. Learning about the field site takes skill, dedication, and effort to do well. But it is always work that will reward you in the end.

4.5 Thoughts on Screeners, Discussion Guides, and Moderators

Recruitment screeners and discussion guides are holdovers from outdated market research practices. Far from being "best practices" they can be detrimental to good research practice. However, once we understand what they actually are—communication documents between a researcher and a commissioning client—then we can begin to see their usefulness.

A recruitment screener is a way to come to an agreement on who should participate in the study as a respondent. It is more of a statement of purpose between the client, the researcher, and the recruiter. It is a practical thing because it allows all three to agree upon a common language, a common set of goals, and share an understanding of who the project will be studying. The problem begins when you put them into practice and realize that the more detailed they are, the more problematic they become. Most screeners work when they outline a very general person—known as the "warm body" screener in less serious agencies and consultancies, and thus leave room for discovery. The more specific they are, the more they outline a person who is the result of an educated guess. The specificity is actually an opportunity for preconceived notions, biases, and mistaken thinking to establish themselves in the study. Paradoxically, the more specific a screener is, the less likely the profile reflects reality. Every project I have participated in that uses a market research style screener has eventually revealed a huge gap between the individual described in the screener and the real, breathing, flesh-and-blood people I spoke to. No one really fits a one-size-fits-all description, and so it is ridiculous to think the description is anything other than a convenient starting point. In most of those projects, my first insight was always how far reality had strayed from the hypotheses set in the screener criteria.

Unless the content is derived from a prior, validated study, recruitment screeners are just a set of hypotheses. The variance of the real people within the outline of the screener presents the first opportunity for real insight into the lives of real customers/users/patients. Their quality depends on how well it works as a hypothesis. This means the screener should be used for what it is good at: to be a way to establish a baseline between the stakeholders and as a sacrificial construct used just to get the process started. It is nothing more than this.

The discussion guide, another mainstay of commercial research, has few redeeming qualities unless you need a structured conversation that is little more than a survey conducted in-person.[2] While this is a legitimate research structure, it is not ethnographic at all. Thus, for any study where you want to understand experience, the details of real life, or the ins and outs of human behavior, the discussion guide is little more than an assumption of how you want the interview to go before you get there. Any experienced qualitative researcher knowsthat closely following discussion guides is a certain way to inject all of the crappy thinking and assumptions you made before fieldwork into every conversation. Its purpose should only be to communicate what will likely be done in interviews between the stakeholders. As a research tool, it is just a set of blinders and should never be used in real ethnography. The purpose of ethnography is to learn what you did not know before and to experience a different way of being. You cannot do this if you hold onto a discussion guide. The guide becomes a set of water wings holding you afloat when you need to learn to swim. Leave it behind and dive into the experience. Let your experience and preparation guide your conversations and plan out the time to sort it all out in analysis.

Finally, in the RHC model, researchers do their own research. There is no place for moderators, translators, or mediation (video recordings, etc.) of any kind. If you cannot conduct the research yourself, in your respondents' chosen language, hire someone who can, and include them in the end-to-end research team as a full participant. Anything less is not really human-centered research.

4.6 Planning for Remote/Online Interviews

Since we established the problems of remote or online research in Chapter 2, we need not spend too much time worrying about it here. If it is not possible to be physically present in field, then there are several things that must be done to mitigate the thinness and lack of engagement remote or online research will bring.

First, you have to plan for having more than one encounter with your respondents. Because the online interview is experientially thinner, and people are less able to sit and answer questions for a long time, you will have to shorten the interviews themselves. It is simply not possible to go for two or more hours on a video chat. This means you need to plan for more than one interview with each person.

Secondly, you have to carefully plan out how you will manage the beginnings of the conversations. You need to establish the kind of back and forth in the dialogue to ensure people speak at length and do not shorten their answers. If you recall, the frame of a particular conversation determines what is possible within that conversation. The frame of a video chat dictates mostly short conversations. Now that most of us have had to endure long days of meetings during the pandemic doldrums, few of us want to say more than we have to in a video meeting. This brevity and desire for short conversations is leaking into remote research. To get the kinds of answers you are looking for, it will be necessary to establish a different frame for the conversation.

Finally, you have to understand that many types of design research are simply impossible without face-to-face interactions. The pandemic situation forced many agencies and researchers online. There are many agencies and consultants who even claim remote research is a positive development. This is wrong. We have to resist the temptation to do what is easy. Remote research is just a format for interviews, it is no replacement for ethnography. This means if remote research is all you are able to do during a study, just remember to scope and scale it smaller. You will not be able to do the same work, with the same quality while on a video chat. You have to adjust your expectations accordingly.

5.0 Entry

The next major step of fieldwork is getting there. While this might seem like it is as simple as a taxi ride to the airport, a flight, and a taxi ride to the hotel, it is actually a period of transition for the researchers. It is a ritual process, like the one described by Victor Turner in his book *The Ritual Process*, and RHC researchers use this time to become something different, someone better suited to the difficulties of fieldwork.

The basic outline of the ritual process describes a transition from one state to another through an intermediary state called the *liminal* state. While this is interesting, the liminal state is not immediately relevant. The shift from one thing to another is where we should focus. Travel is a transition physically and conceptually. It affords us the ability to be something else when we arrive. RHC researchers make the most of this. We use this time in transit to shed the old way of thinking, to transition away from the world of consulting and into the sensitive and vulnerable state of the effective fieldworker. We use the transit as an opportunity to start learning, and to observe the differences we experience and to try to understand how they reveal the first data we need for our project. To do this well, we have to consider some additional key factors.

5.1 Nothing Goes To Waste

The transit itself is not time to be on autopilot. Putting the "radical" in RHC means using every opportunity to learn. This means, even the transit is something we should be recording, and carefully tracking. Even details you see in the airport when you arrive should be indicators of a line of thinking you will use in your observations and interviews.

In the RHC approach, nothing goes to waste. I am sure you have experienced a moment of serendipity where you learned something interesting yet seemingly useless, say the history of Swiss watchmaking, the names of different stiches used in hand sewing, or the name of a professional sports star, only to have it be something you use in conversation later in the day to great effect. The RHC approach tries to force this kind of serendipity wherever possible. Do not leave it up to change. Be a sponge and soak up everything you can when you are entering the field. It might help you in ways you cannot imagine. This involves more than passive observation of your surroundings. An RHC researcher is actively analyzing at every step. Try to capture the experience so you can accelerate your learning process.

5.2 Leaving the Consultant's Ivory Tower

Consultants and businesspeople seem to enjoy denigrating academics with PhDs. One of the favorite insults suggests academics are out of touch because they live in an ivory tower. However, to paraphrase one of my mentors, Dr. David Locke, it is very difficult to hide in the ivory tower when you are eating, sweating, and living with your new friends. It is often the consultants and businesspeople who are in the ivory tower. They live in expensive hotels, conduct research in a way to keep themselves at least at arm's length from their customers/users/patients, and spend as little time in field as possible. An RHC fieldworker, on the other hand does the exact opposite, wherever and whenever possible.

A key part of fieldwork lies in the experience of the context. You cannot "know" something if you do not experience it fully. This means you have to throw yourself body and soul into your new surroundings, even for something like a smart home study. Live in one. Experience it for yourself. All you have to do is work to keep your, and your new friends', experiences separate in analysis.

Live life in the tempo of the people you study. Learn the rhythms of their lives. When I was studying the experience of pain in a study of injection experiences, I even learned to self-inject myself, and learned how time relates to the fear and the expression of pain.

You also have to live outside of the ivory tower physically. More creative housing options are a good solution for this, because living close to your respondents, learning about the smell and feel of their environments helps you understand every word they use.

Now, this is extreme. We are not outlining something called "incrementally better human-centricity." Here, I am talking about a radical take on fieldwork within a commercial context. But when you consider many anthropologists leave their homes for years, speak different languages, eat new food, and live the life of the culture they study, it does not seem radical at all. Instead of a few hours of interviews, all an RHC approach requires of you is a few days of immersion.

6.0 In Field

The practice of being in field is exhilarating, exhausting, and expanding. It is also very, very hard work, taking many years to learn the craft. The skill of doing ethnography is something you have to work on all the time. It is not learned in books or captured in process diagrams and their brief explanations. Anthropologists call fieldwork "a way of being in the world" or "being there" using Clifford Geertz's careful observations in his book the *Interpretation of Culture* as our guide.[3] Whether you are doing an ethnography of practice, a phenomenological hermeneutic exploration, a kinship exploration, a socio-linguistic analysis, or even design ethnography, there is no substitute to just throwing yourself in the mix. The skill comes in how to make sense of what you learn and experience after you come up for air. You close in on what you are after only once you have been there long enough.

Like many aspects of the RHC approach, it is the adherence to a more expansive approach that makes it radical. Commercial research is a process of convenience, but ethnography should not be convenient. It should get in your nose, under your skin, and change you. If you do not experience a shift away from your normal self, then you are not doing ethnography. The researcher must change. And to be human-centric, this change should be incremental movements toward someone else's way of seeing the world and defining their place in it. And while this is wildly out of scope for a commercial piece of work, an RHC researcher does it anyway, because there is a larger purpose behind human-centered research—to learn as much as you can about the world. A single project for a client is just one small piece of a longer process of learning. It is an additional opportunity to learn. So, we do ethnography and do not play the dilletante's game of only dipping a toe in.

A full description of fieldwork practices would take several book-length treatments in themselves. Because it is not the purpose of this explanation to go over the *how* of doing ethnography, we will skip to a few thoughts about how an RHC approach expands beyond what is currently used in commercial settings.

6.1 Recording Fieldnotes

Creating fieldnotes is as much a part of being an anthropologist as incomprehensible jargon and participatory observation. It is one of the three key activities in ethnographic fieldwork. But for some reason, it is minimized, if not entirely forgotten in commercial research. Transcripts provide a literal recording of the words used in an interview. Photos and videos provide a partial account of what it looked like. But if you are there to experience and learn, then the only way to record what happened is to create fieldnotes.

You will notice I did not say "write" fieldnotes. This does not have to be a written process, although it most often incorporates some writing. Firstly, fieldnotes should be a mnemonic device to help a research recall what happened in field. As such, it should be a record of what was experienced, what needs to be recalled, and what the researcher was thinking at the time. This last point currently has no place in commercial research because no one cares what the researcher was thinking. However, a record of one's thought process throughout an interview helps the researcher understand why they asked certain questions and structured the interview in the way they did. This helps them balance their perspective in relation to what the participant provided.

The RHC approach uses fieldnotes to being to outline the trajectory between hypotheses, through learning, to insights. Its radical aspect is in the requirement to be a capture point for the thinking of the researcher and the flow of the conversation, experience, or explanation. This means being reflexive throughout, regardless of the medium used to "record the fieldnote." The researcher needs to be as present in the fieldnotes as the people they are studying in order to be able to make their presence explicit in the story. This way, any biases can be mitigated. They are on the record.

Fieldnotes are also a place to being to craft draft insights and allow them to develop as the researchers progress through the fieldwork. They are the way to begin to incorporate all of the inputs and make sense of the contingent and systemic nature of the knowledge they are receiving and developing.

Above all else, good, thickly descriptive fieldnotes are the antidote to the gimmicks of design research, like the static capture sheet, and the weaknesses of market research, like the dependency on verbatim transcripts. Fieldnotes should be flexible accounts that grow in complexity as the learning progresses. They should not just be the dumping ground of "data" that are so prevalent in conventional "human-centric" processes.

For the reasons discussed in Chapter 3, in the RHC approach, researchers take a minimalist approach to asset capture. Take only what you need and leave the field site better for your presence. In practical terms, this means you should not take more pictures of people and their homes or possessions than you need. You should not take video unless it is absolutely essential. You should always ask before taking these recordings, and ensure people understand exactly what they are for and how they will be stored before you begin. You should also refrain from having people "spy" on themselves and place them in a position where they are obligated to collect these recordings themselves. It is possible to convince people to do this by providing a financial incentive, but it is not ethical to do so. So, the place and value of the recording in a study begins with research design and ends with a simple consideration of what you are taking from them. Nothing in research should be considered benign. Researchers have a responsibility to protect people, even from the impact of the research or the actions of the researchers.

7.0 Leaving

Like the transit to the field site, the way you leave is also a key step. However, this step is less about the research and more about the human side of human-centered research. Leaving is a transition back to the old, familiar context, but this shift is fraught with the burden of new knowledge and new responsibilities.

7.1 Getting Out

Again, the radical aspect of radical human-centricity rests on common sense. How do you leave a field site after you have worked hard, and spent time, effort, and money to get into it? How do you leave a group of people and not leave them feeling like their time and stories were worth the small "incentive" payment you have given them.[4]

The best approach is to consider what you have built and act accordingly. The people who you met in field have given you a piece of themselves. It is important to respect this and pledge to take care of their stories. An ethnographic researcher, and even a quantitative researcher, become stewards of the stories and data they collect. Treating it as a snatch and grab operation, and just leaving abruptly without truly thanking the people you have worked with, is not the best way to be human-centric. It is better to leave your hosts with gratitude and humility.

7.2 Building Lasting Relationships

The implications of this you must consider your engagement with the people in field as one that will last beyond the project. You have worked hard to meet new people, and it is worthwhile to cultivate these relationships and give back to the community that supported you. Give as much as you get, and you will fulfill your role as a radically human-centric researcher.

Notes

1 Being a long-term participant in a recruiting company's panel or list is a marker of this questionable status.
2 This format is not unknown in the social sciences. Sociologists, who often incorporate quantitative methods into a single research program, often use strictly organized interviews in their work. However, there is a big difference between these carefully built interviews, where every question is tested, and the majority of commercial discussion guides.
3 Geertz, Clifford.
4 It is worth noting that the name for the honorarium "incentive" is rather insulting. It is based on the language of capitalism and suggests the only way to get another person to do something is to incentivize their behavior. This is nonsense. The vast majority of people will participate for free—not that businesses should take advantage of this—and do. But the idea they are being greased by money alone is odious and not really in keeping with a human-centric ethos. It is better to leave this terminology in the past.

UNDERSTAND

The understand phase does not usually appear in a lot of service design protocols. It is missing in the "Observe, Generate, Activate" format used in service design and foresight circles. It appears a bit in the "define" stage of the design thinking process, but given that this protocol outlines its actions as "empathize," "define," "ideate," "prototype," and "test," we can see emphasizes problem framing and is not about a true analysis of what is discovered in research. This is a real shame, because this is an omission borne out of the "action-oriented," somewhat antiintellectual phase in contemporary business. There is little appreciation, or time allowed, for the work of sitting and thinking, arguably the key element of any consulting process. Since most consultants and innovation teams use off-the-shelf formats like service design, or design thinking processes, there is very little to differentiate them except their skill as analysts. And yet, the process they adhere to does not really give detailed thinking its due. It is a forgotten skill in any research process, and it is what happens between the "ethno" and "graphy" of ethnography.

The RHC process puts an emphasis on analysis and thinking by giving them their own phase—the Understand phase. What this means is in any RHC engagement, the thinking is not squeezed between the flight home and the production of some deliverable but is given the appropriate amount of room to breathe.

Thinking is an undervalued skill in business and design. It is not something cultivated in cultures that prefer "do" over "think." But without analysis, data is just data, and fieldnotes are just a list of curious observations. Insights do not happen overnight, and so it is important to allow researchers the time to make sense of what they experienced and to translate this into what everyone needs to know about we world they studied. This is a time for experience and expertise. The Understand phase is also a time for conversation, collaboration, and argument between collaborators. It is a time to make mistakes and to correct problems in thinking. Done properly, the Understand phase develops the foundations holding everything coming after. Done poorly, or too quickly, and the entire project is built on quicksand.

The activities of this phase are the least well understood, explained, or explored by UX, design thinking, design research, and commercial research practices. In design thinking models, there is only a discussion of "analysis" and "synthesis," where analysis is "about breaking down complex concepts and problems into smaller, easier-to-understand constituents" and synthesis is "involves creatively piecing the puzzle together to form whole ideas."[1] Where there are practical definitions of analytical procedures in UX, design thinking, and service design we have descriptions of clustering activities or sensemaking games. Often, the analytical and epistemological implications of these activities are left out, and it is rare for any handbook ono design thinking to discuss them. This reveals a big problem. If you do not understand the way you are managing information, or comprehend the epistemological underpinnings of the procedure you are using, you should not be doing it. Post-it grouping is not a legitimate form of analysis. Playing children's games categorizing post-its onto a 2x2 framework called an "empathy map" is not an analytical procedure—or an act of empathy, for that matter. Developing "how might we" questions is not analysis or synthesis. All of these things are the gimmicks of design thinking, which have a practical merit but no standing as a research methodology. No serious human-centered researcher uses these processes.

This might seem to be an extreme position at first. Certainly, it is the strongest statement in this book. But considering none of these processes resemble any of the analytical methods and approaches used in any of the social science disciplines should indicate how far design research, design thinking, and commercial research have strayed from the world of serious, real research. There is no talk of coding transcripts in Atlas, which is a basic analytical procedure in sociology and sociolinguistics. There is no appreciation of the differences between a poststructuralist, deconstructivist, and a hermeneutic analytical method typical in many approaches to cultural and social criticism. There is no reference to the different analytical entry points presented by language, meaning, reference, or signs. Instead, design thinking gives us "analysis" which puts factoids onto post-its, and "synthesis" which groups them together via clustering games.

Analysis is complicated; it is not something that can be learned overnight. It is something taught and developed in the crucible of quality graduate programs over many years. So, there is little gained in trying to provide a step-by-step guide here. This is a time for experts and is better solved in the hiring process rather than at the project level. There are many skilled practitioners who have learned a wide range of analytical procedures, evaluated their results in the literature where they were put to use, and have developed their own approach. In an RHC approach, we depend on their expertise and experience. However, I will spend a little time describing some issues and outcomes that define the move to an RHC approach to analysis.

8.0 Analysis

Analysis is the time for making sense of what was captured in field. This process is not a reductionist one, where you take complex data and try to reduce it to anodyne, simple statements. That is not analysis, it is a violent, destructive act. First it is essential to fully understand what was captured in research. This means a complete overview of everything and an assessment of what was discovered and what was not. The next step is where the researchers develop a perspective on how to maintain the complex web of interactions between all of the artifacts gathered in field. This also includes deciding on a way to mitigate the subjectivity and presence of the researcher themselves— to write the researcher's skewed perspective on things out of the system. Finally, it is time to start describing, defining, and modeling the world you studied.

8.1 Data Management

There is a tradition in anthropology where anthropologists transcribe their own recordings and fieldnotes. This takes hours upon hours to do, particularly when you consider the number of conversations that can be captured in one to two years in field—to say nothing of five-year stints. But there is a reason why anthropologists do this beyond the practical issue of language. Transcribing conversations and checking them against fieldnotes allows the researcher time to reflect, remember, and understand what happened and what it is they captured in field. This period of reflection is essential and needs to become a central part of commercial research from now on.

In the RHC approach, the return to the office is marked by a period of reflection and artifact management. Everything needs to be cataloged, transcribed, typed, and read. This is done without any attempt to analyze. It is an act of circumnavigating the entire research project and understanding the scope and scale of what was brought back. Only once you can understand what it is you have, can you start to make sense of it. Failing to do this, risks any number of part-for-whole type breaks in logic or fatal omissions.

This is also a time to consider the gaps in what was discovered. It is impossible to be comprehensive in just a few weeks of time. Assessing what was missed, what was only partially captured, and what is questionable and weak, will allow researchers to navigate the unevenness of what they have collected.

This is a time to implement a coding process to mark-up transcripts and to translate fieldnotes into documents indented for public consumption. This process facilitates quick access to details and collaboration between colleagues.

All of this might seem to be too difficult to do or requiring too much time to accomplish. When I describe the RHC process at this point, I often get the response that "we don't need that. We just need some quick insights." This kind of response is borne out of the false belief that business does not require real research and that anything that is quick and dirty will do. This belief is a foolish and blinkered way to see the world. It is also insulting to the people who participated in the research. To be human-centric, you have to work with respect. Researchers owe participants careful and considered attention. This process does not have to take long, but it does have to be done well to remain within the promises of human-centric research.

8.2 Actually Managing Complexity

At a minimum, analysis is a practice of making sense, prioritizing what to emphasize in storytelling, and gathering the evidence needed to justify a particular conclusion and prove its validity. It is not, and should never be, a process of simplification or over-complication. In qualitative research, researchers never remove something from its context and never isolates a variable as you would in the natural or experimental sciences. Analysts should not reduce complexity; they should explain it and account for it in their explanation.

For example, during a blue-sky design research project I conducted for a global technology and appliance company, we investigated the social role of different kinds of appliances in people's home. This was only part of the study, but it was a necessary thread of inquiry because it would lead to a way to outline what possible social roles appliances can have within a home context. When I say social role, what I mean is the objects understood the degree of agency within the social network of the family. What we found was that there are "dumb" appliances and there are "smart" appliances at a minimum and that the two roles had a very different set of social affordances. Dumb appliances should be quiet, simple, and forgettable. Smart appliances were allowed to be communicative, carry data, and interact without being asked. However, what we found was that the boundaries of these categories could move, depending on which country you were in. Some dumb appliances could be in the smart category in a different context. This meant that this category had to also account for variations in the cultural context and its attendant expectations. This realization arose in field, but it was not until we began our analysis that we realize how complex these two constructs actually were.

In a design research or design thinking process, all of the details of what are smart and dumb would have been separated, and then regrouped to create a feature list for what goes under the "dumb" post-it and what goes under the "smart" post-it. However, because we were conducting real research, we had to begin with a matrix assessment that correlated the categories, their typology, the tokens that fell under the category headings, and account for the variances to each in different contexts. It meant we had to first overcomplicate the assessment before we could parse out what was directly demarcating dumb/smart, and what was not. Then we had to compare these differences across the different contexts, eliminate the competing perspectives, and arrive at a set of commonalities that survived this process. What we did was eliminate what was oppositional and irrelevant. We did not reduce the complexity of the system.

It is absolutely essential to not break the interconnections, oppositions, and interacting components of a socio-cultural system, meaning, or object. You have to deal with it in the context you find it, at the same level of complexity. Instead of reducing complexity, good analysis is brought up to the same level so it can deal with it as you found it. This means good analysis is a flexible process where the analysts have to be able to change the way they approach a problem.

8.3 Mitigating the Dreaded "Subjectivity"

There are no real established protocols to effectively write yourself out of an analysis completely. This is because as the researcher, your perspective, your assumptions, your biases, and your strengths and weaknesses are part of the research already. The best metaphor to explain this is the distortion effect of a lens. Every single lens warps an image in a particular way. Good photographers or cinematographers understand and anticipate these distortions when they choose which lens to use. Much of the Scoping phase we covered above is really about choosing the right lens and acknowledging its benefits and drawbacks.

When we come to analysis, it is best to see the Scoping and Understanding phases as the two halves of the use of an anamorphic lens in filmmaking. The anamorphic lens allowed filmmakers to have a wider field of view and to predictably compress that image onto a standard 35mm frame. However, the print could not be projected in the usual manner because the image would be heavily distorted on film until it is translated in postproduction or shown through a projector that was the reverse of the camera lens.

Setting up the project is equivalent to filming with an anamorphic lens. The analysis phase is where the image is returned to its undistorted version. The process of writing yourself out of a study in order to minimize the impact of your subjective decisions in field and in analysis requires writing yourself into the research plan and recording your thoughts in a predictable manner.

That way you can trace your effect on what you collected in field in an understandable manner. Then, through a process of deletion, or impact assessment, you can see what is left when you are removed. This requires good set up, and excellent recordkeeping in field. We discussed this in the Scoping and Observe phase descriptions.

9.0 Synthesis

Synthesis is not an act of putting things together after you have disassembled them. It is an analytical procedure to resolve differences between disparate or oppositional ideas, concepts, or contexts. As such, synthesis is an act of creation. This type of synthetic analysis was outlined by F. W. Hegel as his dialectical method, which is a key element of his phenomenology. Originally intended to resolve differences in conceptual models about the world, the dialectics of thesis, antithesis resolving into synthesis, is a linear way to create ever more sophisticated propositions about the world. Since insights are these propositions, the dialectical method is the obvious intellectual tool to build them.

In commercial research, Hegelian dialectics is not something you want to explain to a client, but given that human-centered research is phenomenological research, it makes sense to use it behind the scenes. Practically, it means you must search for differences and commonalities between people, contexts, and events. You explain the commonalities in one set of insights. Then you synthesize the differences by resolving oppositions with a common statement of how the variances are manifestations of similar, or shared meta-processes, beliefs, or meanings. These become the second set of insights. Then finally you resolve any oppositions between the two sets and presto! You have a set of insights.

As an analytical process, this is preferable to the post-it game, because you are not making associations, which can come from misunderstands or outside sources. Instead, you are working only within what you learned in field and making use of agreements and disagreements alike. Nothing is wasted, and you are allowing the differences in experience and opinion to create a deeper understanding and not eliminate differences but embrace them.

10.0 Return-Test-Verify-Edit

In an RHC format, testing and verifying insights is a cooperative process done with the people who know the context best, the research participants. This means you should always plan to return to the field site in some way in order to verify what you learn and test your insights. The benefits of this are multiple. You are able to test what you wrote and continue the process of working out your misunderstandings and omissions. You get to deepen your understanding and strengthen your descriptions. You may learn something new. You also take an ethical position and help the research participants control how they are represented. And you also get to edit and hone the key piece of a commercial research project, the understanding of how a company can enter this space in a positive way.

This short moment in the Understand phase can have a big impact on the success of the work and the validity of the findings. It is also a good way to see your new friends.

Note

1 https://www.interaction-design.org/literature/article/stage-2-in-the-design-thinking-process-define-the-problem-and-interpret-the-results#:~:text=Analysis%20is%20about%20breaking%20down,that%20relate%20to%20our%20users.

At the end of the Understand phase, the principal research part of a commercial research project is almost over. What is left is the generation of insights and the activation of the storytelling process. In the RHC system, these are separated so they neatly map over the more conventional design thinking and service design processes used by most commercial clients. However, they are really part of a single effort.

GENERATE

In research, the generate phase is focused on the articulation of insights and the establishment of a common understanding of the context.

11.0 Insights

In Chapter 6, I established the purpose and structure of an insight, which describes, explains, and predicts a particular phenomenon in context. This describes what they should be, but there are some practical considerations that need to be addressed as they are developed.

11.1 Description

As a descriptive construct, an insight should detail something as thickly as possible. But this description needs to be organized so that it allows the audience to view the content of the insight through the eyes of a cultural insider. This is not the time to foster a clinical perspective. This is important because this description allows the audience to get a visceral sense of the distance between them and their customer/user/patient.

11.2 Define

Insights should raise concepts and terms that are completely new to the audience. It is easy to do this if you draw from the terminology native to the context you studied. However, this means an insight should also help the audience understand the meaning of these terms or the importance of the concepts. Here we are staring to being the translation process and providing the intended audience access to ideas they need to understand.

11.3 Translate

Insights should point towards the culture and perspective of the audience. They should serve as a bridge between the people who were studied and the people who want to learn about them. As such, the fundamental purpose of insight is to be a bridge between these two groups.

This is not an easy thing to do, because it involves an intimate knowledge of both. If one is a consulting researcher, then there needs to be time and effort devoted to learning about the client and their internal politics, knowledge system, and the perspectives they have on the world. One of the most useful tools to use to accomplish this is conducting a set of baselining interviews at the beginning of a project. These interviews should be with the people running the project, receiving the work (e.g., design group, engineering teams, etc.), and the stakeholders who have a voice in determining whether or not the project was successful. These conversations should focus on what people think, what they think they know, what they expect from the work, and what success looks like at the end.

Essentially the baseline is a micro-ethnography of the client and their internal culture. Running this little internal session has big implications for the rest of the project. It allows the researcher to understand where the problems lie, what is likely to be acceptable, how far to push the client, and how to deliver a set of insights that will engage them and force them to act. The baseline is the foundation for the double translation and the best way to understand how the storytelling and rhetorical organization should unfold.

11.4 Actionability

An actionable insight is a statement of truth that is fit for purpose. The actionability of insight depends entirely on the nature of the collaboration between the researchers, the stakeholders, and the intended audience. Actionability is not a quality, it is an outcome. If an insight is descriptive, rich, evocative, pithy, understandable, and acceptable to the intended audience, then it is on its way to being actionable. But that is not enough. The story it tells needs to be memorable, transferable, and exciting. This is not easy to do and is not something that should be the sole responsibility of a researcher. This is only possible when there is a good working relationship and when the project stakeholders have been clear about what they want and need. This means the actionability of the insight is grounded in the work of the first three phases, and not something you can conjure up at the last minute.

NOTES ON ACTIVATION

In a commercial research project, the purpose of the activate phase is to develop the stories that ground the practical work of design or developing a strategy. The activities here are well known, as they are part of established processes. The key issue here is that a researcher's role shifts from research or analyst to become the voice of the people in the study. It is not really possible that a set of insights will capture everything there is to learn in a research study. Having a researcher along for the design, development, testing, and GTM phases of product and/or service design, ensure that new questions can be answered, and that the voice of the customer/user/patient is present to some degree at every stage of this continuing process.

The activate phase is where a collaborating researcher embeds into a different kind of team. This stage is no longer about research, it is where design and strategy begin. What this means is that the researcher ceases to be a voice for themselves and takes on the voice of the people they spoke to in field. In the best-case scenario, the researcher becomes a source of information. Designers, engineers, strategists, and marketers should be using them as a resource, to ensure the project keeps the human side of the story front and center. In the RHC format, the researcher becomes a source for interpreting what was said on the page, what was left off the page that might be relevant, and for guiding the team in a direction where they navigate the possibilities and constraints provided by the stories from the field. This means the research is a guide and is a key player in maintaining the human-centric nature of the work being done.

CONCLUSION

Throughout this book, I have tried to demonstrate why a set of radical shifts in commercial research are necessary and how they should be accomplished. These shifts must begin with a fundamental change in the way business leaders, research managers, engineers, designers, and innovators of all kinds think. They cannot just be an alteration to commercial research for strategy or design purposes. Radical Human-Centricity requires building new cultures of innovation inside companies and governments.

As you have seen, the Radical Human-Centric approach to real research is not a sweeping revolution. It is the application of a higher standard of research practice. But if we consider what I am recommending, it is not radical at all. Instead, Radical Human-Centricity is the first step in fulfilling the promises made by design research and design thinking, at least. It provides insight into the changes in thought and practices needed to deliver the details about the world and the people who live in it, and in doing so, lay the foundation for business strategies and innovations which do not intrude in people's lives, but actually make them better. As a research practice, it stands in direct opposition to all of the overreach and dehumanizing practices of market research. Using an RHC approach will preclude the use of market research practices in innovation design and strategy, and the misapplication of research tools in places where they do not belong. But for design thinking processes and the innovation effort in general, it is an amendment. Radical Human-Centricity is meant to be an intervention into the way design or innovation research are conducted, and help designers, engineers, strategists, and business leaders start to understand their place in the wonderful world of human thought, action, and interaction.

The radical human-centric practitioner is someone who is committed to amending their research approach to do better when studying people, their beliefs, desires, and behaviors in a commercial or applied setting. But as you have seen throughout this book, it begins as a set of adaptations, alterations, and adjustments to existing research practices, whether they come from innovation research or academia. It requires a recognition that things are broken as they stand now and a willingness to change one's own way of working. It is a rejection of the bad habits and poor logic clogging the works of applied and commercial research. It is a statement of belief that everyone can be better, but that it is not necessary to throw everything out. It is a celebration of expertise and experience. And finally, it is a promise to do better with every project.

This task begins and ends with locating oneself within a larger context. To be reflexive about one's place in relation to others and one's impact on this world is central to actually understanding the world as it is. This means to understand another human's thoughts, beliefs, emotions, requirements, desires, and actions, it is essential to understand yourself. And ultimately, this is what is missing in business, design, and innovation. The advancement of technology and capital are not sufficient goals in themselves. We must always remember we live in a much larger, more complicated world filled with human and nonhuman actors. Business activities have a huge impact on this delicate system, and we must wake up and understand how the work of innovation affects everyone else.

It is my intention that this book be a sufficient productive critique of existing commercial research practices to convince people that they are able to make this change. I have outlined how it can be done, but it is up to every researcher and business leader to enact these changes in their daily lives. Once everyone agrees, there will be more to do to replace old, broken, and failed research traditions with rigorous thinking and action. RHC constitutes the beginning, not the end of this effort.

Innovation research can lead to some remarkable things. But if it is done poorly, or with questionable intent, it can also be very damaging. Making no compromises, being honest, and always being ethically minded throughout ensures we are able to innovate using the best of ourselves. This makes the extra effort worthwhile in itself. Research has the capacity to uncover new things about ourselves and our surroundings. In this way, it can expand our lives and make space for the improvement of everyone's lives. Yoked to bare avarice, or to blinkered thinking, research can justify horrors. To fulfill the promise of human-centered research, we must strive to achieve the former while denying the latter. Anything short of that is not radical enough.

So, commit to real research. Think before you act. Research with focus, skill, and intent. And tell the stories that will capture the minds of people capable of making a huge difference in the world. Done well, radically human-centric research can change the world.

REFERENCES

Anderson, L. 2006. Analytic Autoethnography. *Journal of Contemporary Ethnography, 35* (4): 373–395.

Augustine. 2009. *Confessions.* Oxford: Oxford Classics, 10.

Barley, N. 2000. *The Innocent Anthropologist: Notes from a Mud Hut.* Waveland Press.

Barnett, H.J. and Morse, C. 2013. *Scarcity and Growth: The Economics of Natural Resource Availability.* London: Routledge.

Baudrillard, J. 2020. *Simulacra and Simulations* (pp. 230–234). Routledge.

Bateson, G. 2000. *Steps to an Ecology of Mind: Collected Essays in Anthropology, Psychiatry, Evolution, and Epistemology.* University of Chicago Press.

Battarbee, Katja, Jane Fulton Suri, and Suzanne Gibbs Howard. "Empathy On the Edge: Scaling and Sustaining a Human-Centered Approach In the Evolving Practice Of Design." IDEO, 1. https://new-ideo-com.s3.amazonaws.com/assets/files/pdfs/news/Empathy_on_the_Edge.pdf.

Bennardo, G. and Munck, V.C.D. 2014. *Cultural models: Genesis, Methods, and Experiences.* Oxford: Oxford University Press.

Berlin B, Kay P. 1963. "Basic Color Terms: Their Universality and Evolution."

Bhaskar, R. 2014. *The Possibility of Naturalism: A Philosophical Critique of the Contemporary Human Sciences.* London: Routledge.

Boland, R.J. 2008. "Decision Making and Sensemaking." In *Handbook on Decision Support Systems 1*, Springer, Berlin, Heidelberg, 55–63.

Borneman, J. and Hammoudi, A. eds. 2009. *Being There: The Fieldwork Encounter and the Making of Truth.* University of California Press.

Bourdieu, P. 1984. *Distinction: A social critique of the judgement of taste.* Harvard university press.

Brentano, F. 1995, Psychology from an Empirical Standpoint, Trans. Antos C. Rancurello, D. B. Terrell, and Linda L. McAlister, London and New York: Routledge.

Carlyle, Thomas. 2010 (1840). "The Hero as Divinity" In *Heroes and Hero-Worship.* New York: Cosimo Classics.

Chan, J. Dang, S. and Dow, S.P. 2016. "Comparing Different Sensemaking Approaches for Large-Scale Ideation." In *Proceedings of the 2016 CHI Conference on Human Factors in Computing Systems*, May: 2717–2728.

Conklin, Harold C. M. 1955 "Hanunoo color categories." *Southwestern Journal of Anthropology* 11(4): 339–344.

Deleuze, G. and Krauss, R. 1983. Plato and the Simulacrum. *October* (27): 45–56.

Ellul, Jacques.1964. *Technological Society.* New York: *Vintage Books.*

Emerson, R.M. Fretz, R.I. and Shaw, L.L. 2011. *Writing Ethnographic Fieldnotes*. University of Chicago Press.

Engelke, M. 2019. *How to Think Like an Anthropologist*. Princeton University Press.

Foucault, M. 2005. *The Order of Things*. London: Routledge.

Foucault, M. 1972. The Order of Things: An Archeology of Knowledge. New York: Pantheon Books.

Gasparini, A. 2015, "Perspective and Use of Empathy in Design Thinking." In *ACHI, The Eight International Conference on Advances in Computer-Human Interactions*, February: 49–54.

Geertz, C. 1988. "Being There: Anthropology and the Scene of Writing." In *Geertz C, Works and Lives: The Anthropologist as Author*, 1–25.

Geertz, Clifford. 1973. "Thick Description: Toward and Interpretive Theory of Culture." In *Interpretation of Cultures*. Basic Books, 4–30.

Ginsburg, Faye. 1995. "The Parallax Effect: The Impact of Aboriginal Media on Ethnographic Film." *Visual Anthropology Review* 11(2): 65–80.

Goffman, E. 1974. *Frame Analysis: An Essay on the Organization of Experience*. Harvard University Press.

Greenson, R.R. 1960. "Empathy and its Vicissitudes." *International Journal of Psycho-Analysis, 41*: 418–424.

Halse, J. 2020. "Ethnographies of the Possible." In *Design Anthropology*. London: Routledge, 180–196.

Hannerz, U. 2016. *Writing Future Worlds: An Anthropologist Explores Global Scenarios*. Springer.

Hartley, Paul. 2020. "Beyond Design Thinking: Can Design Research Education Unlock a New Foundation for Design?" *Applied Arts Magazine*, April 8. (https://www.appliedartsmag.com/blog/beyond-design-thinking-a17631/).

Hartley, Paul. 2017. "What is a Human Future Anyway?" *MISC: Human Futures* 25:6.

Hartley, Paul. 2017. "Towards a Human Futures Perspective." *MISC* 25:117–125.

Hayano, D.M. 1979. Auto-ethnography: Paradigms, problems, and prospects. *Human Organization, 38*(1), pp. 99–104.

Hess, J.L. and Fila, N.D. 2016. The Manifestation of Empathy Within Design: Findings From a Service-Learning Course. *CoDesign, 12*(1–2): 93–111.

Husserl, E. 2001, Logical Investigations. Trans. J. N. Findlay. London and New York: Routledge.

Ideo.org. 2015. *The Field Guide to Human-Centered Design*. San Francisco, CA, Ideo.org. https://www.designkit.org/resources/1?utm_medium=ApproachPage&utm_source=www.ideo.org&utm_campaign=FGButton.

Irwin, Terry, et al. 2015. "Transition Design." https://design.cmu.edu/sites/default/files/Transition_Design_Monograph_final.pdf (Accessed january 2021).

Kim, J. and Ryu, H. 2014. A Design Thinking Rationality Framework: Framing and Solving Design Problems in Early Concept Generation. *Human–Computer Interaction, 29*(5–6): 516–553.

Knochel, Aaron D. 2017. "Why do conservatives want the government to defund the arts?" https://theconversation.com/why-do-conservatives-want-the-government-to-defund-the-arts-71866.

Kouprie, M. and Visser, F.S. 2009. A Framework for Empathy in Design: Stepping Into and Out of the User's Life. *Journal of Engineering Design, 20*(5): 437–448.

Köppen, Eva, and Christoph Meinel. 2015. "Empathy Via Design Thinking: Creation of Sense and Knowledge." In *Design Thinking Research*. New York: Springer Cham, 15–28.

Lai, Sylvia. 2018. "5 Steps to a Hypothesis-driven Design Process." https://www.invisionapp.com/inside-design/hypothesis-driven-design-process/ (Accessed January 2021).

Liu, Y. Kliman-Silver, C. and Mislove, A. 2014, May. "The Tweets They Are A-Changin': Evolution of Twitter Users and Behavior." In *Proceedings of the International AAAI Conference on Web and Social Media*, May, 8(1).

Lunt, P. and Livingstone, S. 1996. Rethinking the Focus Group in Media and Communications Research. *Journal of Communication*, 46(2): 79–98.

Malinowski, B. 2007. Method and scope of anthropological fieldwork. *Ethnographic Fieldwork: An Anthropological Reader.* London: Wiley-Blackwell, 4–25.

McDonagh, Deana, and Joyce Thomas. 2011. *Design + Empathy = Intuitive Design Outcomes, The Design Journal*, 14(2): 147–150, DOI: 10.2752/175630611X12984592779881.

Merleau-Ponty, M. 2012, *Phenomenology of Perception.* Trans. Donald A. Landes. London and New York: Routledge.

Metz, Ashley and Paul Hartley. 2020. "Development as a Valuation Practice: Implications for practitioners and fields. *Technological Forecasting & Social Change*, 155:C.

Miemis, V., Smart, J. and Brigis, A., 2012. Open foresight. *Journal of Futures Studies, 17*(1): 91–98.

Misak, C. ed. 2004. *The Cambridge Companion to Peirce.* Cambridge: Cambridge University Press.

Norman, Donald A., 2005. Human-centered design Considered Harmful. *Interactions, 12*(4):14–19.

Oberle, B. Bringezu, S. Hatfield-Dodds, S. Hellweg, S. Schandl, H. and Clement, J. 2019. *Global Resources Outlook: 2019.* International Resource Panel, United Nations Envio.

Okely, J. 2020. *Anthropological practice: Fieldwork and the ethnographic method.* Routledge.

Open Science Collaboration. 2015. "Estimating the Reproducibility of Psychological Science." *Science*, 349(6251).

Peirce, Charles Sanders. 1992. *The Essential Peirce, Volume 2: Selected Philosophical Writings, 1897–1913.* Indiana University Press.

Pike, K. L. 1967. "Etic And Emic Standpoints for the Description of Behavior." In K. L. Pike, *Language in Relation to a Unified Theory of The Structure of Human Behavior.* Mouton & Co., 37–72.

Rogers, C.R. 1989. *The Carl Rogers Reader.* Houghton Mifflin Harcourt.

Rogers, R. 2013, May. "Debanalizing Twitter: The Transformation of an Object of Study." In *Proceedings of the 5th Annual ACM Web Science Conference*, May: 356–365.

Rouse, William B., 1993. Human-Centered Design: Concept and Methodology. *Journal of The Society of Instrument and Control Engineers, 32*(3): 187–192.

Roys, N. and Seshadri, A. 2014. "On the Origin and Causes of Economic Growth." *The Social Systems Research Institute (SSRI)*, 4–5.

Rylander Eklund, A. Navarro Aguiar, U. and Amacker, A. 2021. "Design thinking as sensemaking—Developing a Pragmatist Theory of Practice to (re)Introduce Sensibility." *Journal of Product Innovation Management*, 39(1): 24–43.

Short, T.L. 2007. *Peirce's Theory of Signs.* Cambridge: Cambridge University Press.

Standage, T. 1998. *The Victorian Internet: The Remarkable Story of the Telegraph and the Nineteenth Century's Online Pioneers.* London: Phoenix.

Stover, L.E. 1973. "Anthropology and Science Fiction." *Current Anthropology, 14*(4): 471–474.

Tinius, J. 2018. Capacity for Character: Fiction, Ethics and the Anthropology of Conduct. *Social Anthropology*, *26*(3): 345–360.

Walford, G. 2009. The Practice of Writing Ethnographic Fieldnotes. *Ethnography and Education*, *4*(2): 117–130.

Wittgenstein, Ludwig. 1991. *Philosophical Investigations: The German Text, with a Revised English Translation*, 3rd Ed. London: Wiley-Blackwell.

Žižek, Slavoj. 2009. *The Parallax View*. MIT Press.

INDEX

Lightning Source UK Ltd.
Milton Keynes UK
UKHW041830050822
406863UK00002B/74